ALSO BY R. J. HERRNSTEIN

A Source Book in the History of Psychology (with E. G. Boring)

Laboratory Experiments in Psychology (with J. C. Stevens and G. S. Reynolds)

I.Q.
IN THE
MERITOCRACY

I.Q.
IN THE
MERITOCRACY

by R. J. Herrnstein

AN ATLANTIC MONTHLY PRESS BOOK

Little, Brown and Company – Boston–Toronto

FIRST EDITION

T 05/73

The table on page 172 from J. L. Jinks and D. W. Fulker's "A Comparison
of the Biometrical Genetical, MAVA and Classical Approaches to the
Analysis of Human Behavior," *Psychological Bulletin*, Vol. 73, 1970, pages
311–349, Copyright 1970 by the American Psychological Association,
and reproduced by permission of the Association and the authors.

Table 2 from Arthur R. Jensen's "How Much Can We Boost I.Q. and
Scholastic Achievement?" *Harvard Educational Review* 39, Winter 1969,
pages 1–123, and part of Figure 1 from Arthur R. Jensen's "Reducing
the Heredity-Environment Uncertainty: A Reply," *Harvard Educational
Review* 39, Summer 1969, pages 349–383, © 1969 by the President
and Fellows of Harvard College. Reprinted by permission of the publisher.

The table by C. Burt from "Intelligence and Social Mobility," *British
Journal of Statistical Psychology* 14, 1961, page 11, is reprinted with
permission of the publisher.

The letters from the *Harvard Crimson* are quoted with permission
of the publisher.

ATLANTIC–LITTLE, BROWN BOOKS
ARE PUBLISHED BY
LITTLE, BROWN AND COMPANY
IN ASSOCIATION WITH
THE ATLANTIC MONTHLY PRESS

Library of Congress Cataloging in Publication Data

Herrnstein, Richard J
I. Q. in the meritocracy.

"An Atlantic Monthly Press book."
Bibliography: p.
1. Intellect. 2. Mental tests. 3. Nature and
nurture. 4. Social status. I. Title.
BF431.H399   153.9'2   73-304
ISBN 0-316-35864-9

*Published simultaneously in Canada by Little, Brown & Company
(Canada) Limited*

PRINTED IN THE UNITED STATES OF AMERICA

For Roger Brown

ACKNOWLEDGMENTS

This book grew out of an article entitled "I.Q.," published in the *Atlantic Monthly* magazine in September 1971. I owe the editors, particularly Robert Manning and C. Michael Curtis, a debt of gratitude for their interest in the idea of such an article and then, after I wrote a draft, for their criticism and counsel. Later, when the article had swelled about fivefold, I was fortunate to have Esther S. Yntema, senior editor at the Atlantic Monthly Press, as a faithful and deeply insightful critic. Susan Herrnstein has performed her usual but invaluable service as my most objective reader. I have also been fortunate that the preparation and editing of the manuscript rested in the capable hands of Arlene Andrew and Sara Hill.

Others have also been helpful respondents to all or part of either article or book. I am happy to thank V. E. Anderson, E. C. Banfield, T. J. Bouchard, Jr., H. Brooks, J. E. Cohen, B. K. Eckland, M. S. Feldstein, Z. Griliches, E. R. Harwood, G. Homans, C. Jencks, A. R. Jensen, B. Moore, C. E. Noble, R. Nozick, E. B. Page, E. L. Pattullo, D. Riesman, R. Rosenthal, W. Shockley, S. S. Stevens, H. S. Terrace, M. Vernon, M. L. Walzer, J. Q. Wilson, and D. B. Yntema for letting me know their reactions and, in a few cases, for making available unpublished materials. To Roger Brown, who read both original article and book and gave me generously the benefit of his scholarly perspicacity and good sense, I am especially indebted. The undergraduate general education course that we taught together was the occasion, to begin with, for an account of intelligence testing and its social implications, and then it was the setting for much of the peculiar and protracted controversy that followed (recounted here in the preface). I owe him, therefore, not only thanks but apologies. Obviously, none of these people should be held in any way accountable for the use I have made of their help, although they deserve credit where it is due.

The book has a dual goal. First, I hope it conveys a timely collection of facts fairly and reasonably nontechnically. I have tried to restate every statistical conclusion in plain English, for practical decisions in recent years have often been based on too sketchy an understanding of the potentialities and limitations of the kinds of analysis available to social science. Second, I hope the book sheds light on the controversy surrounding I.Q. and social status without again igniting it.

R. J. HERRNSTEIN

CONTENTS

LIST OF FIGURES AND TABLES

I.Q.
IN THE
MERITOCRACY

A True Tale from the Annals of Orthodoxy

In the immediate aftermath of Charles Darwin's epochal *Origin of Species,* social theorists were quick to apply the doctrine to man. If it was true that "survival of the fittest" was nature's rule for selection, could human society do otherwise than obey it, these social Darwinists wondered. For them, nature "red in tooth and claw" became the driving principle of society, replacing the mystical and theological forces of earlier times. The grinding poverty, the brutal inhumanity, the untempered egotism that accompanied the rapid industrialization of the nineteenth century seemed to some to be part of nature's plan, akin to the sufferings of animals in their "struggle for existence." Success in society, measured by wealth and social position, was the human counterpart, to these theorists, of successful reproduction in animals. Human society was seen as evolving insofar as it favored its most able members.

Almost as soon as Darwinism was applied to social theory, there were problems. First, it did not appear that society's "best" were also society's most prolific in producing offspring, as they would have to be to fulfill their biological destiny. The upper classes simply did not think of having babies as the ultimate measure of their worth. Moreover, if a nation was moved by compassion or political expedience to redistribute some part of its wealth for the sake of its suffering masses, it seemed to be trafficking dangerously with nature's prime tool — survival. What would be the result, the Darwinians asked ominously, if those who otherwise would die or fail to have families, except for private or public charity, start surviving and reproducing? The answer seemed unmistakably clear — the impoverishment of man's hereditary legacy. The biological result of charity in one generation seemed likely to be diminished vigor and adaptability in one's descendants.

The solutions varied with the style of their advocates. The laissez-faireists would have allowed nature, in the form of competitive society, to do its cruel work on man as it has on other creatures. Government should stand aside to let the best men (and women) win. In striking contrast, Darwinian theory could also bolster ethnocentrism, particularly for those who happened to believe that their own people were biologically superior in some important way. The political result could easily be just the opposite of laissez-faireism, concentrating power in the state to advance the cause of one's "people." There was also the more direct solution of eugenics, which would have made having babies a matter of public policy. To Francis Galton, natural parenthood looked more like a social privilege than an individual's right, which is an idea that the crisis of overpopulation has renewed. In spite of the differences, none of these alternatives appeals much to modern readers, for we today are on the other side of a great intellectual divide, separating us from those in the nineteenth and early twentieth century who were trying to put political philosophy and biological science together — especially in light of the Darwinian theory of evolution.

For the early Darwinians, the idea of perfectible man had been swamped by the central lesson of the new biology — that all creatures operated within the scope permitted by their structure. For man, the scope might be great, even vastly greater than other animals, but limitless it was not. Furthermore, a man's future was continuously shaped, for good or ill, by the genetic legacy piled up by his ancestors. Instead of a Hegelian evolution towards the one and only perfect society, Darwinians envisioned a host of less promising outcomes, including even extinction. While Darwin himself managed to avoid these troubled political topics, some of his followers relentlessly pressed what they believed to be the logic of natural selection.

Logic notwithstanding, social Darwinism started going out of style in the United States after World War I. Biological determinism doubtless came hard to begin with, running as it did against the American grain. Not only did it challenge our egalitarianism, it also said that Horatio Alger may need more than hard work to get ahead. Darwinian evolution portrays nature as wasteful, disinterestedly selecting a few from among the many. That is hard medicine to swallow for a people whose institutions are conceived, in principle if often not in fact, in precisely the opposite terms — that every individual is precious and unique, *equally* precious and unique. But Darwinism was not only disagreeable, it could also be dangerous, as a rationalization for individual or class or racial advantages. And then, in the 1930's, Nazi Germany proved how lethal the idea of group superiority could become in malevolent hands.

For whatever reasons, then, we today have mostly grown up in an intellectual climate dominated by extreme, unrestrained environmentalism, which is the modern alternative to Darwinism, the religious alternatives having gone into decline also. Virtually all influential political and social theories since the 1930's assume that society, as well as the individuals composing it, are shaped mainly by social forces. Change those forces, the theorists promise, and man in society will change accordingly. It may be no accident that social scientists gravitate towards theories that give them the maximum potential for practical influence. Thus, among experts, the doctrine of environmentalism reigns, not only supreme but virtually alone, in almost every sphere of human affairs. The biological analogies to human matters — as in Robert Ardrey on territory or Desmond Morris on sex or Konrad Lorenz on aggression — have been resisted, although they clearly strike a response among laymen.

To solve our monetary, criminal, medical, economic, educational, emotional, familial problems, we call on environmental solutions — we adjust interest rates, penal practices, health habits, manufacturing processes, school curricula, occupational pressures, parental expectations, and so on. To be sure, no one should object to society's investing resources in the things it can get hold of. If interest rates, penal institutions, medical facilities, capital investment, and so on, are within our control, and if changing them helps, change them we should. But tagging along with that simple and unobjectionable pragmatism comes a conviction that the things we can change are the *only* things that make a difference. In other words, if mortality rates or productivity fail to improve, the remedy is assumed to be more social intervention, often more of the same sort of social intervention. The possibility that society may yield to nonsocial pressures is usually greeted with the reaction one customarily accords astrology, except for the greater hostility we reserve for threatening notions, which astrology is not. By dogma, not by data, it has been decreed that we may safely disregard nonsocial agents that we cannot readily control. And the prime nonsocial agent, to our knowledge, is our own genetic potential. Except for the prevailing orthodoxy, we would want to know how genetic factors interact with our social goals — in medicine, economic advancement, educational innovation, even in the deterrence of crime. While in certain areas of social life, genes may contribute little or nothing, in others their contribution may be both substantial and substantially overlooked, because of the environmentalist doctrine that dominates both our education and our attitudes towards social policy.

As a psychologist submerged for twenty years in the depths of environmentalistic behaviorism, I was slow to identify the current that guided my work, especially since almost everyone around me was caught in the same stream. Behaviorism — that pragmatic, empirical, and distinctly American brand of psychology — has concentrated in the laboratory on the study of the learning process, while its public pronouncements have held out the promise of a science to remake man by applying its "laws" of learning and conditioning. The promises go back almost fifty years, to behaviorism's founder, John B. Watson, and are coming still. But in recent years, the experimental study of the learning process has run into data that fail to square with the prevailing environmentalism. One is, naturally, loath to overthrow what seems to be a scientific consensus for the sake of isolated findings on the behavior of pigeons or rats or monkeys. Moreover, it is easy enough to suppose that even if pigeons or rats or monkeys are less teachable than had been supposed, we could continue to assume perfectibility in society. The environmentalist dogma might be only 80 or 90 per cent right for man — instead of the 100 per cent that its high priests seem to promise — but it would still be the best *simple* truth we have, even if not quite the whole truth.

Eventually, however, my confidence in the environmentalist doctrine broke down, when my study of the subject of intelligence testing (or, more broadly, mental testing) persuaded me that the facts about people, far more than those about animals, point to the role of the genes in human society. Among its other distinctions, mental testing is the only major psychological subject that spans the two sides of the intellectual divide with a more or less continuous line of development. It got started towards the end of the nineteenth century and has prospered since (at least scientifically), so that its roots are in the early post-Darwinian era and its major discoveries in the environmentalist period, with which it has been profoundly out of joint. Over the same interval, other psychological topics have waxed and waned, or vice versa, depending upon how they squared with the prevailing intellectual climate. Theories of insanity, for example, have swung from the organic to the functional — i.e., from the constitutional to the environmental — and now seem to be beginning to swing back. Theories of education have shifted from the assumption of fixed innate mental faculties, which school merely exercises, to the assumption that school is nearly omnipotent in shaping minds. Theories of personality have abandoned their belief in innate temperamental differences — perhaps even correlated with physique — to an unqualified reliance on upbringing for the entire account of personality. While Sigmund Freud himself was keenly aware of the biological roots of personality, the psychoanalytic movement has drifted steadily towards total environmentalism. In contrast to all this, mental testing has evolved in an unbroken, although somewhat meandering, path, starting from the idea that individual differences in mental functioning can be measured, followed by the measurement of many such differences, of which some have proved to be largely genetic. Perhaps because mental testing has had the salubrious additional burden of producing a concrete and visible outcome — the test score itself — it has not waxed or waned with the prevailing dogma. What has waxed and waned instead is people's willingness to accept the hereditarian conclusions that testing unmistakably conveys.

In the early days of mental testing, individual differences in test scores were usually taken to show inherited differences between people. Given the Darwinian bias of the time, that was the natural assumption. Today's scholars see quite clearly the weakness of the early bias — genetics may have nothing to do with the similarity between parents and children. Parents give their children more than genes; they also pass on their outlook, their habits, their cultural milieu. Today, the parent-child similarity in scores usually gets blamed on cultural, rather than genetic, inheritance. Today's scholars do not see that their environmental explanation is every bit as rash a leap as the genetic conclusions of early testers. The similarity among parents and children (and among kinfolk generally) may be cultural, genetic, or both in any ratio of admixture. And to find out requires the methods of quantitative genetics, a set of powerful statistical procedures that can unravel how much the genetic and nongenetic factors contribute to the correlations among kinfolk for any measurable trait.

The first hints of this new statistical technology started turning up towards the end of the nineteenth century, and the pace has greatly quickened since. In regard to individual variations in intelligence-test scores, right from the start the genes predominated. In the early days, before about 1920, that was the expected finding, in accord with the prevailing intellectual climate. Later on, the finding became progressively more out of tune with the times, yet the results came out the same way nevertheless. One can search the scientific literature from one end to the other, as I have now done, and find no significant empirical challenge to the sizable genetic contribution to scores on intelligence tests.

In a practical sense, we all know perfectly well that people's endowments vary and that some of those endowments run in families. No one would be surprised to learn that the children of professional basketball players tend to be taller than average. Since basketball players are tall, since height is somewhat inherited, and since tall men probably marry taller-than-average women, the tall children follow naturally. In fact, we know that height is somewhat inherited only because it runs in families, for no one has seen the genes for height. For height, inheritance reveals itself in the pattern of family resemblances rather than in a direct scrutiny of genes. Of course, resemblances can deceive. If, for example, diet were all-important for height, then the resemblances between parents and children would be entirely nongenetic. However, foster children, sharing the same diet, should then resemble their foster siblings as much as ordinary children resemble their natural siblings, which is of course not the case for height. From just such comparisons, and many others, we gradually build up an estimate of the degree to which height passes through the germ plasm. We know how much to expect tall people to cluster in given families, which occasionally produce a basketball player when height combines with the other requisites.

So it is for any trait that plays a significant social role and has some genetic basis. And if, for the sake of discussion, one grants the possibility that mental abilities do vary at all genetically, then a powerful and surprising conclusion follows — namely, that society may segregate people into social groupings or classes based at least partly on biology. For if mental capacity is to any degree inherited, and if social standing reflects mental capacity, then social standing must be a mirror, albeit an imperfect one, of inherited ability. Moreover, as society equalizes the opportunities for advancement, which is to say as society becomes "fairer," by the ordinary standards of fairness, it will tend more and more to base its social distinctions on genetic grounds. In other words, if parents no longer can pass social and economic advantages on to their children — let us say, because of taxes and welfare and public housing and uniformly excellent public schools — they will instead contribute to their children's success and failure only by their genetic legacy.

The study of mental capacity has made the foregoing argument more than merely hypothetical, but our environmentalist bias has prevented us from noticing that society is willy-nilly subject to the laws of biology. There is evidence not only for the genetic ingredients in mental capacity but also in social status. Many of the means and ends of contemporary social policy fail to take into account those biological constraints, and they may consequently misfire. Equalizing educational opportunity may have the unexpected and unwelcome effect of emphasizing the inborn intellectual differences between people. It may instead be better to diversify education, providing multiple pathways instead of just one. Technology, while lightening some of the burdens of working people, may be creating others, in particular by wiping out those intellectually simple jobs that used to occupy the less endowed portion of the population. Even the effort to encourage social mobility may have its penalties. The biological gap between social classes will grow if the people who rise from lower to higher status are selected for their native ability, as is bound to happen to some extent. All this seemed to me interesting and important enough to set before the general public, hence my article "I.Q." in the *Atlantic Monthly* magazine for September 1971.

It still seems interesting and important, so I herewith press the case further, adding the detail and documentation that would have been inappropriate in a popular magazine. But in this preface I digress, to tell about the uproar that followed my article's publication. Not that tempests in academic teapots are all that noteworthy, but that this one may have some broader relevance as evidence of the power of the egalitarian orthodoxy.

To anticipate briefly: The furor seemed mainly to be the work of the student extreme left. And, indeed, the demonstrations and leaflets and general hubbub usually bore the identifying marks of the Students for a Democratic Society (and its affiliates), which at Harvard in 1971–72 could otherwise hardly muster a reminder of its former campaigns. On genetics and intelligence, however, the campaign raged on and on, as it has for years at Berkeley, where Professor Arthur Jensen teaches. This, however, is because the furor is not just from the extreme left; it is the response of a large segment of the academic community to a cherished orthodoxy threatened by heresy. But to prove my point, I should let the story speak for itself.

2

Within a few days after my article's publication on 19 August 1971, I received a letter from a member of the prestigious National Academy of Sciences, in which, among other things, he wrote: "Your heresy on equality of native intelligence will get you crucified if the experience of those of us who have expressed similar ideas is any indication." His experience was firsthand, dating from when he had written on the heritability of intelligence and had been treated like a moral pariah instead of like the scholar he actually is. I answered, about two weeks after publication, with guarded optimism: "So far, the reactions to my paper have been civil and, occasionally, gratifying. It is too soon, though, to start believing that the subject of inborn intellectual differences can be discussed rationally in the United States. More likely, I am enjoying the quiet of the summer doldrums."

My correspondent and I were not the only ones awaiting the

surge of counterreaction to my "heresy." In a generally accurate account in *Time* (23 August 1971) summarizing the main points mostly by direct or indirect quotation from my article, the writer added: "Many blacks and whites will be angered by his defense of intelligence testing because they believe that the racial characteristics it discloses reflect no real differences in ability but only the cultural deprivation of blacks and the cultural bias of I.Q. tests." That sentence, and the accompanying illustration, showing a white and a black child at school, seemed out of place, since my article took what might be called an explicitly agnostic stand on racial (i.e., black-white) differences in tested intelligence. For technical but compelling reasons, as touched on in my article, I believe that racial and ethnic group differences are hard to pin down as regards inheritance. My interest was not race, but social-class differences. It is true that there was an editor's introduction to my article that mentioned racial differences in I.Q., but that, too, avoided drawing any conclusions.

The *Time* writer was not the only commentator who gravitated towards the racial issue. (In fairness to him, he did write: "Herrnstein avoids the racial issue, concentrating on the relative influence of 'nature and nurture' [heredity and environment] in shaping intelligence.") For example, Alvin Poussaint, associate professor of psychiatry at the Harvard Medical School, appeared on the op-ed page of the *Boston Globe* at the beginning of December, when the uproar started to peak. Fulfilling *Time*'s prophesy of the anger coming, Professor Poussaint said: "Richard J. Herrnstein, professor of psychology at Harvard, may or may not be a racist. Perhaps it doesn't matter. Whether he intended it or not, he has become the enemy of black people and his pronouncements are a threat to the survival of every black person in America." Later on in his article, he asked rhetorically: "Shall we carry banners for Herrnstein proclaiming his right to freedom of speech? Why do these social scientists focus on white-black differences?" Inadvertently, I would suppose, Professor Poussaint was disseminating something other than the article I had written. Not many of my critics seemed to have read it. Perhaps not many people at all read it; it was, after all, rather long and tough going in spots. There seemed, in fact, to be a pattern — those who gave clear signs of having read it rarely got excited, while those who got excited had usually not read it. I spent a good deal of time during these months reciting its contents to people who had gotten upset over something I had not said. In any event, to the people who read Poussaint's précis instead of the original, he conveyed the false impression of an argument for significant, perhaps innate, racial differences. While he may have succeeded in directing the hostility of certain people towards the social sciences in general and me in particular, he was also spreading a message of racial inequality to those who wanted to hear it as well as to those who did not.

What is the relation between individual differences and racial differences? Perhaps this is the place to answer that question, for the temptation to slide from one issue to the other is apparently almost irresistible, yet the issues may not be fundamentally related. For my purposes, inherited individual differences said something interesting about the membership of social classes. To the extent that social groupings draw on heritable talents, they will also reflect biological constraints. Intelligence tests measure something both heritable and socially significant and are therefore the prime example of my point. It may, in fact, safely be said that in any complex, modern society that permits some degree of social mobility — capitalist, socialist, or otherwise — the social classes contain some element of genetic segregation for mental capacity. Or, to put it more simply, social position tends to run in families for genetic, as well as for social, reasons. Moreover, if a society minimizes the *social* inheritance of social standing (by sharply progressive taxes and the like), it will maximize the *genetic* inheritance. The connection between social position and genetic inheritance, intimate and direct as it is, cannot be legislated out of existence by any extant, or even any plausible, social reform. As long as genetic factors contribute to success or failure, status differences will have a genetic component.

In contrast, any statistical connection between race and social position could be a by-product of social forces, rather than of anything genetic. In the United States, for example, blacks bunch disproportionately at the lower end of the social scale (although progressively less so in recent years), as shown in average income and unemployment figures, geographical dispersion, average education level, and so on. But since both inherited and noninherited determiners contribute to a person's average social position, that disproportion could be the outcome of racial prejudice or other social disadvantages, instead of a genetic handicap. Yet, it is not hard to see why so many readers assumed that my analysis of class differences cryptically expressed the racial inferiority of blacks. The stages in that false assumption must have gone something like this: 1) I claim that social classes reflect genetic differences. 2) Blacks turn up in the lower classes out of proportion to their number in the general population. 3) Blacks must therefore have a disproportionate endowment of the genes that keep people in the lower classes. By the same fallacious line of argument: 1) Selection for a basketball team reflects a high genetic endowment for height and agility. 2) College graduates turn up disproportionately often on professional basketball teams, as compared to people who have not graduated. 3) College graduates must therefore be disproportionately tall and agile. The fallacy in both cases is to consider the genetic factor as the only one, so that the outcomes can be due only to genetic differences. Professional teams recruit from college teams; doubtless social classes also recruit less than evenhandedly.

We do not know why blacks bunch towards the lower end of the social scale, or, for that matter, why Jews bunch towards the top. Cultural factors, general surroundings, and racial discrimination complicate the analysis in unknown ways. Given the interest and the data, one might succeed in teasing apart the genetic and nongenetic factors for various groups, but such was neither my goal nor my subject. Instead, I hoped to call attention, first, to the genetic spine running through the social class continuum, giving it a rigidity that few social theorists, let alone ordinary laymen, recognize; and, second, to the likely stiffening of the genetic spine if society manages to wipe out the complicating factors like racial discrimination and varying social inheritance and give everyone an equal chance.

To be sure, not all my readers read the issue of race into my article. *Newsweek*'s writer, in contrast to *Time*'s, got the point and kept it. After summarizing the article carefully and accurately, he wrote: "But even if he carefully skirts the racial issue, Herrnstein's thesis seems bound to attract fervent opposition among both scholars and political radicals." On 23 August 1971, when *Newsweek* carried that sentence, there was still no sign of "fervent" opposition, for Harvard (with its "scholars and political radicals") was still on summer vacation. By the time fall classes began, the September issue of the *Atlantic*, containing my article, had been replaced on the newsstands by October's, and my two hundred offprints quickly were depleted. Nevertheless, on September 20 and 21, flyers were handed out at both Boston University and Harvard University. At Boston University, the leaflet's title was "Defeat the Bosses' Ideas," while at Harvard it was entitled "Fight Harvard Prof's Fascist Lies"; one leaflet was in elite type, the other was pica, but the texts were identical and both leaflets were signed by the "University Action Group," a new name to me at that point. I later identified the UAG as an assortment of SDS members and their elder sympathizers, plus members of the Progressive Labor Party.

The leaflet warrants quoting, for it sets the tone of the furor better than anything I could muster:

PROF. R. HERRNSTEIN SAYS,

"JOBLESSNESS RUNS IN THE GENES"

UNIVERSITY ACTION GROUP SAYS,

Fight Harvard Prof's Fascist Lies

If you are a teamster, riveter, power lineman, or salesclerk, Harvard Professor of Psychology Richard Herrnstein says that you have this type of job because you are not smart enough to do anything else. Further, if you are unemployed or cannot find a job, Herrnstein says it is because you might be part of the "low-capacity residue that may be unable to master the common occupations." In addition, he says that this inability to hold down even a low-paying job is inherited. If you are too stupid to find a better-paying job, chances are your parents had a hard time finding one, and your children will also have this problem. And, finally, since a large part of the low-paid or unemployed people are black, it follows that blacks are at the bottom of this "residue."

Herrnstein presents these fascist ideas in an article in the September issue of the *Atlantic*. (Lest someone think that our use of the term "fascist" is exaggerated, Herrnstein also 1. admits that there is a ruling class; 2. says that membership in this class is increasingly a reflection of superior intelligence; 3. the democratic ideal of equality cannot be realized but the dictatorship of an "intelligent" ruling class must continue; and 4. that this seems good to him. Furthermore, the logic of saying that many people are born too stupid ever to be socially productive is the elimination of these people by genocide or "genetic selection" by enforced sterilization. The only difference between this and Hitler's version is that the racism falls on blacks and other minority workers — currently the most heavily unemployed — rather than on the Jews.)

This article is not simply a new "scientific finding" that someone just stumbled upon. We think its publication is a conscious attempt on the part of the ruling class to justify the intensity of their recent attacks on working people. People are being fired and laid off so that big business can make more profits. Living conditions are going down for masses of people everywhere while business profits are going up. But, most importantly, people are fighting back. People have demanded and won more Medicaid in Boston and the right to strike for higher wages at GE during Nixon's strike ban.

The article in the *Atlantic* is an attempt to divide working-class from middle-class people and divide black workers from white workers so that they will not be able to fight these attacks together. The *Atlantic* is read mainly by teachers and middle-class white-collar workers. This article is a way of telling these readers that unemployment isn't the fault of the big businessmen who fire people; it is the fault of the people who are fired. They are "residue" — too stupid to hold down a job. This article tells the middle class that it makes no sense to ally and fight with the working class. It tells teachers that it is alright if they do not try to teach working-class, and especially black working-class, students anything. It is alright even if they beat them. After all, they are too stupid to ever learn anything anyway. This theory is presented as justification for racist teachers like Tom Boussey in Boston who beat a black student on a scar that was healing from a kidney operation, or the murder of the rebelling prisoners in Attica, and as a way of discouraging other people from supporting these courageous rebellions.

This article is not an honest piece of scientific research. Herrnstein has done no research on this subject. He only reports his ideas. This kind of thing is not new. In World War II, the ruling class needed women to work in factories. To help fill this need, the press published a number of "scientific" articles showing that children grew up better if their mothers spent some time away from home. When World War II was over, returning soldiers needed jobs. The ruling class had to get rid of some workers. Suddenly, the press published "scientific" research that said that children needed their mothers home all day. The ruling class is doing the same type of thing now.

FIGHT THIS KIND OF ANTI-PEOPLE SLANDER!!

These attacks on workers cannot be fought by simply talking about them. We have to build a movement that actively fights back. For example, two years ago, a similar article was published by Arthur Jensen, a professor in California. People made life so miserable for him that his classes had to meet in secret. And because there were masses of people fighting him and showing that his theories only divided workers from one another, people were much less willing to accept his slanders as "scientific truth." We think, in a similar way, that we should attack Richard Herrnstein for writing the present article and the *Atlantic* for publishing it.

Tuesday at 12:00 noon, we are going to demonstrate in front of the *Atlantic* offices on Arlington Street in Boston and make the following demands:

1. No more copies of this article should be distributed.
2. Richard Herrnstein should be fired from Harvard.

We want to build this movement. If there had been a similar movement in Nazi Germany when university professors were "scientifically proving" the inferiority of Jews, it would have been harder for Hitler to have exterminated the Jews.

Demonstrate at
The *Atlantic* Offices

Tuesday   Sept. 21   Noon
Corner of Beacon and Arlington

Fight Racist Lies
— University Action Group

University Action Group is an organization of university staff, graduate students, and faculty who are fighting racism, male chauvinism, and other anti–working class ideas and practices. For further information call 864–1293, 442–5633, or 354–1925.

I was to come to know well the style in the ensuing months. Name-calling — "fascist," "racist" — and paranoia — "We think its publication is a conscious attempt on the part of the ruling class to justify the intensity of their recent attacks on working people" — sometimes interlarded with misquotations and often capped off with unfriendly plans for my future — "Herrnstein should be fired" — are the ingredients of the "radical" literature I provoked. I hedge in "radical" with quotation marks because it was not really *radical*, in the sense of getting at the roots of anything, or even of being politically innovative. On the contrary, my radical critics were quite old-fashioned and doctrinaire, as leftist extremists go, which I will try to prove later on. Meanwhile, I call them radicals because that was how the press referred to them.

The demonstration heralded at the end of the first leaflet was uneventful, judging from the brief article the next day in the *Boston Herald-Traveler.* "Several dozen persons" assembled on the street in front of the offices of the *Atlantic,* but failed to persuade the editor to stop distributing my article or even to meet with them en masse. He did meet with a few representatives in his office, but they remained unhappy with the *Atlantic.* Nor were they pacified later by the *Atlantic*'s efforts at evenhandedness, as in publishing, in the December issue, over seven pages of letters to the editor covering the full range of reactions to my article.

A couple of weeks into the semester, the student daily newspaper, the *Harvard Crimson,* carried the news that the radicals at Harvard had decided to conduct "a fall offensive" against me. By that time, however, I was already well acquainted with the offensive, for the large undergraduate course that a colleague and I teach was attended by radicals at virtually every lecture, handing out leaflets to the two to three hundred students as they entered. One or two new leaflets were prepared each week, setting forth essentially the same points made in the document quoted above, in various permutations and elaborations, and usually calling for a "rally" at some appointed time and place. Most of the time, the radicals entered the lecture hall and took seats, although with one or two exceptions, they were not enrolled in the course. Generally, they were quiet while my colleague or I lectured, but occasionally they would ask questions designed to expose my "racism" or simply make pronouncements to that effect. Often they would approach the front of the lecture hall at the end of a class to denounce me or to accuse me of one thing or another, which, since the accusations were unfailingly false, I would deny. A few times, they hung large, angry placards around the room and scribbled further accusations across the blackboard.

My colleague and I tried to deliver our lectures as normally as we could, but we sensed we were fighting a losing battle. The atmosphere in the room was hardly conducive to the business of education, with students taking sides "for" or "against" the lecturer. My student allies were no more able to respond with proper objectivity to the material being taught than my opposition, even when it had nothing to do with intelligence or other points of controversy. Scholarly detachment proved to be a fragile, but crucial, ingredient of our course, for it was badly damaged, even though the radicals usually refrained from the flamboyant kinds of classroom disruption, which is why the university administration felt it could not do much to help us.

Meanwhile, the campus in general was deluged with the same leaflets, along with posters glued to fences, trees, buildings, and the walls of the local subway station. One of the most widely circulated posters is reproduced here, to exemplify further the level of debate. Each of the five quotations on this poster is to some degree a misquotation (one is not even recognizably from my article), and all are set in false contexts. (Also, I have never trained pigeons to hunt down Viet Cong, although I did for several years serve as a consultant to an electronics company that had contracts from the Defense Department. To my knowledge, that company did not so train pigeons either.) A year later, scraps of posters can still be seen on trees, fences, etc., but only by one with a trained eye.

At first, in the hope that open discussion might calm things down, I scheduled a public session open to all comers, to answer questions about my article. The meeting was widely advertised in the *Crimson* and in leaflets by the radicals. The radicals, plus a few hundred others, came, and some questions were asked and answered. At least at the beginning, the two-hour session consisted mainly of my trying to clarify, or simply explain, technicalities of correlational analysis and the measurement of heritability. Toward the end of the meeting, when the departure of most of the rest of the audience had left a high density of radicals, the tone began to deteriorate. Instead of questions, the comments from the floor started sounding more like accusations — of racism, of connivance with political reactionaries, of dishonesty in my presentation of data. But, even so, this was one of the better meetings of the year, for it was civilized enough to allow an actual exchange of remarks. (The stranger who threatened to stab me "some night in Harvard yard" as I was leaving the lecture hall, I took to be acting impulsively and not reflecting official SDS or UAG or PLP policy.) All in all, the radicals did not seem (at least to me) to have promoted their cause at the meeting, for they had little besides anger to confront me with. Nevertheless, within a few weeks, they were clamoring for another public meeting. I refused because I thought it would waste time, and I think they expected me to. They, in turn, made much of my "unwillingness to discuss the article." However, at no time did any of the more active radicals make any effort to discuss the issues with me privately or by mail or in the seminar on intelligence that a colleague and I were conducting during the fall semester. In fact, fewer than twenty students enrolled for the course, which was a detailed survey of the very issues that were being so hotly and publicly contested.

While intense, the radical campaign appeared to involve fewer than a dozen active radicals and perhaps another dozen part-time participants, not all of whom were Harvard students. Yet in some respects, they had the support of many students and faculty members, especially in regard to the touchy subject of inheritance

WANTED

FOR RACISM

RICHARD HERRNSTEIN
(ALIAS 'PIGEONMAN')

HERRNSTEIN IS A KNOWN ACCOMPLICE OF THE U.S. DEFENSE DEPARTMENT (HE TRAINED
PIGEONS TO HUNT DOWN VIETCONG). MORE RECENTLY, HAS TURNED HIS DUBIOUS
TALENTS TO WHOLESALE ATTACKS ON:

<u>BLACKS</u>: "A LOW-CAPACITY RESIDUE UNABLE TO 'MASTER EVEN THE COMMON OCCUPATIONS'"
"THE SAMPLE" (OF "GIFTED PEOPLE") CONTAINED "A SHORTAGE OF LATINS,
NON-JEWISH EASTERN EUROPEANS, AND NEGROES"

<u>WOMEN</u>: "WHATEVER (INTELLIGENCE) IS ,BOYS MAINTAIN IT BETTER THAN GIRLS"

<u>WORKING PEOPLE IN GENERAL</u>: "THERE IS A PERMANENT LOWER CLASS OF THE
UNINTELLIGENT." "UNEMPLOYMENT RUNS IN THE GENES LIKE ROTTEN TEETH."

HERRNSTEIN IS ARMED WITH THE 'PRESTIGE' OF HARVARD, TRUMPED-UP STATISTICS, AND
NON SEQUITIRS. HE SHOULD BE CONSIDERED EXTREMELY DANGEROUS TO ALL WORKING PEOPLE.

** DO NOT ATTEMPT TO APPREHEND ALONE

** BUILD A MASS MOVEMENT

COME TO HERRNSTEIN'S CLASS
MON., WEDS., 10 AM BURR HALL
HARVARD.

UAG

UNIVERSITY ACTION GROUP

and racism. And, without any doubt, the earnest abhorrence of racism was fueling much of the attack directed towards me, however misguided it may have been. Moreover, there were some well-intentioned faculty members who hoped to keep the facts on inheritance and society obscured behind a smokescreen of controversy, as I will try to show later. As in other recent campus issues, the radicals were acting out, albeit crudely, the sentiments of substantial numbers of "liberals," to use the imprecise, but familiar, designation.

Notwithstanding the sparse ranks, the radicals enjoyed abundant press coverage throughout the autumn and winter, primarily in the *Crimson,* but also in the *Boston Globe,* the *Washington Post,* the *National Observer,* and other major newspapers and magazines. The peak of local news coverage came in the 8 December *Crimson,* containing two full pages of editorial comment and various letters to the editor. The occasion was an ad published in the *Crimson* some days earlier and signed by one hundred and seven members of the Harvard faculty, disapproving of the radicals' tactics. The faculty ad had said, among other things: "The open-minded search for truth cannot proceed in an atmosphere of political intimidation," and "The entire academic community should make it plain that it regards such harassment [of me] as has occurred as not only an unforgivable attack upon legitimate scholarship but also as an assault upon intellectual freedom."

The majority of the *Crimson* staff, as well as a few faculty members, found the ad provocative and were therefore prompted to further commentary. The main editorial drew a distinction:

We are not convinced by the statement of 107 Faculty members which defends Herrnstein on the grounds of a vague "intellectual freedom." This freedom is apparently all-inclusive; at least, its proponents have not taken the time to define it. The boundary between ideas and actions is an academic distinction. The distinction, while fuzzy, is important. Generally, intellectual freedom guarantees that ideas will be opposed only by other ideas, and that a theorist will always have a place in the academic community. But in some cases, when theorists become policy-makers, the distinction between idea and action vanishes. In such cases — for instance, when social scientists commissioned by the government draw up plans to expand the Vietnam war — the phrase "intellectual freedom" no longer applies and the academic community can no longer offer sanctuary.

As these editorialists saw it, then, the question was whether to put my article in the category of reprehensible policy-making, like expanding the Vietnam war, or whether I qualified for "sanctuary." It was, apparently, not an easy choice, for, after all, my "prognosis of a hereditary caste of the unemployable could leave ominous thoughts in the minds of some readers," and, moreover, it was clear that "the threat of [my] ideas is more dangerous than the imagined threat of SDS and UAG [the University Action Group] to intellectual freedom." Furthermore, "by publicizing the uncertainty of the ideas and the potential harm of their implications, SDS and UAG have performed a service." But, even so, the majority of the editorial board concluded that "in this case, the concept of academic freedom applies. Herrnstein's opponents should limit themselves to the arena of ideas." I was awarded a qualified sanctuary.

All in all, the editoral majority had straddled the political center by mixing things up and contradicting itself, a not uncommon phenomenon in factional strife. The dissenting views on either side at least had the virtue of clarity. One hardy soul took the position to the right (by current university standards):

The Herrnstein article on I.Q. has created much genuine intellectual controversy around the country. . . . Perhaps there would be more here at Harvard if SDS hadn't refocused the debate. Far from deserving praise for "raising the issue," the members of the SDS-UAG anti-Herrnstein campaign — though their behavior lies outside the disciplinary reach of any rational system of academic justice — deserve the censure and contempt of all members of this community.

And, on the left, three editorialists saw my article as a call to political action:

> To consider the problem as merely a case of academic freedom is to mask the political implications of that position. The point is this: that it is a political, not a scholarly, act for which Professor Herrnstein is responsible. And it is political considerations that must decide the terms of any debate.

On the possibility that in a university ideas should compete on their merits, the leftists called forth an analogy:

> There is an intellectual Darwinism among us that believes if only all that can be said or thought is permitted, right thinking will out and the best will come to the fore. But history has shown that there is an economics of ideas as surely as there is an economics of goods. And the free marketplace of ideas is no more self-regulating, no more inevitably just than the laissez-faire capitalism which produced it.

I wondered what "history" these young men had learned (and from whom) to turn them against the free expression of ideas. They apparently did not know what history really tells us about a world in which ideas and data must pass tests of political or moral propriety.

In addition to the editorials, the *Crimson* also featured letters and testimonials that day from assorted groupings of students and others, somewhat in the style of resolutions of workers' and soldiers' soviets in Russia in 1917. One letter started off: "The graduate students of the History of Science Department, acting as a body, have voted the following" and then proceeded to enumerate the outcome of its deliberations. First, it said, the "racist, sexist, and anti–working class theories" of Herrnstein (and others) are "dangerous and unscientific." Furthermore, "such theories attack the legitimate aspirations of oppressed peoples for a decent life." Next, the *Atlantic*, the *Harvard Educational Review* (presumably for publishing the work of Arthur Jensen), and the *New York Times* (presumably for reporting the controversy on I.Q.) were to be condemned. And, finally, the faculty statement deploring the radicals' behavior was adjudged "pernicious, insensitive, and misleading." Other letters from individuals and groups, in that issue of the *Crimson* and others at around the same time, struck a similar note of condemnation, for my alleged poor scholarship, for my imputed motives in publishing, and for my supposedly right-wing politics. Various correspondents and articles weighed the suitable punishment for my transgression — should I be fired, censured, repudiated, or just answered. Yet, for all this attention, I waited in vain for a single substantive response to my article that might have led to some revision of my conclusions, or even to some interesting intellectual exchange.

Meanwhile, the handful of radicals plied their chores, leafleting at our class and around the campus. The leaflets added the tragic events at Attica prison to the list of my sinister powers ("Herrnstein's article is a premise for the murders at Attica," said a leaflet on 13 December.) In addition, in leaflets scattered all over the campus, they claimed to have discovered that I had intimidated or badgered students in my course for disagreeing with my article. The tales were false, as the people involved readily agreed, but not before the *Crimson* published a story headlined "SDS Charges Herrnstein Harassed Grad Students." The resulting rumors of my bullying of students were still circulating five months later.

With the Christmas vacation, the reading period (during which classes do not meet), and final exams coming, we were about to have almost a two-month recess, from 15 December to 7 February. Since the radicals used our classrooms as their prime base of operations, I anticipated a substantial, hopefully a lasting, improvement. That optimism proved to be unwarranted, as I first learned in the beginning of January, when a friend from a university not in the Boston area called to ask if I knew anything about the "National Convention Against Racism" scheduled for Harvard University at the end of March. I did not, so I asked him to forward whatever he had on the subject. A few days later I received from him a stack of leaflets including a brochure composed of quotations from my article and from the press commentary on it, followed by a call for a convention which, it promised, "will be an opportunity for people to get together and evaluate what we have been able to do by the time of the convention and make concrete plans to continue the campaign against racism." Some of the material identified itself as being the work of an organization called "Scientists and Engineers for Social and Political Action," which was a new name to me although it listed a Boston mailing address. Apparently sponsored by no particular organization, the convention organizers used as a mailing address only a Boston post office box number under the name "National Convention Against Racism." Whoever they were, I had become their symbol of racism, at least in the Boston area.

Along with the brochure on the convention came a document entitled "A Public Statement on the Herrnstein Controversy," which, my friend said, was also being handed out on his campus. This "statement" pronounced me a racist and proceeded in the now familiar style to misconstrue, willfully or otherwise, my article as a discussion of racial differences and the contemporary causes of poverty. The first topic I barely discuss, the second topic I do not discuss and barely mention. The statement, which was signed by five academics from the Boston area (including a Harvard professor of philosophy who has publicly referred to himself as the only Communist on the Harvard faculty, which I note because the Marxist connection will get some attention later on), ended with a plea for cash, to pay, it said, for further distribution.

Within days after my friend's call, the Harvard-Radcliffe chapter of SDS requested permission to host the annual convention of the national SDS, devoted, it said, to the fight against racism. From that point on, the "National Convention Against Racism" was one and the same as the 1972 national convention of the SDS. The Harvard administration first responded to the request bureaucratically, noting that the SDS had not paid its past debts, that it would have to advance a cash deposit in addition, and that the local chapter of SDS did not appear to be the actual host of the meeting, since the flyers being circulated made no mention whatever of the SDS, local or otherwise. The SDS responded in kind by paying some of its debts, quibbling about others, offering a deposit, changing the flyers to mention SDS specifically, and promising to appoint marshals who would assure good conduct by the visitors. Only the dates remained at issue. SDS was inviting participants for 30 March to 2 April. Harvard, on the other hand, said that since the last two days of March were regular school days, no classrooms could be provided for meetings, at least not until the late afternoon of Friday, 31 March. Furthermore, Harvard added in a brief display of firmness, SDS must prove that it has notified its correspondents of the change in the starting date, and it must revise its posters accordingly, or else forfeit its claim on a permit. To this the SDS would not assent, and, with increased fervor, continued to invite its adherents for Thursday morning, 30 March. The bickering over the date gradually petered out indecisively, finally resolving itself in a Tolstoyan fashion when it turned out that the Harvard administration had no real control over the starting date. A good many Harvard buildings are under the supervision of people who feel no obligation to stand by the central administration's position. In particular, dormitory heads, perhaps yielding to student pressure, issued one invitation after the other to the radical visitors. The convention ran from 30 March to 2 April, with no further response from the administration.

As long as Harvard actively resisted the convention, the radicals directed their efforts against the Harvard administration, but as resistance evaporated, they were back at me. For the two or three weeks of the main debate between the SDS and the administration, we lectured (classes now having resumed for the spring semester) in peace. When SDS had prevailed over the deans, my colleague and I were again lecturing to an expanse of leaflets instead of heads. However, the militancy of the leaflets had escalated, for now the SDS had more than merely a local interest in me. I and a handful of other academics were the theme of their convention. The base of operations had spread substantially, as I was soon to discover.

3

I had a long-standing date to speak to the staff and students of the psychology department at the University of Iowa about some of my research on the learning process in animals. A couple of weeks before my scheduled talk on 25 February, just while SDS was bickering with Harvard about its convention, the chairman of the Iowa department called to say that the radicals at his university were stirring up interest in my impending visit, and that the interest was not friendly. He was calling to give me a chance to think about what he saw as the three obvious alternative courses of action: cancel the visit, come as planned, or come and debate with the radicals to "defuse" the situation. I asked for a few days to think it over and to see the pertinent leaflets and articles in the student newspaper that he offered to send. The stirrings in Iowa City, it turned out, began when the student newspaper published verbatim the "Public Statement on the Herrnstein Controversy" mentioned before, except that their headline writer had retitled it as "Noted Psychologist a Racist, Sexist." Next came some letters to the editor defending my article by pointing out that it was neither about, nor took any position on, racial or sex differences in mental ability or the causes of contemporary unemployment or poverty; then, the inevitable counterreaction from the radicals. And it was also inevitable that at some point in the exchange, one of the radicals noted that I was scheduled to speak at Iowa and that I should be "confronted."

Soon leaflets were drumming up interest among those who might have missed the coverage in the student newspaper. One leaflet started off depicting me as a racist by means of a string of misquotations, ending with the following paragraph:

Right now at Harvard there is a growing student-faculty movement against Herrnstein to remove his cover of "scholarship" and expose him for the racist quack he is. They have made it impossible for him to spread his theory in public without controversy in the entire Boston area. In fact, he has said that he may not teach undergraduates anymore. Now he is coming to the Midwest to speak to students at the University of Iowa. Iowa City SDS has called a Midwest demonstration against Herrnstein, with people coming from all over this region to confront Herrnstein. The next day we'll have a conference to discuss ways to continue the fight against racism on our campuses. Come with us to confront Richard Herrnstein!!!!

The leaflet promised a "teach-in" on Monday before my talk on Friday, featuring the national secretary of SDS, then a rally and march just prior to the demonstration at my talk, followed the next day by the "Midwest Conference on Racism." It also reminded its readers of the national convention at Harvard and offered transportation to Cambridge. Among the stack of leaflets was one of the "Wanted for Racism" posters that had been pasted all over the walls and fences around Harvard Square. It was clear that there was at least enough coordination among these radical groups so that they could swap leaflets.

When I called back, I told the chairman of the department that I would not debate with the radicals, because they were obviously not interested in debating my article with me, as their pamphlets amply revealed. However, I said, I did not like to think that I had lost my right to move freely around the country; consequently, I preferred to come to give my talk on animal behavior. assuming that I could do so safely. And as to safety, it seemed to me and the chairman, the question was strictly numerical: a dozen or so radicals could do little more than shout, while a large angry crowd might be menacing physically. We agreed to wait to see how many turned up for the Monday teach-in, and also to get an impression of their intentions.

While awaiting the next report, I received a call from Princeton University, where I was scheduled to speak about two weeks later, also on my research on animals. As at Iowa, the Princeton radicals were using the student newspaper to let it be known that I was coming to speak and that they were planning to confront me for my "racism." A psychology professor (who had earlier been a colleague at Harvard) was reported in the newspaper to have called my article "at the least . . . evil, elitist, and racist." In another item, a radical was quoted as saying that I would be "forced" to answer questions, presumably if I did not answer voluntarily. I told my caller about the troubles at Iowa and asked to defer a decision about Princeton until after I had had some more experience with the problem. He was more than willing to wait. I also asked him to convey to the radicals my willingness to answer any questions they might care to send me. Although I believe my message was delivered, no questions have ever arrived.

Meanwhile, the teach-in at Iowa proved an uncertain harbinger. About one hundred people turned up, including an unknown number of university administration spies and curiosity seekers. The national secretary of SDS was quoted in the student newspaper as calling for a disruption of my talk, but she did not get universal assent from her partisans. While the speakers at the teach-in generally agreed on my villainy, there was as yet no consensus on a course of action to deal with me. I felt obliged to interpret the news optimistically and therefore agreed to come as planned. The chairman of the department appeared to be glad of that decision, for he did not want it to seem that Iowa had failed to meet the challenge of a couple of dozen radicals out of a university community well in excess of twenty thousand.

When I arrived in Cedar Rapids at about noon on Friday, the professor who met me at the airport conveyed reports of an influx of radicals from as far away as Chicago and Madison. Driving through the late winter countryside between Cedar Rapids and Iowa City, we talked about the crescendo of radical exhortation during the week. It was still not clear what the radicals were going to do, but whatever it was, they would have as much help as they could muster from a radius of at least a few hundred miles. I still felt obliged to continue as planned and spent a quiet couple of hours visiting the psychology department's laboratories and meeting some of the staff and graduate students. The outcome remained uncertain until about 3:45 — forty-five minutes before the scheduled time for my talk. We were then told by a campus policeman that a group of seventy-five to one hundred people had gained entrance to the lecture hall (whose capacity was variously estimated to me during the day as between two hundred and fifty and three hundred and fifty), in spite of the campus police who were supposedly stationed at the door to keep anyone out until just a few minutes before 4:30. By a few minutes after 4:00, the lecture hall was filled, but not with the usual audience for a technical, rather mathematical, talk on the learned responses of pigeons. The legitimate audience for that talk — whose world population falls considerably short of 350, let alone the fraction in and around Iowa City — was unlikely to turn up much before 4:25. And not only was the lecture hall filled, its walls were festooned with placards denouncing me as a racist, fascist, and so on, and speakers were already addressing the crowd — warming them up. The chairman talked by telephone to someone further up in the administration about the impending crisis and apparently received nothing more helpful than a suggestion that we move to a larger lecture hall, a suggestion I quickly rejected.

At the suitable time, the chairman, a professor in the department, and I walked to the physics building which housed the lecture hall. Going in through a back corridor, we could hear the crowd shouting and chanting but not see them. I had earlier been told that if during my talk I should suddenly "feel some urgency" about escaping from the hall, I should go through a particular pair of double doors, then through another single door, whereupon I would find myself in an alley at the end of which a green, unmarked car with a driver would be awaiting me. I was rehearsing those instructions mentally when we arrived at the small preparation room adjoining the hall. In the room were about eight or ten uniformed campus policemen and a smaller group of men in mufti. The crowd next door was noisily chanting "We want Herrnstein." The thought of the equations I needed to scribble on the blackboard to help explain my slides of graphs and data seemed hopelessly incongruous.

It was now clear that I was not going to be able to give my talk, even if I went into the hall and tried. Some observers estimated that there were seventy-five to one hundred active demonstrators in the room, both local and out-of-towners, and most of the rest were spectators attracted by the prospect of the confrontation. No doubt, most of the scholarly audience for my talk was locked out in the front corridor, along with the couple of hundred other people who arrived after the room was jammed beyond its capacity.

In the prep room, I asked the head of the campus police whether he could assure my safety if I went into the lecture hall. In effect, he said no. I asked further if it would help him do his job if I went in and allowed my talk to be disrupted, for it was obvious that the crowd would not accord sixty seconds, let alone sixty minutes, to the mathematical basis of learned behavior in animals. I was thinking of the growing legalism on today's campuses, especially in regard to leftist disruptions. Would my not going in make it impossible to prosecute or discipline the disrupters? Perhaps, I thought, I had a responsibility to allow my talk to be disrupted. The police chief (quite properly, now that I look back on it) answered that I should not concern myself with helping him do his job. "Then," I said, "let's call it off." I did not like calling it off, but I liked still less the bravado of going ahead with it under impossible circumstances. And there did seem to be some physical risk, since the police clearly had no control whatever over the situation. It may really have been quite an innocuous occasion, but at the time it sounded to me not unlike a Colosseum-full of eager Romans. With evident relief, the police hustled me through the door leading to the alley and there was the unmarked car as promised.

Except for some minor sidelights, including a foiled invasion by a couple of dozen radicals of the psychology department's cocktail party and a car ride to dinner during which we were tailed by two young men, in and out of parking lots and around blocks, my day at Iowa City was over. At the request of the university administration, I spent the night in a motel about twenty-five miles down the road instead of at the faculty club where I had been booked, driven there by the same plainclothesmen who had earlier helped me elude my pursuers.

One outcome of the episode was a decision to handle Princeton differently. I called my contact there within a day or two and asked what would be done to assure my safe coming and going, particularly in light of the well-publicized threat to "force" me to answer questions. I reiterated my willingness to answer questions by mail or in a scholarly setting. However, I was determined to give the talk I had been invited to give — on visual perception in pigeons — and not on whatever it was the radicals had in mind. He promised to inquire into the administration's plans for my visit. A call back a few days later provided no basis for optimism. Except for the department chairman's avowed hope that I would be able to give my talk, the university administration was going to do nothing. While I had no reason to doubt the sincerity of the chairman's hopes, I considered them futile and therefore canceled the talk. To keep the record straight, I wrote a letter to the chairman stating my reasons, the main portion of which said:

To put it most simply, I am unwilling to subject myself to an agenda arranged by the University Action Group. I would not speak in a room in which there were offensive placards or disorderly catcalls or other forms of disruption. I will not "debate" my article in the *Atlantic*, or even answer questions about it, in a setting that does not assure a civilized exchange of views. I have debated and discussed my article at numerous meetings of various sorts, but I will not do so with a group that engages in the crude and repellent, not to mention dangerous, tactics of the SDS and the UAG. I am convinced that those radical groups are not much interested in the contents of my article, at least judging by their leaflets and pamphlets. . . . Instead, it has become amply clear that my article is the closest thing to an issue that the radicals have at this time and they are trying to make the best of it. I can see no reason for cooperating. However, if someone at Princeton does have honest questions to ask about my article, he can write to me, and I will probably answer, as I have answered the several hundred people who have already written with coherent questions.

In your letter you distinguish between the expression of political views in a nondisruptive way and a demonstration that would make speaking physically impossible. The first, you said, is regrettable but permissible, in contrast to the second, which is intolerable. While I understand and sympathize with your effort to keep everyone's rights intact, permit me to say that since one cannot be sure ahead of time what form the demonstration will take, your evenhandedness puts on me the burden of risking intense personal harassment and even physical violence, if the radicals are to be taken at their word. (I am not unaware of the burdens on you, but they are different.) I do not think I should be asked to take such risks, especially when the issue is so transparently phony. Furthermore, I think it is Princeton's responsibility to assure a proper setting for my Colloquium. Had you told me that Princeton would take all necessary steps to protect the Colloquium, so that I could speak on the topic I have been invited to speak on, and keep out of, or remove from, the room people who were acting so as to impair the conduct of the meeting, I would be coming still. Under the circumstances, any less of an assurance is asking me to assume all the risks, which I can see no reason for doing.

The first public manifestation of the Princeton administration's reaction was a letter in the student newspaper, the *Daily Princetonian*, a day after my scheduled talk. (At Iowa, too, the administration became publicly active only after the event, perhaps with some justification since it had no obvious precedent to guide it.) Said President Goheen of Princeton: "The administration *can* do nothing 'to guarantee a scholar's right to speak' when the scholar withdraws from an invitation to lecture without exploring the extent to which he could have been assured a fair and uninterrupted hearing." Mr. Goheen was chiding (besides me) not the SDS or UAG, but a group of students (signing themselves as the "USA") for an ad they placed in the *Daily Princetonian* protesting the university's failure to assure my freedom of movement. The president's view of the matter was partly shared by a chemistry professor, who also had a letter in that issue of the student newspaper, identifying himself as a spokesman for the American Civil Liberties Union. Said Professor Jones: "That Professor Herrnstein was unwilling to discuss publicly his views on I.Q. is unfortunate, but does not really cloud the issue. His unwillingness is not grounds for threats and intimidation." Lest there be any doubts about the threats, the very same page of the *Daily Princetonian* featured an article by a spokesman for the radicals stating the plans for my visit: "Herrnstein [would] be allowed to deliver his talk uninterrupted, after which we would use the question period to challenge him on his racist, sexist, and elitist theories. If he refused to debate or answer questions, we would have blocked the doors of the room until he consented to speak on the I.Q. controversy."

Both President Goheen and Professor Jones also expressed some sympathy for me. And Professor Jones even expressed displeasure at the behavior of the radicals, which was, in fact, the main point of his letter. I, however, had begun to see that between the radicals and the liberal intellectual community there was a more subtle connection than I had at first appreciated. Thus, while Professor Jones deplored the conduct of the radicals, he also left some doubts about my character. And so did President Goheen, although the only conduct he publicly deplored at this time was that of the conservative students who placed the ad saying that Princeton had lost something by not assuring my safety.

At Princeton, as at Harvard, administrators could not make too public a display of solidarity with me (although privately I often received unqualified support). Their problem, some would admit, was not to seem to be defending my "views" while defending my rights. And that was a valid distinction, as far as it went. It was all the more compelling if the "views" are unpopular to a large fraction of the university, as the hereditarian case is under any circumstance. However, the radicals had promulgated a truly offensive rendition of my article — as racist, fascist, anti–working class, and so on. Even if an administrator had taken the trouble to read my article and had seen that the accusations were false — as several clearly did — he could ill afford to seem to be associating himself with it. Some of my more knowledgeable colleagues were caught in a similar position. They told me privately that they agreed with the article, but publicly they chose to remain noncommittal. By stirring up an angry controversy, the radicals had thus loaded the dice against the open exchange of argument and information, as President Bok of Harvard finally said publicly, after it had dragged on for seven months. I suspected that many liberal social scientists, wedded to environmentalism, were not keen for open exchange in any event, even when they genuinely deplored the radical tactics.

The aftermath at Iowa betrayed the liberal ambivalence towards me — or rather, towards what I had come to stand for in the public mind. Here, for example, is an editorial from the *Des Moines Register* on 1 March, five days after my visit:

The Hawkeye chapter of the Iowa Civil Liberties Union is distressed because student hecklers at the University of Iowa prevented a speech by a Harvard professor who wrote an article saying blacks are inherently less intelligent than whites. This view is considered "racist" by some critics.

All who value their constitutionally protected right to express themselves must share the distress of the Civil Liberties Union, but especially members of the university community.

Dr. Richard J. Herrnstein was to have talked at a psychology symposium about his experiments with pigeons which have led him to conclude that some groups of people are genetically inferior. One does not need to agree with such a conclusion, but any scientific opinion reached through application of scholarly methods deserves a hearing at a university — which is supposed to be a marketplace for the free exchange of ideas.

A letter to the editor seemed in order, which went off on 9 March:

Your editorial of 1 March takes a firm stand for democracy and free speech, a position of which I heartily approve. Like most decent people, you condemn the assault on civility launched by the SDS at the University of Iowa on the occasion of my visit a couple of weeks ago. Too bad, therefore, that the editorialist apparently used SDS leaflets as a basis for his characterization of my work.

Contrary to his assertion that my "experiments with pigeons have led [me] to conclude that some groups of people are genetically inferior," there is no connection whatever between my research on pigeons and my conclusions about groups of people. Furthermore, my conclusions about groups of people do not accord with his statement that "blacks are inherently less intelligent than whites." I have seen that false accusation in countless SDS leaflets, but it was a new and unpleasant shock to find it on the editorial page of your distinguished newspaper. . . .

On 15 March, most of my letter was published in the *Register*. In a personal letter, the editorial-page editor apologized for blaming my pigeon experiments for anything and denied having relied on SDS leaflets, saying instead that my article itself was the basis of the editorial. He did not, however, explain where in my article he had found a conclusion about racial inferiority.

Far more incompetent than the *Register*'s editorial was the one on KCRG radio and TV (Cedar Rapids) on 29 February:

A Harvard professor, Richard Herrnstein, was to have spoken at the University of Iowa campus last week. Highly vocal demonstrations caused him to think better of the project, and he left the campus without having been heard.

We do not agree with Mr. Herrnstein's theories of racial differences. They are shot through with faults, and his claim of scholarly work is belied by the fact that the article in which he explains his ideas appeared not in a recognized journal that might lend weight to his methods, but rather in a popular mass-distributed magazine.

But suspect as those ideas may be, even more damaging is the denial of any man the right of free speech. And those on the campus whose actions denied Herrnstein that right have done the cause of freedom more damage than the prattlings of a dozen racists.

To that, I drafted a response that brought an offer to read, or have read, a rebuttal over the station, which I did not bother doing.

The editorialist for KCRG was by no means the only person who disapproved of the publication in the *Atlantic*. In the year of Daniel Ellsberg, Jack Anderson, Senator Gravel, and the rhetoric of "the people's right to know," I ran into many others (particularly from the political left) who similarly thought my article was too "dangerous" for the public to see. What's more, my would-be censors were usually decrying the SDS version of my article, rather than mine; consequently, they were in effect popularizing racist conclusions and innuendos that no responsible scholar would countenance.

If the radicals' purpose had been to suppress discussion of the biological factors in society, as in my article, they could hardly have done better. The accusations of racism, fascism, sexism, and so on, plus the clamor over Iowa and Princeton, constituted a form of virtual censorship, directing attention away from the *contents* of my article and towards the issue of having published it.

The radicals had, in fact, felled a small flock of birds with the stones cast at my article. They effectively censored it, at least for a while, by obscuring its actual contents with their misrepresentations. They deterred other scholars from speaking out on the subject. Meanwhile, they won the sympathy, if not the downright approval, of numerous "liberals" for taking on the fight against "racism." An ad to that effect, congratulating the radicals for their antiracism, appeared in the *Crimson* over the names of several dozen Boston-area academics a few weeks before the SDS convention. The signers included some of the people leading the attack on my article, but also a fair number who no doubt took their word for my "racist" sympathies without bothering to read what

I had said. The radicals kept themselves continually in the news, despite their small and diminishing numbers.

The impending convention explains the escalation of activity during February and March. Shortly after the incident at Iowa, new posters started appearing in Cambridge, entitled "Racist Professor Chased Out of Iowa," boasting, in characteristically inflated terms, of their "victory" in Iowa City. In addition, there were some episodes at Harvard. I was shouted down at a meeting with a group of students who had invited me to discuss my article with them. Still more disturbing was an incident one morning after my lecture, when I was physically barred by some radicals from leaving my classroom and then, after I pushed my way out, was followed back to my office by a crowd of a couple of dozen noisy demonstrators. For about thirty minutes they dogged me as I vainly tried to get away from them, all the while shouting questions and accusations, and alarming the secretaries and other employees of the psychology department. Each incident made the *Crimson* and kept the cauldron of controversy vigorously bubbling. It kept up until the convention, and then promptly stopped. Since the beginning of April (1972), I have seen nothing of the handful of radicals who worked so hard to keep the furor going long after it ceased turning up anything new, let alone interesting. With the convention over, and with most of the actual contents of my article long since displaced in the public mind by the radicals' distortions, they have doubtless turned to other tasks, probably with some sense of relief.

Even now, however, it may be worth examining why the militants who knew what they were doing (which I would place at a minor fraction of even the small band at Harvard) bothered with my article. I believe that, for the knowledgeable few, more was at stake than the need for an issue this year or a theme for their convention (although both contributed). For them, deeper concerns were being expressed and these will continue to influence scholarship on the subject of innate human differences for some time to come.

4

The occasional hostility of Marxists towards the study of genetics is neither new nor localized at Harvard, Iowa, or Princeton. Its most egregious manifestation was T. D. Lysenko's domination over Russian biology during the Stalinist era. Starting in the mid-thirties, as Stalin was consolidating his tyranny, classical Mendelian theory and its successors suddenly became targets of political attack masquerading as scientific criticism. For example, in 1937, a Russian agricultural expert denounced the chromosome theory and its application to agriculture as a "fascist distortion of genetics and fascist utilization of genetics for political aims, inimical to the progress of mankind." That particular quotation (given in Zhores Medvedev's *The Rise and Fall of T. D. Lysenko*, 1969) turned up in the journal edited by Lysenko, one of the prime organs in the assault on modern genetics.

Lysenkoism might have remained nothing more than a historical curiosity had it not had the approval, and no doubt also the assistance, of Stalin. Lysenko's targets were both the theory developed by Mendel's successors and certain Russian biologists who were fruitfully developing an indigenous version. As a result, for about twenty-five years, both the subject and its honest investigators fared woefully in Russia. During that period, genetics in Russia was stunted, if not crippled, and the geneticists, particularly the most eminent ones, were driven out of their laboratories and institutes — by lack of support, imprisonment, and even execution. Until at least the mid-1950's, the Russian price for intellectual integrity in the study of genetics came cruelly high.

Genetics was no random victim of revolutionary zeal, for in its case, science and politics were at cross-purposes in Russia. The leaders of the Russian Revolution, committed as they were to remaking society in a hurry, had little sympathy for the idea that the hereditary endowment of living beings — from wheat to man

— was fixed in the germ plasm, largely out of reach of the influence of the environment, even the new socialist environment. Neither the random and unpredictable changes of genetic mutation nor the glacial drift of natural selection suited the purposes, let alone the temperament, of Marxist visionaries. And according to modern genetics, those are the only ways to alter the hereditary makeup of species. Even the ultimate Marxist goal, the "classless" society, was threatened by the possibility of genetic human differences. It is hard to argue that the "class struggle" can be resolved by a redistribution of wealth and capital, if it should turn out that something more than economics distinguishes the contending classes. And the well-established fact that the upper and lower classes differ in their psychological makeup, for example in their measured intelligence, plus the fact that intelligence, so defined, is substantially heritable, can be just such an unwieldy complication for Marxists, though by no means the only one.

The rhetoric of Lysenko and his associates, as recounted by Medvedev, himself a beleaguered Russian biologist, makes the affinity to my radical critics undeniable. Summarizing some of the atrocities committed during the late 1930's against the study of man's inheritance, Medvedev wrote: "The virtual ban on investigations in human genetics had very harmful consequences, not yet fully understood or assessed. The direct responsibility for this lies with those 'critics' who vulgarly identified human genetics with racism and fascism." Not only the vulgar accusations of "racism" and "fascism," but also the political paranoia can be found in both the Russian and the domestic Marxist reactions to the application of biology to the study of man, as shown by the following quotations. The first is from Lysenko, writing in 1947 on the Darwinian conception of human society in relation to capitalist countries:

Bourgeois science had to invent intraspecific struggle. In nature, they [i.e., the bourgeois scientists] say, within each species there is 'a cruel struggle for food, which is in short supply, and for living conditions.

The stronger, better-adapted individuals are the victors. The same, then, occurs among people: the capitalists have millions, the workers live in poverty, because the capitalists supposedly are more intelligent and more able because of their heredity.

We Soviet people know well that the oppression of the workers, the dominance of the capitalist class, and imperialist wars have nothing to do with any biological laws. They are all based on the laws of a rotting, moribund, bourgeois, capitalist society.

Next, a few sentences from a leaflet handed out in my class in October of 1971:

The emergence of Herrnstein as their ideological mouthpiece is itself a sign of the desperate state of the Rockefellers and other racist rulers. For Herrnstein offers only the stalest, exhausted thoughts and data. The thoughts are no more than warmed-over social Darwinism that was concocted a century ago to justify the oppression and class structure of society. . . . Herrnstein's ideas do not stand in isolation; they are attempts to render palatable acts of inhumanity and exploitation. As such they must be fought as hard as those acts themselves.

Lysenko's mentor, a Russian philosopher named I. I. Present, writing in 1962 on "Dialectical Materialism and the Problem of Genetics," further exemplifies the tone of the Marxist suppression of modern genetics, as follows:

The world bourgeoisie mobilized all ideological means of struggle against Marxism and those scientific theories which serve as a basis and consolidation of the dialectic-materialistic outlook. In particular, Weismannism-Morganism with its theory of an immortal hereditary substance was widely utilized. With the aid of this doctrine, attempts are made to justify the exploitation of workers, colonialism, and racial discrimination. At the same time it is used for proving the proposition that the moving force of social development is not the manufacture of material goods, not the class struggle, but the hereditary substrate, above all, of great personalities.

Like their precursors in Russia, my radical critics apparently also felt that one way to fight exploitation, colonialism, and racism was to undermine the study of human genetics. But the American branch struggles under substantial disadvantages, including the lack of official support from the government, the shortage of working cadres, and the unabated flourishing of "Weismannism-Morganism" — i.e., the genetic theory of inheritance — in biology departments. Not surprisingly, therefore, American antigenetics has, at least so far, been far less virulent than Russian. Here, the price for pursuing the study of human genetics is mainly unpopularity; there, it was truly prohibitive.

The boom in the experimental branch of genetics has resulted in a curious American inconsistency on the subject of human differences, not infrequently acute among biologists and geneticists themselves. And not just among Marxists either, for the environmentalism and egalitarianism that made genetics distasteful to the Russians also characterizes a vein within contemporary American liberalism. Thus, the very same people who one day abhor the idea of tampering with people's genes may, the next day, vigorously deny the conclusion that human society involves genetic factors. But if they really doubt the genetic ingredient in human affairs, why do they fret over genetic engineering? For some people, at least, politics explains the inconsistency. Liberals traditionally distrust the government, hence they are keenly reluctant to give away any power over the germ plasm. But, at the same time, contemporary liberals tend towards egalitarianism, which sometimes includes almost as firm a belief in innate human uniformity as Marxism, especially when they are thinking about society's problems. Genetic engineering runs afoul of the distrust of government; my thesis on hereditary classes runs afoul of egalitarianism. Yet, if genes were not socially important, neither would warrant such alarm.

The egalitarian-environmental outlook is the prevailing bias of American intellectuals in general. I doubtless share the bias myself, for I find it far more congenial to hear that some social problem will be solved by new legislation than to be told that society may have to face problems whose roots are biological as well as social. Biology as an instrument of social change — for example, eugenics — strikes me, too, as posing gruesome possibilities that may be worse than the problem being solved. No more than most of my fellow academics do I like the prospect of some people tampering with some other people's germ plasm. But while that awful prospect is, for the moment, hypothetical, my thesis sets forth a contemporary biological reality in society. While the inheritance of intellectual capacity may not be as alarming in principle as direct genetic manipulation, it is clearly more timely.

To make matters worse, I note that as society succeeds in equalizing opportunity, the genetic factors likely become relatively more important, simply because the nongenetic factors, having been equalized, no longer contribute to the differences among people. And to cap it off, my case relies only on well-documented findings, easily available in many standard textbooks. The novelty, such as it is, in my argument is to have brought those commonplace facts into coordination and shown that the outcome is lethal to all forms of doctrinaire egalitarianism, both Marxist and American liberal-academic.

Some of my colleagues at Harvard, like my stymied hosts at Iowa and Princeton, have been earnestly shocked by how crudely the radicals deal with those who write on the heritability of I.Q. Even committed leftists have expressed their sympathy and concern. Yet, the radicals have served well the egalitarian cause by deflecting attention away from the issues themselves. Insofar as public impressions are concerned, the radicals have protected the egalitarian position by isolating it from a confrontation with facts that would destroy its underpinnings. The sequence goes something like this:

1) Radicals denounce me (or others who bring the facts to public attention) as "racist," "fascist," and so on.

2) In response, the liberal "expert" deplores the crudeness of the attack, while expressing apparently scholarly reservations about the "questionable" logic or the "tentative" findings or the underlying "political" biases in the document in question. The lib-

eral expert's position appears to take the middle ground between the radicals at one extreme, and, for example, my article at the other.

3) The public, observing the range of views, also takes the intermediate position — in this instance, the liberal one. It concludes that the prevailing egalitarianism of American political philosophy has not yet run into unequivocal factual trouble. Since the inherent American bias is egalitarian to begin with, the outcome appears both natural and desirable.

An example of the sequence can be found in the exchange of letters between Herbert Kelman, Harvard's professor of social ethics, but a psychologist by training, and me that took place on the editorial page of the *Crimson* (9 February 1972). Professor Kelman's letter was addressed to a group of undergraduates who had criticized both me and those who publicly disapproved of radicals' tactics. Wrote Professor Kelman:

To the Editors of the *Crimson*:

This is a belated response to the letter from the Concerned Members of Dunster House of December 6, 1971, which you sent to the faculty signers of the "Herrnstein" statement, published in the *Crimson* of November 29. Though my name did not appear in the *Crimson* ad, I did indeed sign the statement. I asked to have my name added to the list when I heard about the ad, but by that time the statement was already in the press.

I happen to be critical of Herrnstein's article on many counts (as are at least some of the other signers of the statement). I challenge most of the article's premises; I disagree vehemently with the sociopolitical values that it reflects; I object to the policy implications to which it seems to point; and I feel that not enough was done to clarify the value premises and speculative nature of the article and to avoid its misuse by those who want to believe that Blacks are intellectually inferior.

It is not just despite these objections to the article, but indeed because of them that I wanted to be included among the signers of the statement protesting the nature of the attacks on Herrnstein. First, I am angry that SDS and UAG have (once again) undermined efforts to debate the issues raised by the publication of the Herrnstein article by diverting the attention of the Community to the nature of their attacks on Herrnstein. Second, I feel very strongly that those of us on the Left have the obligation and the self-interest to speak out against threats to academic freedom wherever they occur. As a frequent and active dissenter for more than a quarter of a century, I am only too well aware of the fragility of academic freedom and of the vital importance of maintaining the integrity of this principle.

I am deeply distressed that many members of the Community do not seem to realize what academic freedom means and what conditions are necessary to preserve and enhance it. I share your concern about the assumptions and implications of the Herrnstein article and I believe that it calls for response — including political response. If the form of the response, however, violates the principles of academic freedom — and, I might add, the associated principles of adherence to truth and respect for fellow humans — then it can only result in a net loss for the values that I believe we share.

HERBERT C. KELMAN

My response appeared a few days later, as follows:

To the Editors of the *Crimson*:

Herbert C. Kelman, Cabot Professor of Social Ethics, has answered my Dunster House critics on the editorial page of the *Crimson*. The gist of his statement is that he values academic freedom so highly that he would accord it even to me. "Those of us on the Left," he says to his partisans in Dunster House, must defend academic freedom. The Herrnstein article, he grants, "calls for response — including political response," but within the limits of academic freedom (presumably mine). I appreciate the protective impulse, but have some doubts about both its source and its goal.

First, however, whence the problem? Why does my article bestir our colleague, aside from the Dunster House petition? The answer, it appears, is that he finds much to criticize me for. He hints at six disagreements, which may be worth drawing more sharply than he does in his impressionistic sketch. Here they are, with my answers.

1) He "challenge[s] most of the article's premises." The main premises of my argument are that there are inherited differences in I.Q. and that I.Q. contributes, in some measure, and by some means, to what our society (at least) considers success. To those premises, I know of no significant empirical challenge. I should have heard of some by now if there were any. If some other premises were meant, Professor

Kelman should tell us what they are and how he challenges them, not merely that he challenges them.

2) He "disagree[s] vehemently with the sociopolitical values [my article] reflects." I am not sure I know what my article's sociopolitical values are, and I am sure I do not know what Professor Kelman thinks they are. Could it be that, like some of my other critics, Professor Kelman thinks I advocate that which I am trying to describe? When I call attention to the possibility of a society increasingly stratified according to biological factors, or to the social importance, if not the inevitability, of unequal distributions of wealth and status, I am not approving of them, nor, for that matter, disapproving of them. I consider my sociopolitical values, supposing for the moment that I have some, to be irrelevant. Let Professor Kelman show how my values have distorted, or even affected, my argument before he scolds me for them. Otherwise, he should let them be, as I do his.

3) He "object[s] to the policy implications to which [my article] seems to point." I drew no policy implications in my article because I felt it pointed nowhere very clearly. In other words, I felt that the data on I.Q., inheritance, and social stratification do not, by themselves, settle conclusively any of the weighty policy questions of the day. They bear on many such questions, but do not answer them. Apparently Professor Kelman agrees for note that he complains about what my article "seems" to imply. To whom should he complain, however? Not me, for I refrained from drawing such conclusions. Not the data, for they would be unmoved. The complaint, I believe, must be lodged with the one who draws the objectionable conclusions — in this instance, Professor Kelman himself.

4) He "feel[s] that not enough was done to clarify [the article's] value premises." Are these different from the sociopolitical values in item No. 2? The key value, personal, not sociopolitical, behind the article is my abiding conviction that it is better to know than not to know. In fact, I find it hard, albeit not impossible, to think of counterinstances, but none in regard to my article. If Professor Kelman advocates censorship of information concerning the topics covered in my article, he should say so.

5) He "feel[s] that not enough was done to clarify the . . . speculative nature of the article." Most of the article — the historical and empirical summaries — was not speculative, but as factual as I could make it. I continue to await substantive criticism. The speculative parts of the article were written in the form of conditional propositions — in fact, as a syllogism and several corollaries.

6) He "feel[s] that not enough was done to . . . avoid [my article's] misuse by those who want to believe that Blacks are intellectually inferior." To this accusation I can answer only by quoting myself. On the question of black-white differences in I.Q. scores, I wrote: "Although there are scraps of evidence for a genetic component in the black-white difference, the overwhelming case is for believing that American blacks have been at an environmental disadvantage. To the extent that variations in the American social environment can promote or retard I.Q., blacks have probably been held back. But a neutral commentator (a rarity these days) would have to say that the case is simply not settled, given our present stage of knowledge." Professor Kelman feels that that was "not enough," but he does not tell us what more he wants.

I agree with Professor Kelman that academic freedom is both fragile and precious. Furthermore, I agree that the SDS and UAG have "undermined efforts to debate the issues raised by the publication" of my article. I doubt, however, that Professor Kelman can see his letter as yet another form of intellectual suppression, albeit more polite and less deliberate.

By casting doubt where there are facts, by impugning my values and motives without substantiation, by conjuring up the specter of racism, he makes it all too easy for well-intentioned people to reject my argument without ever coming to grips with it. The obscurantism exemplified in Professor Kelman's letter has done more, in my recent experience, to "undermine efforts to debate the issues" than the SDS or the UAG.

R. J. HERRNSTEIN

In private conversation afterwards, Professor Kelman assured me that he would soon supply the particulars on his "challenges." At this writing, more than seven months later, I have yet to see any further details.

Another Harvard psychologist, Jerome Kagan, provided a good example of a liberal academic obscuring the subject of mental inheritance because its findings are troublesome. His article, "I.Q.: Fair Science for Dark Deeds," appeared in March 1972 in the *Radcliffe Quarterly*, following a statement by the *Quarterly's* editor condemning the "brutish" conduct of my radical critics while registering disapproval of my views. Professor Kagan's article was offered as an answer to those, like Jensen and me, who claim that the I.Q. is substantially heritable. Professor Kagan wrote:

Those who insist that I.Q. is inherited base their conclusions on a mathematical model of heritability which assumes that the statistical variation in I.Q. scores is additive, some of it due to genetic and some to environmental factors. That assumption is questionable and has been criticized by some psychologists and mathematicians. Hence, all one can say at the moment is that the genetic contribution to I.Q. is still unknown.

In other words — relax, for we experts are still scrapping over the technical minutiae. Of course, no layman can understand the points in dispute well enough to draw his own conclusions, for what does he know about "mathematical models" or "statistical variation" or being "additive" or not? But, in this case, it is possible to document just what Professor Kagan is alluding to as "questionable," for he is here drawing on the work of still another Harvard professor, Richard Light, whose then unpublished paper Professor Kagan was kind enough to send me.

In a technical article addressed primarily to biostatisticians, Professor Light grappled with the subtleties of estimating the heritability of I.Q. scores, with special reference to Jensen's conclusions. As Professor Kagan reports, Professor Light worries about questions of "additivity," "mathematical models," and so on. But whether Professor Light's doubts and reservations are well founded is, for this purpose, less important than whether Professor Kagan has accurately conveyed their gist to his nontechnical audience. Does Professor Light really find that the inheritance of mental capacity is questionable, or, at least, currently unknown, as Professor Kagan says in the *Radcliffe Quarterly*, as well as in some other recent articles?

Here is how Professor Light put it:

He [Jensen] is correct also in pointing out the existence of an important genetic component in human intelligence. Whether this component is 60 per cent or 70 per cent or 80 per cent is not clear, but it is quite clear that a large proportion of variance in children's I.Q. scores can be explained by knowledge of, say, their parent's I.Q. scores.

By a statistical argument that would be out of place here, Professor Light concludes that Jensen's estimate of 80 per cent for heritability *could* be too high, that it might, in fact, be as small as 63 per cent! After developing his case, Professor Light says: "The heritability component has now [by Light's special computations] been reduced to .63; the environmental component increased to .37. I have no reason to believe that these new proportions are 'better' estimates than Jensen's."

Professor Light's recalculation used a particular set of data on I.Q. which posed some statistical problems. But as regards the larger question of mental inheritance in general — the question that Professor Kagan was writing about — Professor Light unequivocally supported Jensen and his hereditarian conclusion: "To conclude, I believe that Professor Jensen has reviewed much evidence and argued very convincingly that a large proportion of the variation in children's I.Q.'s is genetically based."

Most people, even most academics, do not have the time, training, or occasion to work through the technical literature on a controversial subject. Instead, they must rely on professionals for a disinterested evaluation. From some professionals, exemplified here by Professors Kelman and Kagan, they learn that the inheritance of intelligence is "questionable." What they fail to find out is that the question is not whether I.Q. is heritable, but whether the heritability is 60 per cent or 80 per cent (or even more, according to some estimates). The public does not discover that the heritability of I.Q. is not a *new* finding, on which the burden of proof suddenly falls, but the standard, virtually uncontested (i.e., by conflicting data) finding since the first decade of mental testing. Estimates of the high heritability of I.Q. started accumulating in the technical scientific literature by 1910. With improvements in the statistical techniques of quantitative genetics and in the quality and quantity of intelligence testing, the heritability of I.Q. has doubtless become psychology's best proved, socially significant empirical finding. As regards the major, long-term social implications, it matters little whether the heritability is 60 per cent or 80 per cent, or even 40 per cent or 90 per cent, for, in any case, the more society equalizes opportunity, the more it will tend to drive the heritability higher, making genetic factors progressively more important.

Fortified by the spurious assurances of experts, other liberal academics plunged into the fray to hold the line against the unwelcome facts. A convenient example at Harvard was provided by an economist, Richard Musgrave. He, too, expressed unhappiness with the incivility of the radical assault on me and my article, but then used the occasion to register dubiety about my thesis and to protest the racial implications he detected. The exchange, again, was on the editorial page of the *Crimson* (20 January 1972), and again, personal conversation turned up no further specifics. The exchange consists of answer and rebuttal from each, as follows:

December 14, 1971

To the Editors of the *Crimson*:

As one of the signers of the recent faculty statement condemning the disturbance of Professor Herrnstein's classes and in view of the continuing discussion, I should like to add these comments to my earlier signature.

I signed the letter to join in reassertion of the principle that disturbance of classes cannot be tolerated and to protest the type of out-of-class agitation (involving misrepresentation of Herrnstein's statements, as reported in the *Crimson*) which evidently occurred. At the same time I feel that the article under debate — especially in association with the slanted editorial introduction — was unwise and to me objectionable. It should have been made clear therefore that the signers of the faculty statement included people (or at least one person) who felt that the article was neither of compelling quality nor merit and — in view of the hurt and disturbance to which it would give rise — of poor judgment.

Not being a geneticist, I will not pass on the question whether ability is inherited or not. Speaking as a layman, it would seem to me reasonable to assume that inheritance is one factor; but speaking as a social scientist with some experience with quantitative work, the evidence mentioned in the article seems to me to be extremely skimpy. Nor do I find evidence of a critical review of the quantitative procedures underlying the alleged findings by the author sufficient to lead me to accept his judgment that the case is indeed proven beyond doubt.

However this may be, the problem would not be conflict-laden if all people had green skin and were members of the same class, but such is not the case, hence the difference between writing on botany and writing on genetics. The crucial point is that propositions about inherited intelligence (applicable to *individuals* within *all* groups) are one thing, while conclusions about differentials in *average* intelligence among racial *groups* are quite another. The latter do not follow the former, yet it is easy to slip into the error that they do. Professor Herrnstein does not explicitly draw the second conclusion, and there is even a small sentence disclaiming it. Yet the whole setting of the article including its slanted editorial introduction leaves an overall impression that such a conclusion is suggested.

I do not see that the empirical data cited support such a conclusion with a degree of probability acceptable in a sophomore paper on statistics, especially if the massive environmental differentials between racial groups are considered. I therefore find it wrong to launch an article of this sort at the very time when the rectification of racial injustices of the past is the overriding concern of our country. Academic freedom, like other privileges, involves obligations as well as rights. These rights, as I see it, do not offer a franchise to write lightly, on the basis of the most sketchy evidence, on propositions which inflict severe injury on others as well as on the prospects of solving our tragic heritage in race relations.

Feeling this way, should I conclude that the type of protests which occurred were indeed justified? The answer is no because the university above all must be a place where discussion can be carried on in civilized terms. Yet it should have been made clear in the faculty statement from the outset that the signers included people holding the above view. Since it was not, I wish to do so through this letter.

RICHARD A. MUSGRAVE

December 14, 1971

Dear Professor Herrnstein:
I think it is fair to let you have a copy of the enclosed letter which I have mailed to the *Crimson*.

RICHARD A. MUSGRAVE

December 20, 1971

Dear Professor Musgrave:
Lest you confuse the skimpiness of the evidence in my article (for heritability of I.Q.) with skimpiness of evidence on the subject in general, I hasten to refer you to the following sampling:

1) Burt, C. The genetic determination of differences in intelligence: A study of monozygotic twins reared together and apart. *British Journal of Psychology*, 1966, 57, 137–153.

2) Gottesman, I. Biogenetics of race and class. In M. Deutsch, I. Katz, and A. R. Jensen (eds.) *Social Class, Race, and Psychological Development*. New York: Holt, Rinehart, & Winston, 1968, 11–51.

3) Honzik, M. P. Developmental studies of parent-child resemblances in intelligence. *Child Development*, 1957, 28, 215–228.

4) Jensen, A. R. I.Q.'s of identical twins reared apart. *Behavior Genetics*, 1970, 1, 133–148.

5) Jinks, J. L. and Fulker, D. W. Comparison of the biometrical genetical, MAVA, and classical approaches to the analysis of human behavior. *Psychological Bulletin*, 1970, 73, 311–349.

6) MacArthur, R. S. Some cognitive abilities of Eskimo, white and Indian-Metis pupils aged 9 to 12 years. *Canadian Journal of Behavioral Sciences*, 1969, 1, 50–59.

7) Noble, C. E. Race, reality, and experimental psychology. *Perspectives in Biology and Medicine*, 1969, 13, 10–30.

8) Vernon, M. Fifty years of research on the intelligence of deaf and hard-of-hearing children: A review of literature and discussion of implications. *Journal of Rehabilitation of the Deaf*, 1968, 1, 1–12.

9) Cattell, R. B. The multiple abstract variance analysis equations and solutions: For nature-nurture research on continuous variables. *Psychological Review*, 1960, 67, 353–372.

10) Erlenmeyer-Kimling, L. and Jarvik, L. F. Genetics and intelligence: A review. *Science*, 1963, 142, 1477–1479.

You should also look carefully at *Environment, Heredity, and Intelligence, Harvard Educational Review*, Reprint Series No. 2. You will find that the high heritability of I.Q. is generally accepted by virtually all workers who are conversant with the data on I.Q. and with the technical concept of heritability. They argue about details, but not about the large points.

As I understand your letter, you feel I should not write on a subject with deep social implications because dissemination of the truth may make certain social goals harder to obtain. I, in contrast, do not agree that the truth will make those goals harder to obtain. Moreover, I believe that the truth should influence our thinking in defining social goals. Now, you may dispute whether or not my article is truthful, but first I suggest you consult the large (and rapidly growing) literature on the subject.

R. J. HERRNSTEIN

January 11, 1972

Dear Professor Herrnstein:

Thank you for letting me have the list of references in the eugenics field. I did of course not intend in my letter to deny the possibility that intelligence is inheritable, but I was rather concerned with the inferences of the *Atlantic* article which might or might not be drawn therefrom for differences in average intelligence in racial groups.

I am sorry if I hurt your feelings with my letter, but sometimes such cannot be avoided in public discussion.

RICHARD A. MUSGRAVE

January 13, 1972

Dear Professor Musgrave:

Your concern for my feelings is generous, but rather beside the point. (I am, incidentally, feeling fine.)

Your letter to the *Crimson* said: "Not being a geneticist, I will not pass on the question whether ability is inherited or not. Speaking as a layman, it would seem to me reasonable to assume that inheritance is one factor; but speaking as a social scientist with some experience with quantitative work, the evidence mentioned in the article seems to me to be extremely skimpy. Nor do I find evidence of a critical review of the quantitative procedures underlying the alleged findings by the author sufficient to lead me to accept his judgment that the case is indeed proven beyond doubt." The fact of the matter is that there has been no dispute, at least among scholars who study the subject, about the substantial genetic component in the distribution of I.Q. scores in any population for which the relevant data have been collected. The main facts were already noted by Cyril Burt in 1910, although the precision of the estimates of sources of variance has improved greatly since then. My article in the *Atlantic* merely stated the scholarly consensus, with some representative findings. I have yet to hear of any significantly contrary evidence.

In your letter to the *Crimson*, you assume the scholarly mantle ("speaking as a social scientist with some experience with quantitative work") and then cast doubt on my description of the scholarly consensus. Given your letter, a lay reader has little alternative other than to conclude that the case for the substantial genetic role in the determination of I.Q. is still a matter of dispute. But that is a false conclusion, as you would quickly find if you surveyed the pertinent literature of the past 60 years, which I assume you have not done.

You also said in your letter: "I do not see that the empirical data cited support such a conclusion with a degree of probability acceptable in a sophomore paper on statistics, especially if the massive environmental differentials between racial groups are considered." To what "conclusion" do you refer? As I said in my article, there is a black-white difference in I.Q. (and school achievement) in the United States. While the difference may be more or less genetic, we do not, at this time, have the data to permit a further conclusion. I would be interested to know what statements on this subject (of a statistical character) you would rather have your sophomores make.

I fear I see too plainly what you are really saying. You would rather that human differences not be studied. Or, if the results come out wrong by your lights, that they not be made generally available. I could not disagree more. The study of human differences (individual and group, environmental and genetic) is an integral part of my subject, and my subject, like any other academic discipline, may properly be set before the general public in an open society. And not only do I disagree with you, I reject the tone of implicit moral superiority in your letter. I do not believe, and you have not proved, that free and honest discussion of human differences will promote racial injustice or retard its termination. And that, whether you recognize it or not, is actually the issue between us.

R. J. HERRNSTEIN

January 18, 1972

Dear Professor Herrnstein:

Your further letter has been received. In response, let me restate the purpose of my initial communication, which was to distinguish between two issues, i.e., (1) whether intelligence is hereditary and (2) whether if such is the case, the additional evidence of differential performance on intelligence tests justifies the further conclusion that there exists an hereditary difference in average intelligence between racial groups. Your responses deal very largely with (1) and you chide me for not accepting what, you say, is the proven fact of heredity, including, I take it, not only that inheritance is a significant variable in explaining intelligence but that it has overriding explanatory power. My purpose is not to debate this, as it is not the crucial point at issue. The crucial part, as I see it, is point (2).

While you did not draw conclusions thereon I was concerned with the tenor of your *Atlantic* article and especially its editorial introduction (which must have had your tacit assent) suggesting at least to this reader that the answer to (2) might well also be positive. The statement in your letter, that "while the difference may be more or less genetic, we do not, at this time, have the data to permit a further conclusion," leaves me with the same flavor. As close reading of paragraphs 5 and 6 of my letter will show, it was the support (or lack thereof) of this second proposition to which my "sophomore" quip referred.

As to the matters raised in your last paragraph, I favor freedom of research as much as you do, but I would suggest the following rule of conduct: When dealing with subjects of investigation other than human beings, let researchers feel as free to advance hypotheses as they wish, whatever the evidence (or lack thereof) may be; but when dealing with propositions so monstrous and destructive to human relations and the cause of human dignity as that of hereditary racial inferiority, let this freedom be tempered by the utmost caution and sense of responsibility. In the case of your *Atlantic* article this, it seems to me, would have called for a careful and extensive discussion of the existing lack of evidence on point (2) and of the considerable difficulties in overcoming it. I do not claim that my morals are superior; but I do believe that a moral as well as a scientific issue is involved.

RICHARD A. MUSGRAVE

There is no shortage of other examples when the radicals' tactics prompted a liberal to reach for the central position between the extremists of the left and the "right" (Jensen, me, or anyone else who publicly states the case for human inheritance). Professor Musgrave started by denigrating my facts, although he shifted his grounds in the face of my bibliography. But not many readers changed their minds, I would guess. In spite of sixty years of confirmation from thousands upon thousands of measurements, the hereditarian case still comes out in the media as a "new" and "provocative" and above all "questionable" "theory" about mental capacity. The hostility of the radicals, the obscurantism of some academics, the public silence of other academics, the one-sided coverage in the news, the increasing reluctance of scientific periodicals to publish hereditarian findings or scientific agencies to support hereditarian research — these are all signs of a political orthodoxy on human equipotentiality to which scholarship has become hostage. I believe it is an orthdoxy whose social costs we can no longer afford, and not just, or even mainly, because it chokes off honest inquiry.

The false belief in human equality leads to rigid, inflexible expectations, often doomed to frustration, thence to anger. Ever more shrilly, we call on our educational and social institutions to make everyone the same, when we should instead be trying to mold our institutions around the inescapable limitations and varieties of human ability.

CHAPTER ONE

Whence Testing?

The measurement of intelligence forced its way into America's public consciousness during World War I, when almost two million soldiers were tested by the army and categorized as "alpha" and "beta," for literates and illiterates respectively. The lasting effect of that innovation has not been the surprise at learning that the average American soldier had an intelligence equal to that of a thirteen-year-old, or that artillery officers were substantially brighter than medical officers, or any of the myriad other statistical curiosities. Even if those facts are still as true as they were in 1918, the lasting effect has been the mere use of the tests and their serious consideration by responsible people. For intelligence tests, and the related aptitude tests, have more and more become society's instrument for the selection of human resources. Not only for the military, but for schools from secondary to professional, for industry, and for civil service, objective tests have eroded the traditional grounds for selection — family, social class, and, most important, money. The traditional grounds are, of course, not entirely gone, and some social critics wonder if they do not lurk surreptitiously behind the scenes in our definition of mental ability.

But at least on the face of it there is a powerful trend toward "meritocracy" — the advancement of people on the basis of ability, either potential or fulfilled, measured objectively.

Lately though, the trend has been deplored, often by the very people most likely to reap the benefits of measured intellectual superiority. More than a few college professors and admissions boards and even professional testers have publicly condemned mental testing as the basis for selection of people for schools or jobs. The I.Q. test, it is said with fervor, is used by the establishment to promote its own goals and to hold down the downtrodden — those nonestablishment races and cultures whose interests and talents are not fairly credited by intelligence tests. These dissenting professors and testers are naturally joined by spokesmen for the disadvantaged groups. We should, these voices say, broaden the range of humanity in our colleges (to pick the most frequent target) by admitting students whose low college entrance examination scores might otherwise have barred the way. For if the examinations merely fortify an arbitrarily privileged elite in its conflict with outsiders, we must relinquish them. The ideals of equality and fraternity must, according to this view, take precedence over the self-interest of the American–western European middle class.

The issue is intensely emotional. It is almost impossible for people to disagree about the pros and cons of intelligence testing and long avoid the swapping of oaths and anathema. Yet should not the pros and cons be drawn from facts and reason rather than labels and insults? For example, is it true that intelligence tests embody only the crass interest of Middle America, or do they draw on deeper human qualities? Can we make practical predictions on the basis of a person's I.Q.? Is the I.Q. a measure of inborn ability or is it the outcome of experience and learning? Can we tell if there are ethnic and racial differences in intelligence, and if so, whether they depend upon nature or nurture? Is there only one kind of intelligence, or are there many, and if more than one, what are the relations among them? If the tests are inadequate — let us say, because they overlook certain abilities or because they embody arbitrary cultural values — how can they be improved? For those who have lately gotten their information about testing from the popular press, it may come as a surprise that these hard questions are neither unanswerable nor, in some cases, unanswered. The measurement of intelligence is psychology's most telling accomplishment to date. Without intending to belittle other psychological ventures, it may be fairly said that nowhere else — not in psychotherapy, educational reform, or consumer research — has there arisen so potent an instrument as the objective measure of intelligence. No doubt intelligence testing is imperfect, and may even be in some sense imperfectible, but there has already been too much success for it to be repudiated on technical grounds alone. If intelligence testing is to change, it must change in light of what is known, and more is known than most might think.

Mental testing was one of many responses within psychology to Darwin's theory of evolution. In fact, the connection here is intimate and direct, for the idea of measuring mental ability objectively was first set forth by Francis Galton, the younger cousin of Charles Darwin. Far more versatile (perhaps smarter) than his great cousin, Galton was a geographer, explorer, journalist, mathematician, eugenicist (he coined the term), and articulate essayist. In 1869, just a decade after Darwin launched modern biology with his *Origin of Species,* Galton published *Hereditary Genius,* which applied evolutionary thinking to the question of intellect. Galton noted, first, that men varied greatly in their intellectual capacity, and second, that various kinds of excellence run in families, suggesting that the basis of the capacities may be inherited. Going back through British history, Galton found that judges, statesmen, prime ministers, scientists, poets, even outstanding wrestlers and oarsmen tended, for each kind of endeavor, to be related by blood. The eminent families of Great Britain were taken as evidence of superior human strains, comparable to the natural biological variations that figure so prominently in the doctrine of evolution. Today, our sensitivity to the role of the environment (not to mention such mundane complications as money and family connections) make us skeptical of his evidence. Nevertheless, in the first flush of Darwinian social theorizing, Galton called for constructive change. The inheritance of human capacity implied "the practicability of supplanting inefficient human stock by better strains" and led him "to consider whether it might not be our duty to do so by such efforts as may be reasonable, thus exerting ourselves to further the ends of evolution more rapidly and with less distress than if events were left to their own course."

Galton was not much more content with the genealogical approach to mental ability than are we today. Within a few years, he was trying to test mental ability directly, but the problem was how to do it. In 1882, Galton set up a small laboratory in a London museum where people could, for a fee, have their hearing, vision, and other senses tested. Galton knew that mental defectives — idiots and imbeciles — often lacked sensory acuity, and he guessed that there might be a reasonably consistent relation between intelligence and sensory keenness in general. The effort to prove his hunch yielded useful and ingenious tests for getting at sensory acuteness — measuring the ability to distinguish between weights differing only slightly, to hear tones of high pitch, to detect heat and cold, to feel pain, and so on. But as it turned out, his hunch was wrong, or at least not right enough to be useful as a way of testing on a large scale.

Galton was soon just one of many scientists searching for a practical intelligence test, with no one much worried at this point about the ultimate definition of intelligence. Intuition and common sense set the standards as the few simple measures of sensory acuity gave way to a host of tests, some sensory and others drawing on other, more complex psychological processes. An American psychologist named James McKeen Cattell coined the phrase "mental test" in 1890 in an article recounting his studies at the

University of Pennsylvania on the mental abilities of students. In addition to simple sensory function, Cattell measured color discrimination, time perception, accuracy of hand movement, and memory, and he collected descriptions of imagery. People no doubt differed, but it was hard to know what to make of the differences. At that stage, interpretation of the data took second place to enthusiasm for gathering them. In 1893, Joseph Jastrow, a professor at the University of Wisconsin, supervised an exhibition at the Chicago Columbian Exposition where spectators could, and did, subject themselves to batteries of tests, including the estimation of the distance their finger had been moved by the examiner while they were blindfolded, and efforts, unblindfolded, at hitting the intersection of a pair of crossed lines with a blunt point, spiking a moving object, dividing a line into as many equal sectors as the examiner requested, naming the color of patches of cloth and paper, and reading letters and words exposed only momentarily.

Psychological measurement naturally took its place alongside anthropological, as, for example, in 1891, when the anthropologist Franz Boas tallied various things about 1,500 children in Worcester, Massachusetts, and included among the usual physical measures a few psychological ones — hearing, vision and memory. The memory test required the child to repeat right back as many as possible of a list of digits he had just heard, to reveal the longest list of numbers he could reliably and correctly repeat. The "immediate memory span" remains a feature on many intelligence tests for children. Another step in the evolution of mental testing was taken by J. A. Gilbert, whose study of 1,200 children in New Haven, Connecticut, two years later gave precedence to the psychological tests over the physical measures. By getting teachers' subjective impressions of the intelligence of the children in his study, Gilbert could look for objective indices of mental capacity that would correlate with common sense. He found that the speediest children in a simple game of pressing a button as soon as a light or sound were presented also tended to be the brightest, according to their teachers' evaluations. While reaction speed and brightness are not highly correlated by the standards of modern mental testing, it was indubitably a relation to be explored.

By the mid-1890's, testing had attracted so much attention that professional organizations began taking note of it. The newly founded American Psychological Association formed a committee in 1895 "to consider the feasibility of cooperation among the various psychological laboratories in the collection of mental and physical statistics"; in 1896 the American Association for the Advancement of Science instructed a committee of its own "to organize an ethnographic survey of the white race in the United States." The quotations in both cases are Professor Cattell's words; he was a member of both committees and was determined that the ethnographic survey for AAAS include some of APA's mental (and physical) tests.

For all the ferment, it was not yet certain that anything useful was brewing. There was spirit and energy in abundance, but there were as yet no indisputably good tests. It took the work of a French psychologist named Alfred Binet to make intelligence testing practical. In a key article written in 1895, Binet and his junior collaborator, Victor Henri, argued for mental testing based not on sensory and motor functions but on the psychological processes thought to be involved in intelligence. Instead of supposing that being smart is the outcome of having keen senses or speedy reactions, Binet argued that intelligence operates at its own level and that, therefore, a proper test must engage the person at that very level. As for what such tests might be, Binet, like everyone else in 1895, was just guessing. The article suggested a variety: tests of memory, mental imagery, imagination, attentiveness, mechanical and verbal comprehension, suggestibility, aesthetic appreciation, moral sensibility, the capacity to sustain muscular effort, and visual judgment of distance.

Binet criticized his contemporaries for their preoccupation with sensory and other simple processes, which, although fulfilling their desire for exactitude in measurement, had sacrificed the still more salient need for relevance. For Binet, exactitude was secondary. His pragmatism directed him to tests that sorted people out — for, whatever intelligence is, it varies from person to person. The sensory data did not distinguish among people as sharply as common sense required for a test of intelligence. Binet committed himself to seeking the tests that would do so, which was an undertaking that occupied the rest of his life. In the following ten years, Binet and his collaborators worked on mental testing in the psychological laboratory of the Sorbonne, using as their subjects mainly children from the schools of Paris and its suburbs.

The use of children was a happy accident, for it focused attention on the chronology of intelligence. Of all the countless ways one may want to distinguish between smarter and duller people, it may not seem especially insightful to choose the simple fact that during the first fifteen or so years of life, age confers intelligence (on the average). Thus, if an intellectual task sorted children according to their age, then it might properly be included in an intelligence test. In one experiment, for example, Binet tested over five hundred schoolchildren by reading them a sentence and then asking them to write down as much of the sentence as they could remember. Between the ages of nine and twelve (the ages tested), each successive grade of student did better, albeit slightly, than the grade younger. From this, Binet knew that the "sentence-reproduction test" could be taken as one measure of mental capacity. And knowing that, he could say that if two children of equal age differed in their sentence-reproduction scores, they were, other things equal, to some degree different in intelligence. One such test was, however, far from a usable measure of general intelligence, as Binet well knew. In another study, Binet was after tests that would capture in particular the difference in attentiveness between bright and dull children. He took some children rated by their teachers as the brightest and the dullest in a grade and subjected them to a lengthy series of tests, going from simple sensory discrimination to arithmetic and perceptual speed tests. A number of the tests worked, which is to say they distinguished between the two groups of children. In later studies, these tests were further refined for the purposes of sorting children. Even Binet's own two daughters were the subject of intensive study, culminating in a book called *The Experimental Study of Intelligence* (1903), in which the vital psychological facts about the teen-age girls were expressed as scores on their father's tests of word-writing speed, mental imagery, sentence completion, and so on.

As the years passed, Binet and others stocked a rich store of norms and measures of mental ability, based on many tests of many children. It was to Binet, therefore, that the minister of public instruction turned in the fall of 1904 when he wanted a better way to spot subnormal children in the Parisian schools. The children were to be put into special schools where they could be helped, but the first problem was to find them. If mental tests were any use at all, here was a task to prove it. Binet and his psychiatrist collaborator, Theodore Simon, decided to use a series of tests graded in difficulty, first standardized on normal children of various ages.

The idea of using mental age as the measure of intelligence has been obvious only since Binet thought of it, not before him, for it was one of those rare and elegant turns that make for historic innovation. First, he devised some tests that distinguished between children of different ages, on the average. However, he knew that at each age some children did better than their exact chronological peers. Those children, he had found, were judged by teachers to be bright or gifted. Conversely, other children did worse than their peers and were judged to be dull. Hence, Binet had established that if all one knows about a child is that he outperforms his age peers, he can be assumed to be bright. If his performance matches his age, he is probably an average child in intelligence. And if he underperforms, he is probably dull. As Binet well knew, the chronological approach to intelligence finessed the weighty problem of defining intelligence itself. He had measured it without having said what it was. It took a while to know whether the sleight of hand had in fact yielded a real intelligence test or just an illusion of one.

For their first practical venture, Binet and Simon drew up a progression of thirty tests covering the range of mental capacity. At the very bottom, the examiner simply noted eye-head coordination as a lighted match was moved across the field of vision; then he observed the making of grasping movements, the imitating of gestures, the following of instructions to touch various parts of the body, the naming of familiar objects, repeating sentences, arranging identical-looking objects in order of weight, constructing sentences to include three given words ("Paris," "gutter," "fortune"), and finally, the ability to distinguish between abstract words such as "liking" and "respecting." After some preliminary trials, Binet and Simon gave their test to about fifty normal children between the ages of three and eleven, thereby establishing the cutoffs for each age. Finally, using children already diagnosed by standard clinical procedures to be idiots, imbeciles, and morons, they found the corresponding criteria for mental disability in their series of tests.

Is a retarded child really the equal of a normal child at a younger age? For example, the average five-year-old passed the first fourteen tests, while the upper limit for an imbecile was to pass the first fifteen tests whatever age he was. Anyone who passed more was not an imbecile. Was Binet saying that a twelve-year-old imbecile equals a slightly brighter than average five-year-old? The answer is no, for Binet specifically denied the charge. The imbecile, he said, is *"infirme,"* the five-year-old is healthy, and their mental processes are in some respects different, even if the difference is not captured by his test. Nevertheless, the test did its job, for a twelve-year-old who tested at the five-year-old level was, indeed, retarded, while a five-year-old who did so was not (or at least did not seem to be at that time). As always, Binet's approach was doggedly pragmatic and empirical. He was picking out the retardates with his test more quickly, cheaply, and for all anyone knew, more accurately than ever before. The social benefits were self-evident.

The Binet-Simon test was put into use immediately, and almost as quickly was criticized for this or that item. But criticism was corrective, for in showing that some item was not, for example, distinguishing between three- and four-year-olds, the critic was opening the test to improvement. An ineffective item could be dropped, a useful one added, without in the least altering the kernel idea, which was to measure intelligence by a graded series of tasks ("stunts," Binet often called them). The tests and the criticisms were rooted in actual experience with ever-growing numbers of children, adding greater and greater empirical stability to the results. In America, Great Britain, Belgium, Italy, Germany, and elsewhere, the tests were being used and perfected. In a cheering counterexample to Gresham's gloomy law, good test items tended to drive out bad ones, and the better the test in sorting out children, the more it was used and improved. In 1908 Binet and Simon published a much-revised series of tests to be used for rating children in general, not just retarded children. In 1911 the final Binet-Simon scale came out; it was Binet's last work, for he died that year at the age of fifty-four. But the evolution of testing continued unabated and still does.

In the 1911 version, there were five problems which the average child of each age could just solve. Here, for example, are the five items for the six-year-old level:

1. Distinguish between morning and afternoon.
2. Define familiar objects in terms of use.
3. Copy a diamond shape.
4. Count thirteen pennies.
5. Distinguish between ugly and pretty faces.

And here are the five problems for the average ten-year-old:

1. Arrange five blocks in order of weight.
2. Draw two designs from memory.

3. Criticize absurd statements.
4. Answer comprehension questions.
5. Use three words in not more than two sentences.

A child who passes all the tests up to and including those for six-year-olds and none beyond has a "mental age" of six, whatever his actual chronological age. Suppose, however, that he passes all the tests up to but not including the six-year level and then passes only three at the six-year level and one at the seven-year level. His mental age is credited with .2 additional years for every item he passes beyond the level where he has passed them all. This child's mental age would be 5 + .6 + .2, or 5.8 years of mental age. If his chronological age were six years, he would be slightly below average; if five years, somewhat above.

Binet did not come up with the "intelligence quotient" (I.Q.) itself; this fell to the German psychologist William Stern to do soon thereafter. Stern saw that a child who is one year behind at the age of six is more retarded than a child who is one year behind at the age of thirteen. It is the *relation* between mental and chronological age that matters, not just their *difference,* and this relation is best expressed by the ratio of the two numbers. To get the I.Q., divide mental age by chronological age and multiply by 100 to get rid of the decimals. Thus, a six-year-old child who comes through with a mental age of nine is in these terms as bright as an eight-year-old with a mental age of twelve, both having the impressive I.Q. of 150. A child whose I.Q. falls as he ages may not be getting *absolutely* duller, only *relatively,* in comparison with his age peers. In fact, his mental age can increase as his I.Q. falls: he is getting brighter, just not fast enough to keep up with his increasing chronological age.

The I.Q. of 100 divides the population into two roughly equal groups. This is not a fact of nature but an outcome of how the tests were made. Binet and his successors picked and chose until they found items that the average child at each age could just pass, thus assuring that the average child's mental age equals his chronological age and his I.Q. is 100. The idea of a mental age assumes that mental growth is accumulative and consecutive, so that a child who has mastered the items at a given age level one year will (barring disease or trauma) continue to do at least that well as he ages. In this case nature, not the test-makers, meets the condition. At each age during childhood we can do intellectually what we have done before, adding competence rather than replacing it. Binet's idea for mental testing would not have worked for grubs and caterpillars, which appear to lose their grasp of burrowing and cocoon spinning as they become competent at flight.

In other respects, too, Binet fruitfully combined nature and artful design in his tests. Items on the test were included only if some children were ahead of their age in solving them, some behind, but the largest number was neither. Overall, the spread of performance conformed to the bell-shaped curve that statisticians call "normal," with about as many superior children as inferior, but with most crowding around the average. Many biological traits display normal distributions, so that the construction of intelligence tests has been guided by the expectation of normality. However, if the expectation were far wrong, I.Q.'s would not show the useful statistical properties of normal distributions to the considerable extent that they do.

Binet's ideas took hold powerfully and quickly. It was not only in France that the average eight-year-old child could just barely repeat accurately five digits read to him, for the Binet scale was readily exported to Belgium, Great Britain, America, Italy, and so on. The remarkable exportability of the tests was probably the first convincing argument for their soundness. Items that drew on bits of specific, seemingly arbitrary knowledge crossed national and linguistic boundaries as easily as the fundamental tests of memory and reasoning. It could be relied upon, for example, that the average nine-year-old would be able to name in order the months of the year. What does this say about the I.Q.? Should we downgrade a Papuan child, raised in New Guinea, if he cannot name the months? Clearly not, if his language has no such names or has some different scheme for cutting up the year. Some of the items on a test are specific to a culture, but that does not make them poor items. A given test is only for people drawn from the same general population that the test was standardized on. Even if it is hard to locate the precise boundaries of this general population, useful intelligence tests incorporate at least some of the material of a culture, lest they risk missing the child's ability to assimilate his surroundings. Virtually every child grows up in some culture or another, and his intelligence score (if that concept is to retain its ordinary meaning) must reflect his sensitivity to it. The Papuan child cannot sensibly be tested on a Western intelligence test. He would do poorly, but he would also do poorly in most other contacts with Western society. It would mean only that he was not meeting the underlying conditions of the test, which assume that he has been drawn from the standardizing population. Analogously, a child who gets a very high I.Q. after being drilled by parents or teachers on test items is probably not all that bright, and for the same reason. Like any other instrument of measurement, the I.Q. test must be used according to the directions. One does not use an oral thermometer after eating hot soup or sucking on ice cubes — not if one wants to know one's temperature. One may have a fever with a cool mouth, but the thermometer will not reveal it. So, the Papuan child may be bright or dull or average, but only a test applicable to his cultural environment can show which. It is not that "intelligence" itself is peculiarly European or North American, even if the instrument for gauging it is.

If virtually everyone shares substantially equal exposure to the opportunities for learning the answers, then culturally specific questions belong on intelligence tests. Consider, for example, the learning of month names. If "January," "February," and so on, turn up in essentially everyone's environment, a child who learns them early may be brighter than one who learns them later. To be sure, one child may have had a lucky early encounter with month names to put him at an advantage, but then such bits of luck should balance off. The sheer bulk of the typical intelligence test assures that lucky encounters will have minimal impact on the overall scores. The obvious and familiar counterargument to this holds that "lucky" encounters are not just luck, and that they account for most, if not all, of the differences in test scores between individuals and groups. For example, it might be said, some children learn month names early simply because their parents, aware of the importance of vocabulary items on intelligence tests, habitually drill their children. Or even if their intentions are not so cold-blooded, some parents doubtless tend to direct their children's early learning along the very lines assessed by intelligence tests. If those habits and tendencies in child-rearing turn up in certain social classes or ethnic groups or races more than in others, the counterargument goes on, perhaps group differences in tested intelligence are explained away.

In brief, this issue locates one battle line — the question of cultural bias — between environmentalist and nativist interpretations of intelligence. Even at this point, before evidence has been marshaled one way or the other, it should be clear that, given equal opportunities for prior learning, the answers to culturally specific items may tell us something about a person's mental capacity. Or, to put it negatively, cultural *specificity* is not prima facie evidence for cultural *bias*. On the other hand, different scores on an intelligence test are, in and of themselves, equivocal. They may reveal different genetic endowment or different past opportunities for learning or some combination of both. The issue can only be resolved by further information, bearing, in particular, on two distinct and fundamental questions. Can it be shown that the scores on intelligence tests reflect inheritance more or less than environment? Does a person's intelligence score make reliable predictions about his general intellectual performance beyond the test itself? Later on, we will survey what is known regarding both questions.

A person's I.Q. is a different sort of fact about him than his

height or his weight or his speed in the hundred-yard dash, and
not because of the difference between physical and mental attributes. Unlike inches, pounds, or seconds, the I.Q. is entirely a
measure of relative standing in a given group. No such relativism
is tolerated for the conventional measures. Gulliver may have
looked like a giant in Lilliput and a mite in Brobdingnag, but he
was just about seventy inches tall wherever he went. Relativism
is tolerated for the I.Q. because, first of all, we have nothing better. If the testers came up with something like a platinum yardstick for mental capacity, it would quickly displace the I.Q. But
more than this can be said for the I.Q. Because the group with
which a child is implicitly compared is effectively the entire population of Western society, there is great stability to the comparison. The I.Q. gives one's standing among the people with
whom one will live. And if it can be assumed that so large a
sample of mankind is reasonably representative of the whole, then
a relative measure is quite informative. An I.Q. of 100 would then
indicate average intelligence, compared to people in general and
not some small group; an I.Q. of 150 would denote high intelligence, and so on.

At around adolescence, people seem to stop acquiring new intellectual powers, as distinguished from new information or interests. For example, immediate memory span grows until the age
of fifteen, but not thereafter. The average person can repeat seven
digits at fifteen or at fifty. Other items in the Binet scale similarly
level off at about the same age. Thus, if one were to continue
calculating I.Q. in the same way, dividing a fixed mental age by
a growing chronological age, one's score would plummet, reaching (for the average person) I.Q. 50 at about the age of thirty
and I.Q. 25 at the age of sixty (assuming that the mental age is
stuck at fifteen). To avoid such nonsense, some other measure of
relative standing is often used for adults. Thus, instead of saying
that a man has an I.Q. of 130, say instead that he tests higher than
96 per cent of his peers, and then define the peer group. It can be
all American adults, or Caucasians, or college graduates, or mem-

bers of the United Auto Workers or the League of Women Voters. In fact, since the I.Q. is itself standardized on groups of peers (usually children), it and the percentile score are directly and simply translated one into the other.

Notes to Chapter One

The interest in human differences and their inheritance triggered by Darwin's epochal work, *On the Origin of Species by Means of Natural Selection, or the Preservation of the Favoured Races in the Struggle for Life* (1859), stayed with his cousin, Francis Galton, through most of his active intellectual life. Galton's most directly relevant works as regards mental testing are *Hereditary Genius: An Inquiry into Its Laws and Consequences* (London: Macmillan, 1869) and *Inquiries into Human Faculty and Its Development* (London: Macmillan, 1883). The early days of testing, following Galton's first efforts, have been recounted in J. Peterson's *Early Conceptions and Tests of Intelligence* (Yonkers, N.Y.: World Book, 1925), in F. L. Goodenough's *Mental Testing: Its History, Principles, and Applications* (New York: Rinehart, 1949), and, more briefly, in R. J. Herrnstein and E. G. Boring's *A Source Book in the History of Psychology* (Cambridge: Harvard University Press, 1965). The primary references for the works mentioned in the chapter — by Cattell, Jastrow, Boas, Gilbert, Binet, Simon, Stern — plus those for many others not named, can be found in these three secondary sources.

Except for the voluminous Binet and Simon, the primary references are as follows:

Cattell, J. McK. "Mental Tests and Measurements." *Mind* 15 (1890): 373–381.

Bolton, T. L. "The Growth of Memory in School Children." *American Journal of Psychology* 4 (1891–92): 362–380. (Containing a report of Franz Boas's work.)

Gilbert, J. A. "Researches on the Mental and Physical Development of School Children." *Studies of Yale Psychological Laboratory* 2 (1894): 40–100.

Philippe, J. "Jastrow — Exposition d'anthropologie de Chicago — Tests psychologiques, etc." *L'Année psychologique* 1 (1894): 522–526.

Stern, W. *Die psychologische Methoden der Intelligenzprufung.* Leipzig: Barth, 1912.

A biographical sketch of Binet can be found in G. A. Miller's *Psychology, the Science of Mental Life* (New York: Harper & Row, 1962).

Binet's technical papers are generously sprinkled throughout the first seventeen volumes of *L'Année psychologique* (1894–1911), of which he was editor. His obituary appears in Volume 18.

The use of mental tests by the armed services during and after World War I has been voluminously described in R. M. Yerkes's "Psychological Examining in the United States Army" (*Memoirs of the National Academy of Sciences* 15 [1921]), and in C. S. Yoakum and R. M. Yerkes's *Army Mental Testing* (New York: Holt, 1920).

expressed in a single number? Even granting that I.Q. is a measure only of relative standing, can relative standing be given in a
single number? Is Jimmy really altogether brighter than Johnny if
his I.Q. is higher? Perhaps Jimmy is brighter as regards A, B, C,
and D, but Johnny has him beaten on E, F, and G. Even Binet
admitted that intelligence was not just one thing; otherwise his
labors in creating a test would have been far easier. Once, when
he was speculating about the nature of intelligence, Binet mentioned the attributes of directedness, comprehension, inventive-
ness, and critical capacity, which he thought may vary somewhat
independently from person to person. Usually, however, he was
too busy with his practical goals to dwell on hypotheses.

Common sense, however, insists on a multiple conception of
intelligence. Some people are adept at words, some at numbers,
some at spatial imagination, some at visual or auditory remember-
ing, some at deductive reasoning, some at inductive inference,
and so on. We expect some people to be broadly talented, others
to be narrowly so, and still others not to be talented at all. To see
how such constellations of ability can be charted, imagine an
enormous number of different tests, covering the entire con-
ceivable range of mental abilities. And also imagine that large
numbers of people are willing to sit through them. Scores on some
tests would correlate with the scores on others. For example,
people with good visual imagery would tend to excel on pictorial
tests; those unendowed would do poorly. The correlation would
be imperfect because the tests would not call on visualization
alone, but visualization plus other things — knowledge of various
sorts, vocabulary, reasoning, speed, and so on. People who match
each other in visualizing may or may not match in those other
mental attributes. Yet, to the extent that people vary in their
visual imagery, and to the extent that some tests are better done
with the help of a keen mind's eye, there will be a cluster of intercorrelated scores. So it would go for other kinds of mental
ability as well. Tests calling on general vocabulary would give
high scores to people with large vocabularies, low scores to

people with small vocabularies. Tests calling for the inductive leap would favor those so talented and discriminate against the overcautious.

Given enough of this kind of data, the structure of intelligence would reveal itself in the pattern of correlations. But the hypothetical experiment has not been done, nor is it very likely, for it is simply too big and too costly. We do not have hundreds of tests covering every corner of mental functioning, and, if we did, there would not be thousands of people willing to sit through them. Instead we must sneak up on the answers, using the data collected mostly in practical settings — army classification, school and job placement, and so on. And we must rely on advanced mathematical procedures to help compensate for the inadequacies of the coverage of the tests.

Though well beyond the scope of this work, it may be worth noting that the mathematics grew out of another of Galton's inventions, a simple, albeit ingenious, measure of the degree of correlation between parents and their children as regards physical traits like height and eye color, for which there were already ample, reliable data. Galton's student and eventual biographer, Karl Pearson, refined and formalized his mentor's method into a quantity known since as "Pearson's product-moment correlation coefficient," a name that says something only for those few who need hardly be told anything about "product-moments" and the like. Unfortunately, anyone who wants to inform himself about intelligence testing must know at least a little about the correlation coefficient.

The correlation coefficient measures the correspondence between pairs of things in a less than certain, but not entirely chaotic, world. We may, for example, wish to know the degree to which men's hair length correlates with their ages. The relation obviously falls someplace between direct causality and sheer independence, and the correlation coefficient tells us where within that range. Imagine a group of men varying in age from fifteen on up, with hair varying in length from nothing on up. The question of correlation is really a question of whether the two traits — age and hair length in our example — go together in some systematic way. Are the men with long hair in general older than those with short hair, or vice versa, or do the two traits vary independently?

To answer the correlation question requires converting the measures of the two traits into comparable forms and seeing whether they do, in fact, vary together or separately. The comparable forms are deviation scores — numbers that measure how far above or below the average of each trait every individual falls. Age is expressed as deviations from the average age in the group; hair length as deviations from the average hair length in the group. Thus, a man whose age falls at the group average and whose hair length also falls at the group average would get deviation scores of zero and zero on the newly defined scales.

The hypothetical average person just described is identified as a in Figure 1, right at the average for both traits, which is set arbitrarily at 0. Figure 1 shows, in general, how age and hair length might spread out in a typical sample. Both traits follow the familiar bell-shaped curve of natural variation (the "normal" distribution, or the "law of error," to give two of its many names), in which the most common values cluster around the average, while the less common values fall off symmetrically above and below. The two distributions are marked off in units: -3, -2, -1, 0, 1, 2, 3 of "standard deviations." In all normal distributions, whatever they are distributions of, a span of one standard deviation above and below the average covers about 68 per cent of the cases. Two standard deviations above and below the average include about 95 per cent; three, about 99.7 per cent, or virtually all. In Figure 1, another hypothetical person, b, is shown at one standard deviation above the average age, but right on the average for hair length. A third possible case, c, is at one standard deviation above the average for hair length but at one standard deviation below the average age.

If the two traits were perfectly correlated, then each individual would fall at the same point for both distributions. Age and hair

Figure 1

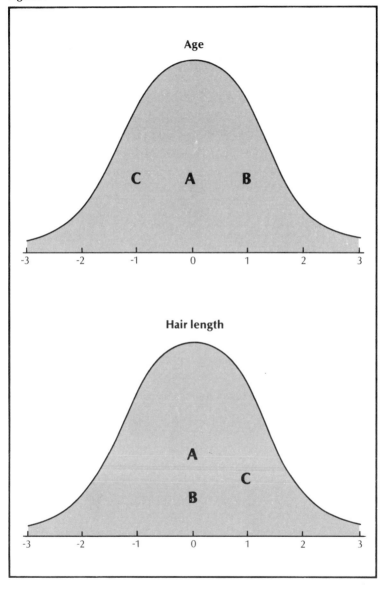

Normal distributions of age and hair length in a hypothetical group of men. The letters A, B, and C locate, in units of "standard deviations," three men in the sample.

length clearly do not covary so perfectly, for while *a* does turn up at equivalent points, *b* and *c* do not. For perfectly correlated traits, knowing the deviation score for one trait predicts exactly the same deviation for the other. When traits are perfectly, but *inversely*, correlated, prediction is still for the same deviation score, except that the sign is reversed. A value of $+1$, for example, would then predict a corresponding value of -1 for the other trait. But this perfect inverse correlation also does not hold for our example, even though one person, *c*, does fall on equal and opposite sides of the two traits.

Perfect positive correlation yields a coefficient of 1.0; perfect inverse correlation yields a coefficient of -1.0. In general the correlation coefficient connecting any pair of traits is the average prediction factor needed to get from the deviation scores for one trait to the deviation scores for the other. If, for example, the correlation coefficient between age and hair length comes out .5, then we must multiply the deviation score for hair length by .5 to predict best the deviation score for age, or vice versa. Hence, if some man's age is 1½ standard deviations above the mean age of the group, then the best bet for his hair length is ¾ of a standard deviation above the mean hair length for the group ($1½ \times .5 = ¾$). To get back to actual years and inches requires only a reversal of the original transformation of the scores into deviation scores.

The actual correlation between age and hair length would probably go just the other way, with increasing ages more often associated with shorter hair (especially if the group includes some baldness). If so, the coefficient would come out as a negative number — $-.5$, let us say — but would still be interpreted as before. To predict the deviation score on one scale, multiply the deviation score on the other scale by the correlation coefficient, following the ordinary rules of arithmetic as regards positive and negative signs. A man measuring 1 standard deviation *above* the mean in age most likely has hair ½ a standard deviation *below* the mean in length ($1 \times -.5 = -½$); a man (or rather, a boy) 2 standard deviations *below* the mean in age may be expected to be sporting hair measuring a full standard deviation *above* the mean $(-2 \times -.5 = 1)$.

For reasons that may not be obvious, the correlation coefficient simply cannot be less than -1.0 or more than $+1.0$. Those limiting values represent perfect correlation, with the two attributes invariably and exclusively linked together. In our contingent and complex world, we must usually put up with lesser degrees of correlation. Even if two attributes were perfectly correlated in actuality, we would likely not find out, since the inevitable measurement errors tend to push the obtained (as distinguished from the actual) correlation coefficient towards zero.

Zero correlation stands for independent attributes, or — to stick with the rule for interpretation given before — a deviation score for one measure, multiplied by zero, makes our best bet for the other measure a deviation score of zero, which is the average itself. As long as the coefficient falls short of perfect, the predicted quantity will be closer to the average than the predicting one, which is just another way of saying that when we multiply any number by a fraction less than one, we diminish it. Multiplying by zero, of course, diminishes it most of all. And since on the deviation scale, we measure in units above and below the mean, the process of prediction brings us back toward the average value.

This curious property of prediction across less-than-certain relations was Galton's crucial insight into correlation, which he called the Law of Regression, by which he meant regression towards the mean in prediction. The insight is as valid now as when Galton first noted it, and just as hard to accept. For example, no one doubts that height and weight have some substantial correlation — the taller the heavier and the shorter the lighter — or that the correlation is imperfect — some short fellows weigh quite a lot and some tall ones are built like bean poles. But it is not so easy to accept the logical implications of the foregoing: that a person who exceeds the average height is most likely to exceed the average weight by a smaller margin. And, at the same time, a person who exceeds the average weight is, similarly, most likely to exceed the average height by a smaller margin. Yet, the regression towards the mean is statistically unavoidable for imperfectly correlated attributes. It is not so much a law of nature as a logical necessity. The amount of regression for any instance depends on both the size of the correlation coefficient and the distance from the mean. With small coefficients and extreme cases, regression is maximal. As a given case gets closer to the mean, the regression effect for it diminishes. Or, as the coefficient gets larger, regression also diminishes, but for all cases involved.

One way to view regression is as a measure of the contribution of other sources of influence on the two attributes being interrelated. If the other sources are nil, then correlation is perfect and regression absent. However, as other sources (which we often cannot identify) impinge, the coefficient approaches zero and regression grows. In fact, given the coefficient, it is possible to state precisely the extent to which the two attributes covary, as compared to how much they vary independently of each other. It can be proved mathematically that the square of the correlation coefficient (i.e., the coefficient times itself) gives the proportion of covariation. With a correlation of .5 (plus or minus), the proportion of mutual covariation is .5 × .5, or 25 per cent, which means that 75 per cent of the variation in each attribute is unaccounted for by variations in the other attribute. With perfect correlation, the mutual covariation is complete, since one squared is one. The correlation coefficient and its square each has its own, somewhat distinct, purpose. For prediction across attributes, the coefficient is called for, since it tells us by how much to multiply the deviation score. But if the goal is to state the extent to which the variation in either attribute can be blamed on (or explained by) variations in the other, the coefficient must be squared.

Clearly an instrument of great power and broad applicability, the correlation coefficient nevertheless has its dangers, to which even "experts" occasionally succumb. First is the possibility that the attributes covary in some more complex way than the direct manner assessed by the coefficient. Suppose, for example, that an actual, detailed tally of the relation between age and hair length would reveal that the two go together for those now between the ages of fifteen and twenty-five, that they go in opposite directions for those between twenty-five and forty, that they are independent between forty and fifty, and that thereafter they again vary together. Pearson's correlation procedure misses all this detail as it cuts blindly through the thicket of complexity, coming up with a single index that expresses the average degree of direct and proportional interrelationship. To the extent that the interrelationship is neither direct nor merely proportional, it will be underestimated by the coefficient. Thus, note that the coefficient expresses the *least* association between the attributes, since it misses any complexity in the interrelationship.

The second danger, probably worse than the first, concerns the range of variation in the individuals being measured. The correlation coefficient measures *covariation* in two attributes. If one or the other attribute in a sample happens not to vary, then the coefficient will be zero. For a group varying little in, for example, age, the correlation between age and hair length would be minimal. It would be minimal even if in the population at large there were a respectable association between the two. Similarly, the correlation between I.Q. and professional success among college professors is also small, because of the restricted range of variation in I.Q. among professors.

In most statistical problems, we are trying to draw inferences about large numbers of cases based on the characteristics of much smaller samples. The Nielsen ratings, for example, strive to tally television viewing in the United States as a whole from the behavior of just a few thousand representative families. Much of the statistical theory — and the complex mathematics that supports it — concerns the procedures and limitations in reasoning from sample instances to general conclusions. In the case of correlation, the problem of limited variation looms large. One does not have to be a statistician to see why. Yet even statisticians and other experts sometimes forget that restricting the range may hide a correlation that a broader sample would reveal.

Knowing even this little bit about correlation should give some insight into how scores on different mental tests may be used to tease out the underlying structure of abilities. Consider, as a homely concrete example, a test of vocabulary on the subject of gasoline-driven engines. Someone who gets a high score obviously knows something about the subject. But given how people's interests go, such a person is also likely to do well on tests about other kinds of mechanical systems. Not in every case, to be sure, but often enough so that among a typical group of people there should be a statistically detectable correlation. Correlation among tests of mechanical subjects constitutes the prime evidence for the existence of what psychologists call "mechanical aptitude," although the correlation does not say how much aptitude a given individual might have. That comes later. Next, suppose doing well on the engine test turns out to be correlated with doing well on tests of three-dimensional imagery in general, which is not an unlikely outcome. Such correlations signify a "spatial aptitude," which permeates a wider range of mental activities than a specialized mechanical aptitude, yet the two both contribute to a person's score on the test. And, finally, since the engine test is a vocabulary test it may correlate with other vocabulary tests, reflecting verbal aptitude, general or otherwise.

Any number of aptitudes, of all degrees of specificity or generality, may contribute to one's score on a given test. A test that concerns only narrow and specific abilities will yield scores not very highly correlated with scores on other tests, except when the others focus on the same range. In contrast, the scores on a test that taps broad abilities should yield many notable correlations. As representatives of the two extremes, consider what one might expect from a test of musical pitch as compared to one of reading comprehension. But our expectations would be fulfilled only given certain tacit conditions, which it would be well to make explicit.

The prime condition is variation, for correlations can be found only where attributes vary. If a variety of tests are given to people who all happen to have the same level of verbal aptitude, then no correlation corresponding to that key factor will emerge. The reason is the range effect noted earlier, here applied concretely. If everybody is very good at words (or very bad, or all average — just as long as they are the same) then they will all do about the same on word tests. Whatever differences they manifest would, by assumption, arise in differences in other aptitudes — spatial, numerical, musical, and so on. Correlations between test scores would betray the covariation between individuals for those other traits. The musical ones would do well on music tests; the tin ears poorly, and the mediocrities mediocrely — which is a wordy way of saying that there would be a correlation.

Tables 1 and 2 are hypothetical correlation tables, consisting of fictional, albeit more or less plausible, results for two groups of people on six similarly fictional tests. Test 1 supposedly measures the intensity of a person's enthusiasm for professional sports; test 2, the person's position on the political continuum going from conservative to liberal; test 3, the person's command of standard literary information; test 4, the person's knowledge of the date of birth of famous historical and contemporary figures; test 5, the person's ability to identify the name and composer of a piece of music, given a few seconds' sample; test 6, the person's tonal precision in singing back a note struck on the piano. The made-up correlations in Table 1 supposedly summarize the test interconnections in a large, heterogeneous group of people chosen at random from the general population in the American Northeast. (Six tests can be arranged into precisely fifteen correlation pairs, no more and no less, occupying just half of the table minus its diagonal.)

One would expect a reasonably high correlation between tests 5 and 6 (music identification and intonation), for the score on one should predict that on the other, based on the individual's musicality. Hence the .8. The .4 correlation between tests 4 and 6

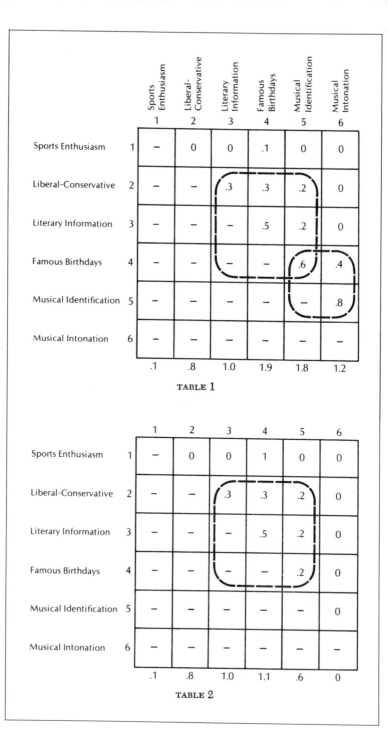

		Sports Enthusiasm 1	Liberal-Conservative 2	Literary Information 3	Famous Birthdays 4	Musical Identification 5	Musical Intonation 6
Sports Enthusiasm	1	–	0	0	.1	0	0
Liberal-Conservative	2	–	–	.3	.3	.2	0
Literary Information	3	–	–	–	.5	.2	0
Famous Birthdays	4	–	–	–	–	.6	.4
Musical Identification	5	–	–	–	–	–	.8
Musical Intonation	6	–	–	–	–	–	–
		.1	.8	1.0	1.9	1.8	1.2

TABLE 1

		1	2	3	4	5	6
Sports Enthusiasm	1	–	0	0	1	0	0
Liberal-Conservative	2	–	–	.3	.3	.2	0
Literary Information	3	–	–	–	.5	.2	0
Famous Birthdays	4	–	–	–	–	.2	0
Musical Identification	5	–	–	–	–	–	0
Musical Intonation	6	–	–	–	–	–	–
		.1	.8	1.0	1.1	.6	0

TABLE 2

HYPOTHETICAL CORRELATION TABLES,
SHOWING RANGE EFFECT

(famous birth dates and intonation), while not large by some standards, would catch the eye of any alert investigator. The explanation might well prove to be the substantial number of famous composers on test 4, which establishes a bridge of musical concern between the two tests. That bridge also makes contact with test 5 (musical identification) for the same reason. Why the test 4–5 correlation (.6) exceeds that for test 4–6 (.4) next calls for interpretation. The answer may prove to be the contribution of general educational level to scores on 4 and 5, but not on 6. If more educated people do better than less educated people on 4 and 5, then there would be a second bridge between those two tests, in addition to the musical one that they have in common with the 4–6 pair. In fact, general educational level seems to account reasonably well for most of the remaining correlations. Tests 3 and 4 (literary information and famous birth dates) both tap one's general knowledge, and so the expected moderate correlation. It is not as large as the correlation between 4 and 5 (famous birth dates and musical identification) because it lacks the common ingredient of musicality. The low correlations involving test 2 (conservative-liberal continuum scale) reflect the oft-claimed liberal bias of the northeastern American intelligentsia. From that bias, it follows that tests of, or related to, educational level (like tests 3, 4, and 5) will correlate with test 2. The unexplained .1 correlation between sports enthusiasm (test 1) and famous birth dates (test 4) proves to be due to nothing more than the smattering of famous sports heroes on test 4.

So much for the individual correlations. In general, the table reveals two main capacities or traits — musicality and general educational level — and a third minor one — sports interest. The main ones, enclosed in loops, overlap at 4–5 (birth dates and musical identification), where the correlation measures both common education and common musicality. The marginal totals at the bottom simply sum the correlation for each test. (Every test enters into five correlations, which are summed to give the totals.) They tell us how much a given test captures of the mental domain encompassed by the table. Test 1, on sports, captures little; test 4 (birth dates) captures most, for it reflects both educational level and musicality. Test 5 (musical identification) does too, but it reflects educational level less strongly. Tests 2 and 3 (political position, literary information) tap only educational level here, and test 6 (intonation) only musicality.

The hypothetical sample of people for Table 1 was assumed to have no special distinction other than being Northeasterners, resulting in correlations between political position (test 2) and measures of educational level (tests 3–5). Had our sample been from some part of the country where political position bears no relation to educational background, test 2 might well have turned up a string of zeros.

Table 2 sets forth yet another set of hypothetical correlations, differing from the foregoing in that the sample of people is presumed to be all musical prodigies of equal talent and training. The correlations in Table 1 have been revised accordingly, as one might expect for a group of people lacking any musical variation. Test 6 now correlates with nothing else, for the essential precondition for correlation — predictive covariation — is absent. Since everyone in the group has perfect intonation (let us suppose), we gain no predictiveness over intonation by knowing, for example, a person's birth-date score (test 4) or musical-identification score (test 5). And a correlation, it should be recalled, is just an index of predictiveness. Hence, test 6 now turns up a column of vacancies, not because the group lacks musical *ability*. On the contrary, it has lots of ability, but it lacks musical *variation*. Similarly, the correlation between tests 4 and 5 (birth dates and musical identification) has dropped from .6 in Table 1 to .2 here, because now only the covariation in educational level affords predictiveness, whereas before it was both educational level and musicality. Everyone in the group does reasonably well on test 5, with the better educated only slightly outperforming the poorly educated. Hence, the small, and equal, correlations between test 5 and the tests that relate to educational level (tests 2–4).

Table 2 turns up only a single major cluster — educational level — plus the small factor for sports interest. The column totals reflect the change, as tests 4, 5, 6, which had captured the musical factor before, have decreased to what they encompass of education and sports interest. Musicality would have passed silently through the correlational net for such a group of prodigies. Needless to say, it would also have been missed if the group had been uniformly nonmusical or uniformly middling-musical. The point is not where on the scale they are stuck, but that they are stuck somewhere.

The hypothetical examples should convey the potential of a correlational analysis, as well as its limitations. From a purely objective, statistical procedure, applied to data from groups of people, we can get the lay of the mental landscape in any given individual. When scores on different tests go together to some degree, we can safely conclude something psychological in common between them. How much in common, and what the something is — these are questions that would take us into even deeper technicalities, so we can note the questions without venturing to answer them. Suffice it to recognize that a test that taps many attributes will correlate with many other tests, but the correlation will rarely be large, unless the other test happens to tap substantially the same attributes. A correlation, as already said, measures mutual covariation. A test that covaries with many different attributes cannot covary much with any one of them. In Table 1, the highest correlation was in the column for test 6 (intonation), which measured the relatively narrow ability of musicality. In the construction of mental tests, one must choose between the sharply focused, narrowly predictive instrument and the broadly applicable, but relatively blunt one. Of course, the easiest compromise is to have both, but that may not always be an option.

The main limitation of a correlational analysis has been implicit throughout the discussion of Tables 1 and 2. Because of the range effect, the mental landscape depicted might omit some towering peaks if the sample chosen happens to contain no variation in respect to it. The hypothetical subjects for Table 2, being all equally musical, would have left no clue to their main talent. Only caution in the selection of subjects can defend against such oversights in real experiments. And, indeed, it may well be supposed that truly universal traits of mind have been, and will continue to be, overlooked and undefined in the study of intelligence. But that is hardly a great loss, for a truly universal trait lacks pragmatic relevance. If everyone has the same amount of it, why bother measuring it? However, between the implausible uniformity of a special talent, as in Table 2, and the fixed universal talents that we can overlook with impunity fall the actual problems of psychometricians. When someone says that I.Q. does not predict success, pointing to such eminences as the starred names in the *American Men of Science* (essentially the *Who's Who* of science in America) or to the membership of the National Academy of Sciences (the *Social Register*, on the same scale), they are falling victim to the main danger of a correlational analysis. The starred names in the *American Men of Science* and the members of the National Academy may not, in fact, be much brighter in I.Q. terms than their less successful colleagues in the sciences, but the entire group of scientists is recruited from a relatively narrow slice off the top of the distribution. Like the prodigies in Table 2, their brightness passes through the correlational net because of its relative uniformity. Among a more heterogeneous group — let us say, grown-ups who as fifth-grade children expressed some enthusiasm for science — one would doubtless find evidence for the predictiveness of I.Q., as a later section documents in some detail.

The other significant limitation of the correlational method has to do with interpretation of traits. In discussing Table 1, it seemed fairly clear that we were encountering evidence for the impact of educational level and musicality. But those designations do not emerge from the numbers themselves; they came from our prior insight into the composition of mental abilities and traits. Because we know that educated Northeasterners are liberal, that a good sense of musical pitch goes with a fondness for music, and so on, we can carve up the mental terrain in some plausible way, giving suitable names to the traits we identify. There is probably no great practical harm in our making the most of our intuition, but we should know what we are doing. In particular, we should know what the correlational analysis, in all its stark objectivity, tells us, and what we, subjectively, add thereafter. The analysis spots clusters of correlations, clusters of clusters (about which more later), and even beyond, if one cares to go after them. To this, subjective insight adds the familiar designations — "musicality," "educational level," "sports interest," and so on.

Even as Binet was developing the first intelligence scale, others were grappling with the conceptually tougher problem of the structure of intelligence. The entire story would be out of place here, but highlights may be worth noting. An Englishman named Charles Spearman resigned a commission in the British Army after serving in the Boer War and set to work on the problem. Taking the intercorrelations between scores on simple mental tests as his basis, he concluded that there was a "universal" intellectual capacity — which he labeled g for "general" — plus a host of minor, unrelated capacities of no great scope. Performance on any mental task — whether the learning of classical Greek in grammar school or the discrimination between musical tones in the laboratory — depended on two factors, Spearman thought, g and whatever else may be peculiar to the task (the s factor, for "special" or "specific"). Thus, for him, the universal factor permeated all intellectual activity in varying degrees, while the other factors were variously absent or present in any given task. To be smart, for Spearman, mainly meant having lots of g.

The universality of g, his theory's most notable feature, rested on an inference from correlation tables like the ones above, except Spearman used real data. It had caught his attention that the correlations between test scores for different sorts of tasks fell into a pattern that would make sense if the common ingredient were always the same underlying capacity. Hence if a given test entered into a few high correlations, it tended to have all high correlations, as compared to the other tests. Inversely, a test with a few low correlations tended to have all low correlations. In practical terms, Spearman found that the order of size of the marginal totals (see above tables) across the bottom of the columns pretty well matched the order of the size of the correlations across any row, clearly not the case in either Table 1 or 2. Such an orderly pattern of correlations suggests, although hardly proves, that some common factor accounts for all correlations, and some tests have more of it than others.

Going boldly beyond his data, Spearman concluded that the common factor exhibited not only suggestive, but absolute and quantitative universality, which meant that there could be only one capacity underlying any correlation between mental tests. The leap was reckless but not pointless, for Spearman was impelled to create the mathematical tools to extract from the scores on each of the various simple tests of the schoolchildren in his study how much could be attributed to g. While the findings have little importance now, the tools he invented proved to be the essential link between Francis Galton's insights into assessing correlation and the vastly more complex methods of "multiple-factor analysis," which is the contemporary term. It has hardly damaged Spearman's reputation that the evidence for a single, universal factor was soon overtaken by evidence for more complex theories of intelligence.

Following Spearman, the next big step was taken by L. L. Thurstone, an American electrical engineer who left a job in Edison's laboratory in East Orange, New Jersey, to work on psychological measurement. A long and illustrious career, covering the measurement not only of intelligence but also of attitudes, personality, sensory capacity, motivation, and the learning process, was the result. For intelligence, Thurstone effectively turned Spearman's method on its head. Instead of committing himself beforehand to a simple, general factor, he scrutinized the correlation table to discover how many general factors are implied by the pattern of intercorrelations. What was done loosely and verbally for the hypothetical numbers in Tables 1 and 2, Thurstone devised how to do rigorously and mathematically — thereby creating multiple-factor analysis. With the greater resolving power of his new technique, Thurstone subdivided Spearman's general factor, g, into a set of Primary Mental Abilities (PMA): spatial visualization, perceptual ability, verbal comprehension, numerical ability, memory, word fluency, and reasoning (inductive and deductive). These are just verbal labels tagged on at the end of a mathematical procedure that really has no verbal labels on it. It would be more precise (if less informative) to say that Thurstone found evidence for seven or eight separate factors or aspects of intelligence, and to leave it at that. Or better still, that Thurstone's method, when applied to the test batteries that make up a complete intelligence test, turns up eight or so factors contributing to the numerous intercorrelations.

An ordinary test battery may include as many as a couple of dozen separate tests — word definition, synonyms and antonyms, verbal and spatial analogies, arithmetic problems, number series, block assemblies, form learning, geometry problems, use of artificial languages, and so on. In Thurstone's first study of the Primary Mental Abilities, there were over fifty such tests, requiring fifteen hours to take. Factor analysis of the resulting giant correlation table located fewer than ten clear primary abilities, contributing variously to the scores on each test. A test heavily "loaded" (to use the standard jargon) on the word-fluency factor, such as a vocabulary test, gave scores highly correlated with all other tests similarly loaded, such as antonym-synonym. Some tests, in contrast, intersected several factors simultaneously, showing no single high loading, but several small or moderate ones. By trial and error and by calculated guess, tests are now chosen to give higher loadings on the primary factors. Fifty-odd tests can be replaced by a much smaller number with no significant loss of information and great savings of time and effort, if the new tests cover the mental domain with less redundancy, perhaps more directly, than the old ones. Factor analysis provides the guidelines for winnowing out the uninformative tests.

Once the tests themselves get calibrated, the people who take them are next. From the jumble of test scores, boiled down to their essential components, the person's mental profile can be constructed. The numbers measuring the various primary abilities reveal the person's strengths and weaknesses, relative just to each other or to other people. With more powerful mathematics and more abundant data, Thurstone's successors have teased out new factors. Like nuclear physics with its proliferation of elementary particles, the study of intelligence has suffered from its riches. Now there are experts who find evidence of over one hundred components in intelligence, and there is no sign of a limit.

Thurstone noted some intercorrelations among the Primary Mental Abilities. People who excelled, for example, in verbal comprehension were often high in word fluency. Other constellations also kept turning up. Such correlations among the factors themselves could signify that mental abilities are hierarchical, arranged in layers. At the very top, there may be a general intellectual power, like Spearman's g, pervading all mental activity. To be smart means having the power in abundance, to be stupid means having a shortage, so that all of Thurstone's PMA's will be to some degree correlated. At the next level down, the PMA's break into clusters involving either verbal abilities or numerical or logical abilities. Then there are the separate PMA's themselves, which vary somewhat independently despite their intercorrelations. In addition to being generally bright or stupid or average, people are verbal, numerical, imaginative, and so on. People can be so strong in one factor or another that they excel in some areas without any special abundance of g. And, inversely, some people may be so poorly endowed in one or the other factors that they appear occasionally incompetent, notwithstanding substantial g. Although the hierarchy seems like a plausible theory of intelligence, it will remain hypothetical until the experts agree on its specific features — which has yet to happen.

At best, however, we should expect no more than a convenient and useful approximation to the whole truth in any theory of mental faculties. The ascending layers, essential to the idea of a hierarchy, emerge only from statistical procedures that, to some degree, assume their existence in the first place. The mind is not really organized like the church or the army, with lines of authority and areas of responsibility. Instead, there is evidence, suggestive but not overwhelming, that the intellectual competence of many people in many intellectual pursuits can be reasonably well summarized by scores estimating their effectiveness in a variety of traits. Furthermore, the evidence reveals traits in generous and confusing abundance, at greater or lesser degrees of generality, all the way from g to solving anagrams, with an unknown number of levels between and beyond them.

For example, many studies, Thurstone's and others, uncover a verbal factor in mental competence. This shows up as a significant correlation among scores on tests involving words in some way. While such findings are beyond doubt, a large number of different sorts of word tests would soon show that verbal ability is not unitary — people may be better at some sorts of word tasks than others. Finding antonyms, doing anagrams, responding to nuances of meaning, completing sentences, and so on, reveal more than one-dimensional differences among people. Not surprisingly, therefore, verbal ability has been itself subdivided further. Thurstone, after his first pass through, offered three subdivisions of the verbal factor, distinguishing among the sheer understanding of verbal materials, fluency in fitting words to restricted contexts, and general ideational facility with words. The evidence for the subdivisions was found, as usual, in tables of correlations, showing that understanding varies somewhat independently of fluency and facility, fluency independently of understanding and facility, and so on. They do not vary entirely independently, of course, since they must at some level combine into the more general verbal factor out of which they emerged. Other studies find four verbal abilities or eight verbal abilities, more or less recognizably articulated into Thurstone's three.

People who are themselves not engaged in empirical sciences often find it next to impossible to picture, therefore to accept, the penumbra of uncertainty surrounding most scientific generalizations. The universal certainties of Euclid and Newton provide the irresistible, doubtless instructive, exceptions in science; that is why they call attention to themselves. More common by far, especially in the inchoate science of psychology, is the theory whose virtue is a pragmatic predictiveness over some more or less limited range of events, beating out vying theories by a hairsbreadth of accuracy or elegance here and there. It is only at this more modest level that we can claim to have made sense out of the complexities of the intellect with the model of the hierarchy.

The sheer complexity of mental capacity guarantees room for alternative descriptions. A recent and promising substitute for the hierarchy is J. P. Guilford's "structure-of-intellect" theory. A long series of studies of mental aptitude during and after World War II persuaded this eminent student of psychological measurement that there was a more useful way of expressing the relation between the various aspects of intelligence. While granting that abilities varied somewhat in scope, Guilford remained skeptical that the narrower ones were in any meaningful sense included within the broader ones, which seemed to be implicit in the notion of hierarchy. Thus, the narrow ability to do anagrams may be correlated with the broader one of verbal facility in sentence completion, yet not be a subdivision of it. If both activities call on various skills, then their correlation may be traced to some common ingredient, rather than to a hierarchical ordering. Furthermore, Guilford remained unimpressed with the evidence for universal g, the keystone of the concept of hierarchy.

In place of the hierarchy, Guilford offered the insight that the factors extracted by the mathematical procedures created by

Thurstone and his successors could be classified three-dimensionally, by answering three questions about each factor. First, what sort of mental *operation* is involved in the factor? The answer, Guilford claimed, could be reasonably approximated by a choice among five alternatives. Either the factor called upon (1) cognition — the immediate awareness of information, or (2) memory — the storing or fixation of new information, or (3) divergent production — the generating of logical alternatives from given information, or (4) convergent production — the generating of a logical conclusion given some information, or (5) evaluation — the comparing of items of information as regards their appropriateness to some standard.

The second question asks what sort of information gets processed by the operation in the first question. When we are cognizant of something or memorize something, what are the *contents*? Here the answer gets chosen from among four alternatives. Guilford suggested a choice among (1) figural — information organized sensorily, like visual images or scenes, sounds, impressions of movement, and so on, or (2) symbolic — information carried by arbitrary signs, like numbers, letters (not combined into words, which turn up in the next alternative), codes, musical notation, and so on, or (3) semantic — information of the conceptual variety most often, although not necessarily, carried by words, or (4) behavioral — information arising from nonverbal sources in human contacts, pertaining to the state of people around us. The last category, the "behavioral," used to be called "social intelligence" in the early days of mental testing and has been relatively neglected in comparison with other categories.

Having sorted out the mental *operations* from their *contents*, Guilford completed the analysis with the list of mental *products*. These embody the alternatives that answer the third and final question: what sort of outcome follows from operations upon contents? The products may be either (1) units — segregated items of mental work like a specific word or a certain image, or (2) classes — collections of units sharing some property, or (3) relations —

the connections between items at any level, such as "bigger than" or "next to," and so on, or (4) systems — a coherent body of information bearing upon something like, for example, a knowledge of baseball, or (5) transformations — changes in preexisting information, or (6) implication — the association of previously unrelated items of information.

With his three-dimensional scheme, Guilford hoped to harness the burgeoning diversity of mental factors to a relatively simple and acceptable framework. The five operations, four contents, and six products yield one hundred and twenty distinct abilities ($5 \times 4 \times 6 = 120$) to be uncovered by testing and factor analysis. If the scheme has merit, it should be possible to garner evidence for a distinct ability to, for example, see the relation between words (i.e., *cognition* of a *semantic relation*) as distinguished from seeing the relation between visual figures (i.e., *cognition* of a *figural relation*). In fact, that particular distinction is old hat in mental testing. The capacity to pick up verbal analogies (man is to animal as oak is to tree) can be, and has often been, separately tested from that of spatial relations (|||| is to □ as ||| is to △). The two abilities, by Guilford's scheme, differ only in regard to contents, the one semantic and the other figural. Yet they should be, and are, somewhat distinct in the sense that people may be adept at one or the other without being adept at both.

Some pairs of abilities differ only in the operations involved, or the products, instead of in the contents. For example, the task of naming as many round and hard things as possible in a given time exemplifies the *divergent production* of *semantic units*. If, instead, the task is to pick from a list of words — e.g. "cross," "button," "tennis ball," "yardstick" — the one best qualifying as round and hard, the ability changes to the *evaluation* of *semantic units*. The change from the operation of *divergent production* to that of *evaluation* defines a measurably different task. Still other pairs of tasks differ only in the third dimension, i.e., in the products.

Even as it answers some questions, Guilford's system of classification raises others, to which he is by no means insensible. Any real mental activity almost invariably calls on various sorts of operations and contents simultaneously, and yields somewhat equivocal products. But the powerful procedure of factor analysis, brought to bear on the outcome of carefully conceived tests, has uncovered so far ninety-eight of the one hundred and twenty abilities predicted by the model. All twenty-four abilities involving the operation of cognition (the four contents times the six products) have been empirically demonstrated, some more exhaustively than others. For the operation called memory, only eighteen of the twenty-four have been demonstrated, for none of the abilities involving both memory and behavioral contents have yet been pinned down. Doubtless, some of those gaps, as well as some of the others, will be filled by new studies, but some may prove obdurate. It may well be that mental activity simply does not sort itself into a distinct capacity for the *divergent production* of *figural relations* or the *evaluation* of *behavioral systems* (to pick two gaps as of 1971).

Like any application of factor analysis, this one too presupposes some of what it later uncovers. The selection of the various dimensions and their components guides the design of tests and the interpretation of results. Guilford could have conjured up other dimensions in addition to, or instead of, his three, or other components for them, and have done perhaps as well in finding evidence for the resulting abilities, which could be quite different from the ones he has chosen. In that sense, the "structure-of-intellect" theory can be accused of arbitrariness. In its defense, however, it could be noted that getting any new form of measurement off the ground — physical as well as psychological — requires a hefty tug on the bootstraps. A theory of measurement receives support when someone actually engages in putting it to use, but the practical use calls on the theory to prove its worth. Without practical use, the theory may seem vacuous; without the theory, practical use may seem trivial or meaningless. Guilford's ninety-eight factors successfully plugged into the operations-contents-products scheme amply shows that the theory has merit. Knowing people's strengths and weaknesses in those factors could be usefully informative, and not just in the obvious practical applications of intelligence testing for school and job placement. While predictive power is bound to be somewhat enhanced by batteries of scores instead of a single index like an I.Q., the long-run gain from Guilford's taxonomy may be more abstract, especially if the practical gain cannot justify the extra cost and time involved in administering and grading the many extra tests that his scheme calls for. The theoretical issues surrounding intelligence — its relation to heredity and environment, its variation among individuals and groups, its growth in childhood and decline sometime thereafter, its contribution to social stratification — take on added depth and complexity with intelligence broken down so finely. Abilities doubtless vary in their heritability, their development, their social impact, and in other ways too, even though the I.Q. as a whole can be fairly simply characterized. The beginnings of a fine-grained analysis can already be discerned in the recent technical literature on intelligence. One should therefore bear in mind that beneath the picture drawn concerning the I.Q. in later chapters dwells the potential for great complexity. The two levels of description do not exclude each other, any more than classical mechanics in physics has been replaced by the laws of thermodynamics. Psychology, like physics, should eventually provide a series of descriptions of its subject, varying in fineness of detail, but meshing together coherently.

As noted before, Guilford's skepticism about the universality of g contributed to his dissatisfaction with the hierarchy of abilities. While not questioning the evidence for broad, general factors in correlation tables, he did challenge their import. He noted that the g that emerged from a factor analysis depended on the particular group of tests being analyzed. In one study, the verbal analogies score might come out being correlated with g by .6, while in another, the correlation might be only .3. The differences were not just the usual sampling errors, either. Instead, the problem clearly had to do with the collection of tests in the various studies. Verbal analogies combined with, for example, tests of number series, vocabulary, antonyms and synonyms uncovered a different g from that obtained when combined with tests of, for example, visual analogies, form-block problems, picture classification. Because of the difference, the test common to the two situations — verbal analogies — appears to be equivocally expressive of g. How, Guilford argued, could g be considered universal and pervasive if each set of tests gives us a unique characterization of it?

The criticism, while trenchant, does not lead inexorably to Guilford's theory. Raymond Cattell has formulated his own original and significant explanation of the instability of g, within the framework of a theory of intelligence. This British psychologist — no relation to James McKeen Cattell, the American who coined the phrase "mental tests" in 1890 — studied under Charles Spearman at London before settling in the United States. As early as 1940, Raymond Cattell advanced the hypothesis that his mentor's g in actuality combined two distinct, albeit related, general capacities. One of the g's, he claimed, embodied "crystallized" intelligence, while the other embodied "fluid" intelligence. Both kinds, he maintained, had great breadth and relevance to everyday life. The apparent instability of g arose because any given set of tests is likely to intersect the two g's idiosyncratically, drawing more or less on each. However, if the investigator expects the single Spearmanian g, he will treat the factor analysis accordingly. In the example outlined above, verbal analogies appeared more g-full in the first study than in the second. Cattell could account for the inconsistency by noting, first, that the initial set of tests tied more heavily into crystallized than fluid intelligence while the other set did the reverse, and, second, that verbal analogies themselves draw more on crystallized than fluid intelligence. A single g extracted in the initial study would actually be mostly g_c (i.e., crystallized intelligence), while in the second it would mostly be g_f (i.e., fluid intelligence). As a result, verbal analogies would be highly endowed with g in the first case, but not in the second.

The investigator, not knowing that he had inadvertently extracted different g's, would be plagued by the apparent ambiguity of his analysis. Cattell has developed the mathematical procedures for extracting both g's and has shown that at least some, if not all, of the wobble thereby vanishes.

As for what the two g's might be, Cattell tells a plausible tale. What he calls crystallized intelligence contributes especially to good vocabularies, word usage, numerical skills, mechanical knowledge. A high g_c means a facility with, and well-stocked memory of, the items of cultural knowledge that turn up in conventional intelligence tests. In contrast, fluid intelligence seems relatively, if not absolutely, culture-free. It contributes to inductive reasoning when the material being reasoned about consists of arbitrary nonsense figures or objects. It shows up in spatial or graphical tasks, especially those which do not draw on specific academic skills. It shows up as speed in perception and reasoning. In contrast to g_c, g_f does not draw very much on a well-stocked memory of factual or cultural information. Also, g_f passes through its peak in one's early twenties, while g_c may continue rising long after. Cattell has created a number of tests that gauge people's g_f the way some conventional intelligence tests gauge g_c.

The distinction between g_c and g_f has something to do with educational history. As Cattell conceives of it, people vary in intellectual potential and also in their opportunities for fulfilling their potential. Someone with high g_f and g_c has had high potential fulfilled. High g_f and low g_c mean that high potential has not been fulfilled. Low g_f and high g_c mean that excellent training has done unusually well with low potential. And finally, low g_f and low g_c mean that a low potential has crystallized into meager intellectual attainments. If we take conventional intelligence scores as estimates of g_c, then the correlation between g_f and g_c typically falls in the region of .5.

If Cattell is correct in thinking of g_c as the product of educational opportunity and intellectual interest working on g_f, then the correlation between the two may vary for different groups of people. For people whose potential has been realized, the correlation should be high, for variations in g_c would be directly linked to variations in g_f. In contrast, people whose intellectual potential has been left more to chance, the correlation should be low. A low g_c could result either from lack of potential or lack of fulfillment. Cattell has evidence for just such diversity in correlations. Adults with little education show less of a correlation in g_c and g_f than young schoolchildren, for whom diversities of educational background are not yet potent factors, at least relatively speaking. Moreover, personality traits and motivational factors show a greater correlation with g_c than with g_f, again in accord with Cattell's view that g_c is g_f subjected to extrinsic factors.

By some standards, g_f is the "real" measure of intelligence, inasmuch as it presumably cancels out noncognitive factors like motivation, personality, and exposure to cultural influence. But that view presupposes a prior definition of intelligence which calls for canceling out those factors. While such a definition is defensible, it is not unassailable. It could be argued that a proper measure of intelligence should include precisely the noncognitive factors ruled out by g_f. This counterargument would hold that if motivation, personality, and exposure to cultural influence make a difference to one's verbal, mathematical, and mechanical competence, then omitting them spoils the measure. A counter-counterargument can readily be framed, pointing out that a measure of intelligence should reveal *potential*, not achievement. As in most questions of definition, there is no right answer, only competing sets of criteria. Whatever one's preference, the facts remain clear. Cattell's two measures of general capacity, although correlated, define distinct entities. Compared to g_c, g_f is relatively free of cultural influence and noncognitive aspects of personality. It is somewhat less predictive of success in school than g_c, but it may not be less predictive of success in nonacademic pursuits. The range of g_f among the general population exceeds substantially the range of g_c. One interpretation of this difference in range is that cultural influences tend to reduce the differences among people in intelligence. The common experiences in society may well serve to diminish somewhat the impact of innate differences in capacity. As expected, the evidence suggests that g_f depends relatively more on genetic factors than g_c, although both betray a substantial inherited component.

For now, we cannot say which, if any, of the foregoing approaches to mental measurement will prevail, but perhaps further consensus is unnecessary. The I.Q. cuts across the fine structure of the various theories, coming up with what is a weighted average of a set of abilities. Any modern intelligence-test battery samples so broadly that most of the abilities get tapped. And since the abilities themselves tend to be intercorrelated, an omission here and there will have little effect. The high correlations among full test scores for different sorts of intelligence tests bear this out. When the task is to get a single number measuring a person's intellectual power, the I.Q. still does the job, even with the proliferation of theories and tests. When the task is something else — a diagnostic profile or an occupational inventory — the fine-grained analysis should take over.

The experience of sixty-five years of testing converges on certain kinds of measurement rather than others. Whatever the theory, the resulting intelligence test requires the grasping of relationships, the use of information for induction, some capacity for assimilating new information. Usually, although not always, the test calls on linguistic skills — vocabulary, similarities in meaning, antonyms and synonyms, and the like. The reason for this convergence in technique should be sought in the impressive extent of underlying agreement about intelligence, notwithstanding the air of controversy. The major figures in the study of intelligence have called it "a capacity for abstract reasoning and problem solving," "the ability to educe relations," "general mental adaptability," "the capacity to act purposefully, to think rationally and to deal effectively with the environment," and so on. The general idea is clear, even if the details and implementation of studying it are not. The statistical, factor-analytic methods outlined here tame some of the inherent complexity of the subject, though by no means all of it. Successful mental testing, by itself, neither replaces nor impedes the study of cognitive growth and development, the psychology of language, the principles of the learning process, nor any of the other efforts to chart the intellect. Indeed, if it were not for the contentiousness of psychologists, the various bits and pieces would doubtless fit together nicely.

Writing in the *New Republic* in 1923, Professor Edwin Boring of Harvard said, "Intelligence as a measurable capacity must at the start be defined as the capacity to do well in an intelligence test. Intelligence is what the tests test." Once we agree on a test, that is doubtless true, just as well-defined physical concepts like force and work can be identified with the instruments that measure them. But how do we get to that kind of agreement on the defining instrument? At some point, it becomes a matter of prior definition, arising in theory or common knowledge. For example, we would reject any intelligence test that totally discounted verbal ability or logical power, but how about athletic prowess or manual dexterity or the ability to carry a tune or qualities of heart and character? More data are not the final answer, for at bottom, subjective judgment must decide what we want the measure of intelligence to measure. So it is for all scales of measurement — physical as well as psychological. The idea of measuring length, weight, or time comes first; the instrument comes thereafter. And the instrument must satisfy common expectations as well as be reliable and practical. In the case of intelligence, common expectations center around the common purposes of intelligence testing — predicting success in school, suitability for various occupations, intellectual achievement in life. By this standard, the conventional I.Q. test does fairly well. The more complex measures, such as Thurstone's PMA's or Guilford's three-dimensional taxonomy, add predictive power that is sometimes essential. As for what intelligence "really" is, the concept still has ragged edges where convenience and sheer intuition set boundaries that will no doubt change from time to time. The undisputed territory has, however, become formidable.

Notes to Chapter Two

In a single early volume of the *American Journal of Psychology,* Charles Spearman contributed not only to the analysis of mental ability, but also to the mathematics of correlation. See "The Proof and Measurement of Association between Two Things" (*American Journal of Psychology* 15 [1904]: 72–101), and " 'General Intelligence,' Objectively Determined and Measured" (*American Journal of Psychology* 15 [1904]: 201–293). For the mathematical concept of correlation, he acknowledged the prior work of Francis Galton ("Family-likeness in Eye Colour." *Proceedings of the Royal Society of London* 40 [1886]: 402–415) and "Co-relations and Their Measurement, Chiefly from Anthropometric Data." *Proceedings of the Royal Society of London* 45 [1888]: 135–145) and Karl Pearson ("Mathematical Contributions to the Theory of Evolution. III. Regression, Heredity and Panmixia." *Philosophical Transactions of the Royal Society of London* 187 [1896]: 253–318). Spearman's two-factor theory of intelligence received further elaboration in his book, *The Abilities of Man* (New York: Macmillan, 1927).

The extraction of distinct factors from a table of correlations was greatly refined by L. L. Thurstone, as described in a series of articles and books. The series was launched in an article by Thurstone — "Multiple-Factor Analysis" (*Psychological Review* 38 [1931]: 406–427) — elaborated more fully a few years later in his short book, *The Vectors of Mind* (Chicago: University of Chicago Press, 1935), and exhaustively presented in his much longer work, *Multiple-Factor Analysis* (Chicago: University of Chicago Press, 1947). Thurstone was, however, by no means the only contributor to the evolution of the statistical procedures of multiple-factor analysis. In Great Britain, Spearman's countrymen pushed ahead with their own statistical refinements. In particular, Godfrey H. Thomson (*The Factorial Analysis of Human Ability*. Boston: Houghton Mifflin, 1939) and Cyril Burt (*The Factors of the Mind*. New York: Macmillan, 1941) deserve special acknowledgment, for their innovations were not purely technical. Each of these men, from Spearman to Burt (plus numerous others) implicitly shaped our concepts of intelligence by forging instruments to measure it. The interplay between method and theory goes on, as for example, in the work of David Wechsler (see his *The Measurement and Appraisal of Adult Intelligence*. 4th ed., Baltimore: Williams & Wilkins, 1958), designer of the famous Wechsler-Bellevue and Wechsler Adult Intelligence Scales, consisting of verbal and "performance" subtests.

A readable, mostly nontechnical, recapitulation of the early days of factor analysis in relation to mental ability is Philip E. Vernon's *The Structure of Mental Abilities* (London: Methuen, 1950). Vernon promoted and developed the hierarchical approach to intelligence, but he credited his predecessors, Thomson and Burt (in the books already cited, plus Burt's "Alternative Methods of Factor Analysis and Their Relations to Pearson's Method of 'Principal Axes.'" *British Journal of Psychology, Statistical Section* 2 [1949]: 98–121). Thurstone's notion of Primary Mental Abilities ("Primary Mental Abilities." *Psychometric Monographs* 1 [1938], 1–121; and "Psychological Implications of Factor Analysis." *American Psychologist,* 3 [1948]: 402–408) he found somewhat less congenial. The margin of substantive or technical disagreement would probably be of little interest to the general reader, but Vernon's book is a good point of departure for deeper probings.

The taxonomic approach to the structure of intelligence has recently been explicated in two books: J. P. Guilford's *The Nature of Human Intelligence* (New York: McGraw-Hill, 1967), and Guilford and R. Hoepfner's *The Analysis of Intelligence* (New York: McGraw-Hill, 1971). R. B. Cattell's contrasting approach, postulating a "fluid" and a "crystallized" intelligence, has also been recently expounded in his *Abilities: Their Structure, Growth, and Action* (Boston: Houghton Mifflin, 1971). For a broad, contemporary survey of the state of the general field of mental testing for aptitude, achievement, and personality see L. J. Cronbach's *Essentials of Psychological Testing* (3rd ed. New York: Harper & Row, 1970).

In some polemics against intelligence testing (see, for example, *The Humanist,* January/February 1972), the statistical approach is denigrated to the advantage of less quantitative efforts, which are doubtless more accessible to a layman's intuition. It is not hard, and it usually is rewarding to the critic, to fan the untrained reader's latent hostilities towards incomprehensible mathematical formulas. But as in so many of psychology's controversies, there is less here than meets the eye. While there are obvious differences between the highly quantitative analyses of, for example, Cyril Burt and, to pick the work of the pre-eminent nontester, the naturalistic, qualitative theories of the prolific Swiss psychologist Jean Piaget, the still more profound similarities regularly get overlooked.

Piaget has created a major modern school of psychology by showing (in several dozen books, summarized in J. H. Flavel's *The Developmental Psychology of Jean Piaget.* Princeton, N. J.: Van Nostrand, 1963) how a child's intelligence passes through stages from sensory and concrete to more and more abstract and objective and also how adult knowledge has an internal structure that was largely unsuspected. Un-

CHAPTER THREE

The Uses of Intelligence

Most of us get our first, sometimes our only, I.Q. test in school; the predictive power of the I.Q. is encountered first in our school grades; our teachers know our I.Q.'s even when our parents (let alone we ourselves) do not; the intelligence test was, to begin with, created for, and tested against, the criterion of scholastic achievement. But for all these connections, I.Q. and education are only correlated, not identical. Because the original goal of I.Q. testing was to be a measure of academic *potential*, not just performance, some divergence was inevitable. The correlations between standard intelligence tests (in other words, I.Q.) and school grades fall in the middle range, a substantial but not overwhelming .5, more or less. By using intelligence tests with greater emphasis on verbal abilities instead of ordinary I.Q., and standardized school achievement tests instead of teachers' grades, the correlation may get as high as .8. The increase should cause no surprise, for teachers' grades are not as rigidly or reliably focused on the purely academic as are achievement tests.

The correlation between I.Q. and schoolwork rises through the successive grades, at least into high school. At some point, the rise stops and even reverses, for the range effect on correlation interferes. The low end of the I.Q. scale begins to vanish from the school population in high school, thereby truncating the correlation coefficient. Two reasons, at least, cause the correlation to rise during the initial years. First, both intelligence-test and achievement-test scores are more reliable with older children, and as the random perturbations settle down, the connection between the two measures reveals itself more positively. Second, and more significantly, the demands of the successive years in school become progressively more like the skills called on by conventional intelligence tests — reasoning, reading comprehension, sensitivity to semantic nuance, general information. In general, the most predictive factor in the intelligence tests is *g*, the Spearmanian general intelligence, and the second most predictive factor is the purely verbal one. Of course, there is nothing eternal, or even essential, about the exact correlations. If school curricula change so as to include more music, art, mechanical skills, and so on, then special-ability factors will perforce become more predictive of school success than they are now. But since these special factors themselves covary with *g*, no foreseeable school curriculum can totally mask the importance of the I.Q., which is itself heavily dependent on *g*.

At each level of education, the I.Q.'s span a broad range, and at each level of I.Q. among adults, the amount of education completed also spans a broad range. A not uncommon finding is that the children in an ordinary third-grade class span a range of competence in reading comprehension equivalent to the norms for the second through the eighth grades, or that those in the fifth span the range from the third through the tenth. The mere fact of equivalent education by no means assures equivalent intellectual mastery, from the lowest to the highest grade levels in primary and secondary school. Even college freshmen in large state universities display an extraordinarily broad range in tests of such basic intellectual skills as written composition, as almost any college instructor who reads their productions will ruefully confirm. Other sorts of evidence further show the divergence of level of schooling and I.Q. For example, studies of foster children indicate that the cultural ambience of a home has a bigger effect on the foster child's success in school than on his I.Q. In the next chapter, that significant discovery gets some more attention. For now, it is intended only to establish further the point that intelligence tests, while a useful predictor of school success, measure something more, or at least, something different. Nor can it be said that the I.Q. is merely the outcome of schooling, for the correlation between them shows up even when the I.Q. is obtained from six-year-olds just starting school. Of course, once a child is known to have a high or low I.Q., he may live up, or down, to his teachers' expectations, but even granting that complication, the I.Q. could hardly predict how much schooling there is going to be in someone's life if it were itself just a result of schooling.

The discrepancies between I.Q. and school grades are instructive, because they follow a definite pattern. It is not just that the I.Q. is not an exact predictor of grades, but that children with low I.Q.'s almost always do poorly in school, while children with high I.Q.'s cover the range from excellent down to poor. For schoolwork, as for many other correlates of the I.Q., intelligence is necessary but not sufficient. Another way to put this is to say that a low I.Q. predicts poor performance more reliably than a high one predicts good performance.

Figure 2 shows a much-idealized representation of how this happens. The shaded triangle depicts the full range of grades and I.Q.'s in a hypothetical school. Scanning from left to right shows that children with low I.Q.'s fall within a fairly narrow band of grades, but as the I.Q.'s rise, the band thickens. Scanning the graph from the top down casts another revealing light on it. Children who do well in school come from a narrow band of high I.Q.'s, but with lower grades, the band thickens to include lower I.Q.'s. Either way, the average grade rises continuously with the average I.Q., as the ascending dashed line shows.

The triangular shape of the relation in Figure 2 says that a high I.Q. offers merely the opportunity for scholastic achievement, but something more is needed to exploit it. We can guess what the something more might be — interest, emotional well-being, energy — but we do not know. Other activities that are correlated with I.Q. — such as success in business — also seem to call on something more, although perhaps not the same extras as good school-

Figure 2

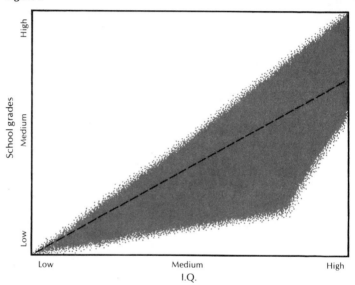

An impressionistic, idealized rendition of how grades may relate to I.Q. The shaded region shows the spread; the dashed line, the average.

work does. No doubt it takes physical strength and stamina to be a champion athlete, but for many sports it takes some intelligence as well. To be a successful actor may take a good appearance or voice, but no doubt also intellect. The examples could be multiplied almost endlessly. I.Q. seems to be the *sine qua non* for an extraordinary variety of successes, but for virtually nothing practical is it the sole requirement.

But still, what is it? Even if it is not just schooling, may it not be a cryptic index of membership in the middle and upper classes, as many critics argue? We often hear that both I.Q. and success- ful education, and all the other correlates, follow from the more basic fact of social origin. To this criticism there is no short and simple answer. The correlation between I.Q. and social class (usu- ally defined in terms of occupation, income, and patterns of per- sonal association) is undeniable, substantial, and worth noting. A cautious conclusion, based on a survey of the scientific literature, is that the upper class scores about thirty I.Q. points above the lower class. A typical member of the upper class gets a score that certifies him as intellectually "superior," while a typical member of the lower class is a shade below average (that is, below I.Q. 100). Precise values cannot be taken too literally, for they depend on somewhat arbitrary definitions of social class and on which par- ticular I.Q. test is used, but the basic finding is beyond dispute.

Dozens of studies, since the earliest days of mental testing, have shown that the average I.Q. keeps pace with the class level, whether the adults or the children in the family are tested. For example, Tables 3A and 3B show the average I.Q.'s of adults (men only) and children sorted into seven occupational categories that correspond reasonably well to most definitions of social class. For this particular sampling (Table 3A), the children were tested in separate studies in America, England, and Russia sometime be- tween 1920 and 1935, but then brought together for purposes of comparison by D. M. Johnson in 1948. For the American and En- glish samples, it was possible to line up the seven occupational categories exactly, but, for technical reasons, the Russian data could be broken down into only six categories over roughly the same range. Nevertheless, the extent of agreement among these children from eleven American states, Northumberland, and the Ukraine makes an impressive case for the link between I.Q. and class level.

For the adults, too, the link is evident, even more so, in fact. American men tested during the two world wars, although sep- arated by more than a generation, give about the same I.Q.'s at

		CHILDREN		
FATHER'S OCCUPATION		*United States*	*Great Britain*	*Soviet Union*
I.	Professional	116	115	117
II.	Semiprofessional and Managerial	112	113	109
III.	Clerical, Skilled Trades, and Retail Businessmen	107	106	105
IV.	Rural Landowners and Farmers	95	97	101
V.	Semiskilled Minor Clerical Workers and Minor Businessmen	105	102	97
VI.	Slightly Skilled	98	97	
VII.	Urban and Day Laborers	95	96	92

TABLE 3A

I.Q.'s of Children in Three Countries

		AMERICAN ADULTS	
		World War I	*World War II*
I.	Professional	123	120
II.	Semiprofessional and Managerial	119	113
III.	Clerical, Skilled Trades, and Retail Businessmen	108	108
IV.	Rural Landowners and Farmers	97	94
V.	Semiskilled Minor Clerical Workers and Minor Businessmen	101	104
VI.	Slightly Skilled	98	96
VII.	Urban and Day Laborers	96	95

TABLE 3B

I.Q.'s of American Adults Separated by a Generation

each level of occupation (Table 3B). The scale for adults, it should be noted, spans a slightly broader range than that for children, a finding that turns up regularly in studies like this. In the next chapter, this regression back toward the I.Q. of 100 from parent to child gets further attention. Another finding is that the I.Q.'s for both farmers and their children undershoot the level that would be predicted by most measures of social status. Probably the main reason for this is the heavily verbal emphasis of most I.Q. tests, which, as Chapter 2 noted, is to some degree, although not entirely, arbitrary. But even so, Johnson pointed out that when the farmers in the World War I group were further subdivided into three categories from "apprentice" to "expert," the top group had an average I.Q. of 102, not far from the value that their social status seems to call for.

Depending on whether one is for or against testing, one will see the class difference as a weakness either in the intellect of the underprivileged or in the tester's definition of intelligence. But in either case, there is no basis for assuming that *no* people from the lower strata have high I.Q.'s. On the contrary, many members of the lower class must have superior I.Q.'s, notwithstanding the low overall average. Recall that, by design, there are as many people above I.Q. 100 as below. In contrast, the social scale is definitely lopsided, with many more at the bottom than at the top even in affluent America. Only about 10 per cent of our people meet the criteria for the upper and upper-middle classes, while about 65 per cent are in the working class and below, with the remainder in between. But only 50 per cent of the people have subnormal (below 100) I.Q.'s. And so, there must be at least 15 per cent of our population in the bottom classes with supranormal (above 100) I.Q.'s. It is therefore not surprising that in a British study after World War I, it was found that over 60 per cent of those intellectually capable of a college education were not getting it, largely because of class barriers. By now, with the liberalization of higher education, that percentage has doubtless shrunk.

It is one thing to note the correlation between social class and I.Q. but something else to explain, or even interpret it. It does not prove that the I.Q. is caused by social class, any more than it proves the reverse — that social class is caused by I.Q. More information is needed to sort out the possibilities. Since a family's social standing depends partly on the breadwinner's livelihood, there might be a further correlation between I.Q. and occupation. Many studies, from World War I on, have confirmed that hunch. One of the most detailed, relatively modern, assessments of the occupational ladder is Naomi Stewart's, published in 1947 in the periodical *Occupations*. She obtained the intelligence-test scores (Army General Classification Test) and preinduction civilian occupations for about 90,000 enlisted men in the United States Army, which was just about 2 per cent of the total at that time, April-June, 1944. Taking only the 67,254 men who reported recognizable occupations in which there were samples of at least 24 other men, there were 226 separate occupations, whose median test scores are shown in Figure 3. The rest of the men were either in occupations so rare that the samples fell below 25 or had no occupations listed in their military records.

Figure 3 shows the median test score for each occupation, grouped into ten categories. Thus, the median lumberjack (which is to say, the lumberjack who had as many above him as below him) was somewhere in the interval between scores of 85.3 and 89.9, while the median electrical-engineering student was at the other end of the range, in the interval between 126.7 and 131.3. In general, occupations calling for more education turn up in higher categories than those calling for less. It would, however, be a mistake to conclude that education is the whole story, for there is more than that to be learned from Figure 3. Men at similar educational levels are dispersed widely across the chart. For example, the median academic high school student fell in the 112.9–117.5 interval while the median agricultural high school student fell in the 99.1–103.7 interval. Or, the median optician was in the 103.7–108.3 interval while his fellow optical craftsman, the median photographic laboratory technician, was in the 117.5–122.1 interval. Or, finally, the median laundry-machine operator was in the 89.9–94.5 interval while the median addressing-embossing machine operator was far above him in the 117.5–122.1 interval. The longer one stares at the chart, the less plausible is the argument that occupational level is a simple and direct outcome of education, at least for the population sampled here.

In several respects, the sample cannot be taken as representative of the population as a whole, even granting that it is over twenty-five years old. First and foremost, it includes only men. Second, it includes only whites. Third, it includes only enlisted personnel, no officers. Fourth, it includes only those who met the army's minimum requirements for induction. And, finally, it includes mainly young men, averaging about twenty-five, who had not yet found their ultimate occupational niches. Certain kinds of occupations — doctor, corporation executive, professor — do not even appear in the chart, because of the age factor. Other occupations — such as personnel clerk, statistical clerk, perhaps also accountant and auditor — may be elevated because young men with high test scores on their way up, occupationally speaking, are caught passing through. Nevertheless, none of those shortcomings can reasonably explain away the evident stratification of occupations with respect to tested intelligence.

The average occupational median fell at 108.3. Refrigeration mechanics, toolroom keepers, railway car mechanics, machinists' helpers, locomotive firemen, and meat cutters, among others, straddled that average value. In contrast to the average occupational median, the average man in the sample had a score of about 103, more than five points lower. The reason for the discrepancy is that there are, in general, more people per occupation for occupations with lower median scores. The line superimposed on the chart shows how many individual men fell into each of the ten categories. There were 8,497 men who were either teamsters, miners, farm workers, or lumberjacks — the four occupations in the bottom category — 15,603 men in the ninety-three occupations

Figure 3

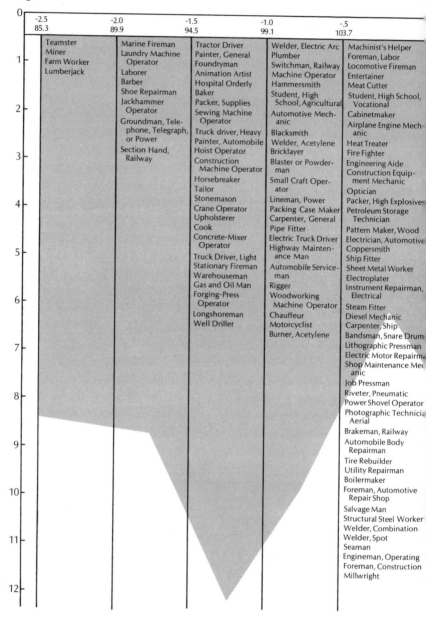

Median AGCT scores for common occupations, sorted into ten categories. The superimposed line shows the number of individuals per category, with the scale at the left reading in thousands of cases.

Mean 108.3	+.5 112.9	+1.0 117.5	+1.5 122.1	+2.0 126.7	+2.5 131.3
Carpenter, Heavy Construction	Switchboard Installer, Telephone and Telegraph, Dial	Bookkeeper, General	Writer	Accountant	
Dispatcher, Motor Vehicle	Cashier	Chief Clerk	Student, Civil Engineering	Student, Mechanical Engineering	
Gunsmith	Stock Record Clerk	Stenographer	Statistical Clerk	Personnel Clerk	
Musician, Instrumental	Clerk, General	Pharmacist	Student, Chemical Engineering	Student, Medicine	
Tool Maker	Radio Repairman	Typist	Teacher	Chemist	
Nurse, Practical	Purchasing Agent	Draftsman	Lawyer	Student, Electrical Engineering	
Photographer, Portrait	Survey and Instrument Man	Chemical Laboratory Assistant	Student, Business or Public Administration		
Photolithographer	Physics Laboratory Assistant	Draftsman, Mechanical	Auditor		
Rodman and Chainman, Surveying	Stock Control Clerk	Investigator	Student, Dentistry		
Airplane Fabric and Dope Worker	Manager, Production	Reporter			
Multilith or Multigraph Operator	Boilermaker, Layer-Out	Tool Designer			
Shipping Clerk	Radio Operator	Tabulating Machine Operator			
Printer	Linotype Operator	Addressing-Embossing Machine Operator			
Steward	Student, Mechanics	Traffic Rate Clerk			
Foreman, Warehouse	Salesman	Clerk-Typist			
Bandsman, Cornet or Trumpet	Athletic Instructor	Postal Clerk			
Instrument Repairman, Non-electrical	Store Manager	Bookkeeping Machine Operator			
Boring Mill Operator	Installer-Repairman, Telephone and Telegraph	Meat or Dairy Inspector			
Projectionist, Motion Picture	Motorcycle Mechanic	Photographic Laboratory Technician			
Dental Laboratory Technician	Dispatcher Clerk, Crew	Teletype Operator			
Laboratory Technician, V-mail or Microfilm	Tool Dresser	Student, Sociology			
Foreman, Machine Shop	File Clerk				
Stock Clerk	Embalmer				
Painter, Sign	Brake Inspector, Railway				
Machinist	Airplane and Engine Mechanic				
Photographer, Aerial	Shop Clerk				
Engine Lathe Operator	Artist				
Parts Clerk, Automotive	Band Leader				
Cook's Helper	Photographer				
Railway Mechanic, General	Geologist				
Office Machine Serviceman	Airplane Engine Service Mechanic				
Student, High School, Commercial	Cable Splicer, Telephone and Telegraph				
Electrician, Airplane	Surveyor				
Student, Manual Arts	Student, High School, Academic				
Policeman	Blueprinter or Photostat Operator				
Sales Clerk					
Electrician					
Lineman, Telephone and Telegraph					
Watch Repairman					
Receiving or Shipping Checker					
Car Mechanic, Railway					
Toolroom Keeper					
Refrigration Mechanic					
Cameraman, Motion Picture					
Telephone Operator					
Hatch Tender					

straddling the mean, and only 511 men in the six occupations in the top category. This lopsided dispersion of men and jobs tells us that labor gets more differentiated towards the high end of the scale. For sufficient reason or not, social scientists, as well as people in general, usually distinguish between auditors and accountants, or dentists and doctors, or electrical and mechanical engineers, but not between those who use spades and those who use shovels, or those who farm beans and those who farm cotton. That greater differentiation at the top is why most occupations have medians above I.Q. 100, the population average.

The occupational medians spread from 129 for accountants to 85 for lumberjacks, with the rest forming the familiar bell-shaped distribution in between. The standard deviation of the distribution was 9.2, which means that about 68 per cent of all occupations fall between 99.1–117.5 (from one standard deviation below the mean of 108.3 to one standard deviation above, abbreviated −1.0 and +1.0 in Figure 3). Because this sample is somewhat unrepresentative — e.g., sex, race, age, truncation at the top (lack of officers) and at the bottom (army rejects) — and out-of-date, we should not take the specifics of the distribution too literally. In a general sort of way, however, it tells us that the greatest number of common occupations are plied by a median person well above the population average of I.Q. 100. By and large, only for menial, manual, and socially simple occupations do we find the median case drawn from the lower half of the population.

This does not yet tell us about the range of individual test scores within occupations, for each occupation has its own range: not-so-bright accountants and very bright bakers are far from unknown. But just as for good grades in school, a high I.Q. is necessary for some occupations, even if it is not sufficient. For example, among accountants, 80 per cent of the scores fell between 114 and 143, leaving out 10 per cent at each extreme. In contrast, for lumberjacks, 80 per cent of the scores fell between 60 and 116. The difference between the two occupations at the bottom boundary was 54, while at the top, it was half of that, 27. Throughout the range of occupations, there was a comparable pattern, with most of the difference across occupations occurring at the lower boundary, which is to say that the higher occupations seemed to have a minimum score more than the lower occupations had a maximum. (Stewart does not provide the full ranges of scores within occupations, but only these 10 to 90 per cent figures, which tend to underestimate the effect noted here. Other studies which do give full ranges, such as Harrell and Harrell's [1945] show a still larger tendency for the lowest score to distinguish best between occupations.) Hence we would expect the variation within occupations to shrink towards the top of the scale, an expectation fully confirmed in these data. The correlation between the median score in each occupation and a common measure of the variation therein (the so-called "semi-interquartile range") was an impressive −.80, saying that the higher the median of an occupation, the smaller the spread around it. As far as I.Q. alone is concerned, virtually anyone can be, for example, a welder, but half of mankind (roughly the half below I.Q. 100) is not eligible for auditing, even if the brightest welder may test as high as the brightest auditor.

In this characteristic way, then, I.Q. affects one's occupation. And it is obvious that occupation affects one's social standing. It then follows logically that I.Q. affects social standing. When people are asked to rate the prestige or social standing of different occupations, they turn up with lists that look very much like the lists based on average I.Q.'s — the professionals at the top, the laborers at the bottom, and the minor businessmen and white-collar workers in the middle. A variety of occupational indices have been constructed, some based purely on subjective evaluation of social standing, some on impressions of the necessary intellectual demands of the job, and still others on mixtures of subjective judgment and vital facts concerning education and income. Such scales all correlate highly with each other and with the average I.Q. of people in the occupations. Although the precise correlation depends on details of any study, a value of .7

can be taken as a reasonably conservative estimate of the correlation between the average I.Q. in a job and how people rate its social standing, across a broad sampling of the occupations generally available to most people. Moreover, these ratings have been about as stable as the corresponding data on the I.Q., in both America and Europe and according to people up and down the social scale, since the 1920's.

The ties among I.Q., occupation, and social standing make practical sense. The intellectual demands of engineering, for example, exceed those of ditch digging. Hence, engineers are brighter, on the average. If virtually anyone is smart enough to be a ditch digger, and only half the people are smart enough to be engineers, then society is, in effect, husbanding its intellectual resources by holding engineers in greater esteem, and on the average, paying them more. The subjective scale of occupational standing that virtually everyone carries around in his head expresses a social consensus both powerful and stable, particularly in its impact on the occupational choices of individuals. It may well be that more people are moved more by that scale than by income, which is merely a correlate of it (and a rather imperfect one at that). More and more these days, young people at the top of the I.Q. scale seem to be choosing the honored occupation, rather than the remunerative one, to the extent that those two aspects can be disentangled. If appearances do not deceive, the correlation between I.Q. and social esteem may be growing even larger than it already is.

The critics of testing say that the correlations between I.Q. and social class show that the I.Q. test is contaminated by the arbitrary values of our culture, giving unfair advantage to those who hold them. But it is no mere coincidence that those values often put the bright people in the prestigious jobs. By directing its approval, admiration, and money towards certain occupations, society promotes their desirability, and hence, competition for them. To the extent that high intelligence confers a competitive advantage, society thereby expresses its recognition, however imprecise, of the importance and scarcity of intellectual ability.

If the .7 correlation between the average I.Q. in an occupation and its subjective prestige rating is taken as a measure (albeit a crude one) of how society values intellect, then the correlation between individual people's I.Q.'s and the prestige rating of the jobs they actually land is the measure (also crude) of how well society succeeds in fulfilling that value. Because we already know that each occupation encompasses a range of I.Q.'s, we can infer that the actuality falls short of the principle. The most thorough recent estimate of the correlation between occupational prestige and individuals' I.Q.'s, published in 1968 by the sociologist O. D. Duncan, is .45, indeed lower than .7, but still substantial. In fact, both figures are probably underestimates of the true value in the population as a whole. Because the estimates come mainly from studies of soldiers and military veterans, they exclude the lower tail of the I.Q. distribution, which is, as noted before, the most predictive part. Given that intelligence is necessary, but not sufficient, for occupational success, a low I.Q. is more predictive than a high one, and precisely that deficient sector of the population gets omitted from the military population. (Duncan's estimate of .45 contains correction for the nonrepresentative population, but almost certainly it does not correct enough.) Also, most studies, including Duncan's, survey only young men (women are typically omitted altogether), so that the most prestigious occupations — high corporation executives, top-level professionals, financial experts, major public officials, and so on — simply do not turn up, truncating the scale at the top and therefore probably further reducing the correlation.

Duncan found that education (measured as number of years of formal schooling, which is itself highly correlated with grades in school) predicted occupational level even better than tested intelligence — .64 as compared to .45. Most other studies agree with Duncan's, for both occupational level and average income. Occasionally, the superior predictiveness of schooling is taken as evidence that education, instead of I.Q., determines success, but that is just faulty inference. Since schooling itself is correlated with I.Q., the question is not whether the one *or* the other predicts occupational success, for if one does they both likely do, but whether the impact of I.Q. on success is *via* schooling or not. The evidence from the sample of young (aged twenty-four to thirty-five) military veterans in Duncan's study indicates that I.Q. works mainly, although not entirely, through schooling to influence career success. On the average, I.Q. appears to make some further contribution, even after schooling is taken into account. Whether the success of all other parts of the general population may be similarly explained is debatable, as shown below for a sample of people with exceptionally high I.Q.'s.

There are good reasons why schooling should, in most cases, be a better predictor than I.Q., even though the two are intimately linked. There is first the obvious fact that occupationally useful skills are learned in school. A student who has the intellectual wherewithal to make it through law school or engineering college, and who does so, is converting his high I.Q. into high occupational status via school. His equal in I.Q. who, for one reason or other, drops out after high school, is treading a riskier path and may not fare so well thereafter. School may help in less concrete ways too. To the extent that college or postgraduate degrees advance one's social standing automatically and without regard to skill or competence, amount of schooling will predict status better than I.Q. Many people with adequate intelligence no doubt get blocked in their climb up the ladder for want of a formal education, even when the formal education would have provided no relevant skills in their line of work. And, finally, recall that I.Q. appears to be only necessary, not sufficient, for both educational and occupational success. If the extra requirements are at all similar for those two correlates of intelligence, then success as a student augurs success thereafter for more reasons than just intellect. If both call, for example, for health, vigor, drive, ambition, then the school is in part a simulation of life thereafter as well as a preparation for it. Someone with I.Q. lacking those traits may fall short in both school and at work, making the correlation between school and work even higher than that between either and I.Q. Of course, the extras may not all be so obviously admirable as the ones just listed, for compliance, stubborn doggedness, disingenuousness, and perhaps even unimaginativeness, may sometimes advance one's cause in school and beyond. In any case, however, the point is that in various natural ways in our society, school is the main channel through which most people's I.Q.'s, and other relevant endowments, carry them to their place in society.

If it is right that education predicts success because it is our society's main way of channeling high intelligence towards the prestigious and lucrative occupations, then we should expect childhood I.Q. to be particularly predictive of later success, since it is a significant determiner of education. In his study, Duncan addressed himself to precisely that issue by comparing the predictiveness of a person's childhood I.Q. with that of his father's education, his father's occupational level, and the number of siblings in his family. These last three factors — father's education and occupation and number of siblings — may be viewed as estimates of the family social background, since family size is known to correlate (negatively) with social class particularly for the generation represented in Duncan's data. While each of the four factors plays some role, childhood I.Q. turned out to be by far the best predictor of all, whether for a person's ultimate educational attainment, his occupational level, or his annual income in early adulthood (i.e., twenty-five to thirty-four years). In fact, the variance in each of those adult outcomes accounted for by childhood I.Q. was greater than the *sum* of that accounted for by father's occupation, his education and the family's size.

An explanation of Duncan's complex statistical procedures for partialing out the various factors has no place here, but his conclusions are both clear and relevant. While children are most likely to end up in roughly the same social class as their parents, a substantial fraction rises or falls, as statistics on social mobility consistently show. Most often, the transmission of social class from parents to children is ascribed to the environmental factors in a home. However, Duncan's findings imply that a child's I.Q., in and of itself, affects his ultimate social mobility, or lack of it.

The existing data, which are still rather skimpy, bear out Duncan's analysis. For example, the eminent English psychologist Cyril Burt reported a study of 200 London children from a sampling of homes up and down the social ladder. He found that children who had higher I.Q.'s than characteristic of their fathers' occupational level were relatively likely to rise in their own occupational level when they grew up. In contrast, children who had lower I.Q.'s were relatively likely to fall in their occupational level. Burt found that the children's attitudes — particularly those reflecting their "industry, ambition, and educational and vocational aims" — also foretold ascent and descent on the social ladder, in comparison to their fathers' position. Estimates of either the parents' attitudes or the children's educational achievement predicted little, after a child's intelligence and personal attitudes were taken into account. Along these same lines, A. R. Jensen describes a study showing that "when siblings in the same family changed their social status as adults, it was the more intelligent who moved up and the less intelligent who moved down the SES [socioeconomic status] scale." Presumably, the siblings in a family share a common set of parental attitudes and environmental advantages or disadvantages, but then rise or fall depending (no doubt, only in part) on their individual intellectual capacities.

Whether a person's I.Q. makes a difference above and beyond its contribution to his education can be examined by looking at extreme cases, particularly at the upper reaches. There is just so much formal schooling to be had in our society, and an I.Q. of 130 or so is probably enough to get a person through, assuming the other attributes are present. Would more I.Q. points beyond 130 confer any advantage, even if not in the form of more schooling? We can answer that question more or less positively because the top of the scale provided the subject of a massive longitudinal study by Lewis M. Terman and his associates at Stanford University. For almost forty years, they followed the lives of a large group of gifted people, publishing their results in five volumes between 1925 and 1959 under the general title of *Genetic Studies of Genius* and in a monograph by Melita H. Oden in 1968. The plan of the study was simple: find a large group of young children with exceptionally high I.Q.'s, record as many potentially interesting and useful additional facts about them as practicable, and then follow the course of their lives. Terman and his staff found slightly more than 1,500 California children whose I.Q.'s averaged about 150. (Because they used different intelligence scales for some of the children, no precise average figure can be given.) This was no small achievement in itself, for an I.Q. of 150 or greater is a rarity possessed, on the average, by the smartest child in a randomly selected group of about three hundred. Most of the children were between the ages of eight and twelve when chosen, but there were also some younger and some recruited in high school.

Right from the start the findings were informative. For example, highly bright boys were easier to locate than highly bright girls. And the disparity increased slightly with age, suggesting that whatever I.Q. is, boys maintain it better than girls. Other studies, too, have found girls relatively scarcer at the extremes of I.Q., both top and bottom, as well as a similar tendency, among girls as compared to boys, to lose I.Q. points with age. No one, however, can yet say anything certain about the origins of those minor sex differences. In any event, the final sample had 857 boys and 671 girls. The children, mainly from urban public schools, definitely did not represent the ethnic or social composition of their communities. Compared to the population from which they were drawn, there was an enormous (over tenfold) excess of children of fathers in the professions and an even more marked scarcity (only .013) of the children of laborers, echoing once again the correlation between I.Q. and social class. In addition, the sample contained an excess of western and northern Europeans and Jews, and a shortage of Latins, non-Jewish eastern Europeans, and Negroes. Since the communities sampled had relatively few Orientals, it was hard to tell whether too few, too many, or just the right number of gifted Oriental children turned up, statistically speaking.

It would nevertheless be an error to conclude that high-I.Q. samples, like Terman's, comprise simply the children of the upper class, for all social strata produce children covering the full range of I.Q.'s. Only the proportions differ. A study by Cyril Burt of over 2,000 children in London schools exemplifies the point admirably. For his random sample of children, Burt tallied the social-class origins of those whose I.Q.'s were 110 or over, 120 or over, and 130 or over. The results are given in Figure 4 for the five standard classes: I — "higher professional, administrative, or managerial"; II — "lower professional, administrative, or managerial"; III — "clerks, typists, shop assistants, and foremen as well as skilled manual workers"; IV — "partly-skilled workers"; V — "unskilled labour."

In the total sample, over 1,100 children came from level III backgrounds, while only 74 came from I and 285 came from V, reflecting the class distribution in London. With successively narrower slices off the top of the I.Q. distribution, the *relative* numbers from the higher classes soared. For example, while the total had about 52 per cent from level III and less than 4 per cent from level I, the slice above I.Q. 130 still had left about 20 per cent of the level I's, but only 1 per cent of the level III's. However, because there was so large a preponderance of level III children to begin with, the absolute numbers give quite a different impression. Of the 54 children whose I.Q.'s were 130 or better, 15 came from level I and 13 came from level III. For children whose I.Q.'s were 120 or better, level III contributed almost four times as many as level I (96 to 25).

In its shrinking sectored disks, Figure 4 shows how the representation from each class level shifted around with higher I.Q. slices. The trend is clearly towards the higher classes. Presumably, Terman's sample of children with I.Q. 140 and above would be the next slice up, weighted still more towards the top of the social scale, but still including cases from a broad range. That supposition is hard to test precisely, for Terman's data cannot be plotted on the same chart as Burt's, given the six thousand miles and thirty-odd years separating the two samples. Nevertheless, Terman noted that about a third of the families of his

Figure 4

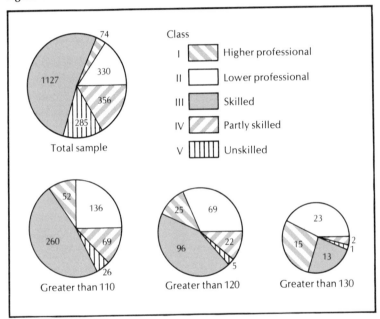

How 2,172 London children spread into five socioeconomic levels at three successively higher slices of I.Q.

gifted children earned less than the average for skilled workers in 1923 in California (i.e., twenty-five hundred dollars), which confirms the expected broad economic range.

Terman's children were nonrepresentative physically as well as intellectually, ethnically, and socially. They tended to be taller, heavier, more broad-shouldered, stronger in hand grip, larger in the vital capacity of their lungs, and somewhat earlier in their sexual maturity than children in the general population. The physical differences, though not large, were large enough to counter the stereotype of the fragile bookworm. Not surprisingly, the gifted children did better in school than their classmates, but mainly in subjects — like reading and arithmetic — that seem to call on intelligence. In subjects like woodworking or sewing, the gifted children enjoyed no particular advantage. They most often liked precisely the subjects that the other children most often disliked, such as reading and arithmetic. At seven years of age the gifted children were already reading books at a higher rate than the average child of fifteen. And even in sports they outdid their classmates, knowing more about the games of childhood and knowing about them earlier. Finally, even in tests of "character" — honesty, tendency towards overstatement, trustworthiness, and the like — the gifted children showed their precocity. At nine or ten years, they had reached the "moral development," by those no doubt quaint standards, of the average child of thirteen or fourteen.

Children with I.Q.'s of 150 or so are, then, special. But the big question is whether they mature into something special, for that would be the proper test of intelligence testing. Did the I.Q. make the difference it should have made? At last assessment, the subjects in the sample had reached their late forties, almost forty years after their selection for the study. The death rate in the sample has been less by almost a third than that in the general population, with fatal accidents relatively uncommon. Childhood delinquency, criminal convictions, and alcoholism are all strikingly rare in the sample. More common and benign maladjustments are not so rare, with the women showing slightly more emotional trouble than the men. It may be a psychological burden to be so bright a woman in our culture, but this is pure speculation. In any event, not much can be made of the differences in minor mental disturbance between the sample and the general population.

About 70 per cent of the sample *finished* college, men ahead of women by a couple of percentage points. This should be compared with the 8 per cent of their contemporaries in the general population who finished college (the 1930–1940 college generation). Out of the more than 1,500 in the sample, only eleven did not finish high school, and of these, eight went to professional or trade school. 40 per cent of the male college graduates earned law, medical, or Ph.D. degrees, and over half of all the college graduates have at least some postgraduate training. There are, proportionately, five times as many Ph.D.'s in the sample as in the population of college graduates in general. As expected, the sample excelled in college, 80 per cent averaging B or better in their courses, and more than 35 per cent graduating with honors (Phi Beta Kappa, *cum laude,* or the like). In addition to the academic degrees, the sample has earned a disproportionately large number of professional licenses — CPA's, Fellows of the American Board of Surgery, Fellows of the American Institute of Architects, and so on.

The ten most common occupations among the men are not the common lot in our society: lawyers first, followed by engineers, college faculty members, middle-level major business managers, financial executives, scientists, physicians, educational administrators, top business executives, and accountants. All told, over 85 per cent of the working men became either professionals or managers in business or industry, with the first category the larger. At the other end of the occupational scale, only about 3 per cent became semiskilled laborers or farmers, and virtually none, unskilled laborers. The men are bunched at the top of the scale of occupations just as they are at the top of the scale of I.Q. And the sample outperforms not only the population in general, but also the average college graduate. The run-of-the-mill college graduate has a 5 per cent chance of becoming a semiskilled or unskilled laborer; the sample's college graduate has a chance of only .5 per cent, a tenfold reduction.

In 1960, a panel of judges selected the 100 men in the sample

most successful in their vocations and the 100 men least successful, to see if differences between them provided any clues to the
requirements for occupational achievement besides I.Q. While
the two groups differed markedly in their careers, the less successful group still outperformed the general population, containing 80 per cent who were in retail business, skilled trades or
higher in the occupational scale, and 40 per cent who had earned
at least the bachelor's degree.

The more successful group had, on the average, more schooling, came from homes higher in social standing (although both
groups covered the range), and had slightly higher intelligence-
test scores in both childhood and adulthood. The main difference
seemed, however, to be in their personal traits. Even in childhood and adolescence, the successful group had been judged
more well-adjusted, more directed towards concrete accomplishment, were more involved in high school extracurricular activities and were younger in finishing college, where they had done
better. In early adulthood, they had been rated by judges to be
more poised, attentive, attractive, curious, and original. In later
adulthood, they enjoyed better health, and not surprisingly, a
greater sense of accomplishment. None of these numerous differences was overwhelming, but the overall picture reveals a
pattern of consistent physical and emotional well-being in the
more successful group, as compared to the men in the other
group.

In addition to everything else, a high I.Q. pays in money. The
average professional or managerial man in the sample was earning about $10,500 in 1954, compared to a national average of
about $6,000 for those occupations. Even the semiskilled and
clerical workers in the sample were outearning, by about 25
per cent, the general averages for the same jobs. The total family
income for the sample was more than double that of white, urban
American families of roughly the same socioeconomic status.
About 30 per cent of the families in the sample earned more than
$15,000 a year in 1954, compared to only 1 per cent for ordinary

families in the same general socioeconomic class. The sample shows the economic advantages of a high I.Q., after discounting education, race, occupation, and geography.

In the general population, income and education correlate highly. One encounters, from time to time, estimates of how much a high school diploma or a bachelor's degree should add to one's paycheck. No doubt about the facts — more highly educated people make more money — but the interpretation is arguable. The usual interpretation assumes that a given man with some higher education would earn more than the same man *without* the education. But that is not really what the data show, for we know that the people who have the extra education are usually not the same in other ways as those who do not. Among other things, they usually have higher I.Q.'s and they may tend to come from the upper class. Suppose, for the sake of relevance, that income *really* depended more on I.Q. than on education. Suppose further that the amount of schooling also depended on I.Q. Educated people would then earn more not because they were more educated (which they would also be), but because they were smarter (had a higher I.Q.). To disentangle the complex factors in society at large and find out what causes what, simple correlations are not enough. We need to know if income would be correlated with I.Q. if education were held constant, or conversely if income would be correlated with education if I.Q. were held constant. Terman's high-I.Q. sample is a step in this direction, for it allows us to see whether income depends on education when I.Q. is held constant at the virtual top of the scale.

High school graduates in the Terman sample were earning about as much as the college graduates with a bachelor's degree. Further schooling beyond the bachelor's did improve income somewhat. However, of the six men with the highest incomes (ranging upward of $100,000 a year) only one finished college. The highest annual income of all, $400,000 for the last year reported, was earned by a man who had had no college education whatever. In other words, if *very* high income is your goal, and you have a high I.Q., do not waste your time with formal education beyond high school. For this particular sample, education did not unequivocally add to income, as most often claimed. No doubt, for people of more ordinary talents the connection is straightforward, but the study shows that at the upper extreme, I.Q. may get converted into income without the benefit of formal schooling.

The study did not gather just the economic facts of life. When the men were asked about their state of mind, almost 90 per cent said that they were at least fairly content, and virtually half were finding "deep satisfaction" in their lives. Only 6 per cent reported discontentment. The more prosperous men were generally the more contented. When the men were asked to estimate how well they were living up to their intellectual abilities, there was again a correlation between satisfaction and income. The average yearly wage of those who said they were "fully" living up to their capacities was almost $12,000, while the group least satisfied was making less than $5,000 per year. Money, of course, is not the only measure of success, for the more prosperous tended to be the more successful by other criteria as well.

Women's salaries were substantially lower than the men's and did not correlate with contentment. Notwithstanding their poorer salaries, on an average, the women reported greater satisfaction in their lives than the men. The housewives, who were earning less money than anyone else, expressed about as much satisfaction as any other group in the sample, although they were more likely to credit their families as the source of satisfaction than the working women who were caught up in careers. There is little here to support the feminist argument that a housewife's life is intolerable, especially for educated, intelligent women. It would be hard to pick a brighter group than the women in this study, yet they seemed to be adjusting easily to their lot. To give but one example of the many striking cases, a woman whose

I.Q. of 192 places her close to the top of the entire sample, and whose retested intelligence at maturity was again virtually at the top, was raising eight children, including three sets of twins. According to the account at the latest report, she had no outside activity at that time other than an interest in the PTA, but was apparently content, if not serene. Of course, such tranquility may be gone now, fifteen years later.

The enormous harvest from the sample by their late forties included about 2,500 scientific and technical articles, more than 200 books and monographs, 400 short stories or plays, 400 miscellaneous publications, 350 patents, not to mention hundreds of radio and television scripts, newspaper stories, and achievements in art and music. Their names turn up disproportionately often in compilations of our effective people — in *Who's Who, American Men of Science*, the National Academy of Sciences, and so on. They are active in PTA, clubs, hobbies, and various forms of public service. They vote far more faithfully (over 90 per cent of the time in national elections) than the general population (and are somewhat more conservative). By the mid-1950's, they had spawned (with spouses who were themselves significantly brighter than average) about 2,500 children whose average I.Q. appears to be above 130 — not as brilliant as their exceptional parents, but still among the top 5 per cent of the population. Even in their mid-forties, the sample continued to test within the top 1 per cent of the general population in intelligence, whether or not they had been successful in their careers, and whether or not they had been to college. No doubt the predictive power of the I.Q. is outlasting the first forty years of the study.

No single study is beyond criticism, not even this massive enterprise by Terman and his associates. Critics can point to the possibility of hidden biases in the original selection of the children. Not *every* child in the California schools was tested, only those who looked "promising" for one reason or another. The final selection employed just the I.Q., but the prescreening may indeed have been a source of bias. Later estimates uncovered, however, only a few children missed this way, certainly not enough to change the general conclusions about the predictiveness of I.Q. Critics may also wonder how people are affected by being included in this select group. Are they impelled to excel, or are they stunted by anxiety? Judging from all the other data showing correlations between I.Q. and achievement, the sample seems to be psychologically normal for an I.Q. of 150.

Whatever the flaws in the study, there can be no reasonable doubt about its main conclusion. An I.Q. test can be given in an hour or two to a child, and from this infinitesimally small sample of his output, deeply important predictions follow — about schoolwork, occupation, income, satisfaction with life, and even life expectancy. The predictions are not perfect, for other factors always enter in, but no other single factor matters as much in as many spheres of life.

Terman was unapologetic about where he thought I.Q. came from. He believed in the inheritance of I.Q., at least to a considerable degree, but by no means did he rule out the possibility of environmental influence. Bluntly, but not dogmatically, he wrote in 1925:

There are . . . many persons who believe that intelligence quotients can be manufactured to order by the application of suitable methods of training. There are even prominent educators and psychologists who are inclined to regard such a pedagogical feat as within the realm of possibility, and no one knows that it is not. If it is possible it is time we were finding out. Conclusive evidence as to the extent to which I.Q.'s can be artificially raised could be supplied in a few years by an experiment which would cost a few hundred thousand or at most a few million dollars. The knowledge would probably be worth to humanity a thousand times that amount.

The opening paragraphs of the disturbing and controversial article by Professor Arthur R. Jensen of the University of California, Berkeley, could be taken as the equally blunt answer to Terman's challenge, forty-four years later:

Compensatory education has been tried and it apparently has failed. Compensatory education has been practiced on a massive scale for several years in many cities across the nation. It began with auspicious enthusiasm and high hopes of educators. It had unprecedented support from Federal funds. It had theoretical sanction from social scientists espousing the major underpinning of its rationale: the "deprivation hypothesis," according to which academic lag is mainly the result of social, economic, and educational deprivation and discrimination — an hypothesis that has met with wide, uncritical acceptance in the atmosphere of society's growing concern about the plight of minority groups and the economically disadvantaged.

The chief goal of compensatory education — to remedy the educational lag of disadvantaged children and thereby narrow the achievement gap between "minority" and "majority" pupils — has been utterly unrealized in any of the large compensatory education programs that have been evaluated so far.

And the reason, Jensen goes on to say, why compensatory education has failed is that it has tried to raise I.Q.'s, which, he argues, are more a matter of inheritance than environment, and therefore not very amenable to corrective training. What evidence has he for this unexpected and unpopular conclusion?

Notes to Chapter Three

Useful secondary sources of information on the relations between school performance and intelligence tests are the textbooks: L. J. Cronbach's *Essentials of Psychological Testing* (3rd ed. New York: Harper & Row, 1970); and L. J. Tyler's *The Psychology of Human Differences* (3rd ed. New York: Meredith, 1965). On the triangular shape of the scatter diagram relating school performance and I.Q., see, in addition to Tyler, J. Fisher's "The Twisted Pear and the Prediction of Behavior" (*Journal of Consulting Psychology* 23 [1959]: 400–405). In a somewhat different context, A. R. Jensen also discusses the effect of necessary, but not sufficient, relations between ability and school performance. In particular, see his "Hierarchical Theories of Mental Ability" (in *On Intelligence*, edited by B. Dockrell. London: Methuen, 1970).

The I.Q. separation between social classes is virtually a universal finding wherever it has been examined, and Tyler's book is again a convenient secondary source. The data on the American, English, and

Russian children, and on men during the two world wars, were assembled in D. M. Johnson's "Applications of the Standard-Score *IQ* to Social Statistics" (*Journal of Social Psychology* 27 [1948]: 217–227). A summary of class differences in I.Q. among English children over a thirty-year interval can be found in J. Conway's "Class Differences in General Intelligence: II" (*British Journal of Statistical Psychology* 12 [1959]: 5–14). The presence of large numbers of people with high I.Q.'s in the lower classes, notwithstanding the average differences, was alluded to in C. Burt's "Class Differences in General Intelligence: III" (*British Journal of Statistical Psychology* 12 [1959]: 15–33). See also his *Mental and Scholastic Tests* (London: King, 1921).

On the intelligence-test scores found in various occupations, see N. Stewart, "A.G.C.T. Scores of Army Personnel Grouped by Occupation" (*Occupations* 26 [1947]: 5–41); T. W. and M. S. Harrell, "Army General Classification Test Scores for Civilian Occupations" (*Educational and Psychological Measurement* 5 [1945]: 229–239); R. L. Thorndike and E. Hagen, *Ten Thousand Careers* (New York: Wiley, 1959); and R. B. Cattell, *Abilities: Their Structure, Growth and Action* (Boston: Houghton Mifflin, 1971).

Occupational standing has been variously estimated, although the resulting scales are highly correlated with each other. The "Barr scale," based on subjective estimates of the intelligence required in over 100 common occupations, is described in L. M. Terman's *Genetic Studies of Genius: I. Mental and Physical Traits of a Thousand Gifted Children* (2nd ed. Stanford University Press, 1926). This book also briefly characterizes the familiar five-level "Taussig scale" of occupations. The correlation between the Barr scale and measured intelligence can be found in R. S. Ball's "The Predictability of Occupational Level from Intelligence" (*Journal of Consulting Psychology* 2 [1938]: 184–186). Comparable results are reported for an English sample by C. Burt, "Intelligence and Social Mobility" (*British Journal of Statistical Psychology* 14 [1961]: 3–24). The stability of prestige rankings of occupations across time and geographical distance is discussed in Tyler's textbook, which also gives the references to the primary sources.

The interrelations of family background, I.Q., education, and occupational status — along with other matters — are discussed in O. D. Duncan's "Ability and Achievement" (*Eugenics Quarterly* 15 [1968]: 1–11). For occupational status, Duncan used his own index, as described in "A Socioeconomic Index for All Occupations" (in *Occupations and Social Status*, edited by A. J. Reiss, Jr., et al. Glencoe: Free Press, 1961).

Aside from Burt's "The Gifted Child" (*British Journal of Statistical Psychology* 14 [1961]: 123–139), the material on the high-I.Q. end of the distribution comes from Terman's longitudinal study, which is reported in the series under the general title of *Genetic Studies of Genius* and published by the Stanford University Press (Volume I cited above): C. M. Cox, *II: The Early Mental Traits of Three Hundred Geniuses* (1926); B. S. Burks, D. W. Jensen, and L. M. Terman, *III: The Promise of Youth: Follow-up Studies of a Thousand Gifted Children* (1930); L. M. Terman and M. H. Oden, *IV: The Gifted Child Grows Up: Twenty-five Years' Follow-up of a Superior Group* (1947); L. M. Terman and M. H. Oden, *V: The Gifted Group at Mid-life: Thirty-five Years' Follow-up of the Superior Child* (1959). One additional report is M. H. Oden's "The Fulfillment of Promise: 40-Year Follow-up of the Terman Gifted Group" (*Genetic Psychology Monographs* 77 [1968]: 3–93).

The quotation from Terman comes from the first volume of *Genetic Studies of Genius,* pp. 635f. The "response" by Jensen comes from the opening paragraphs of his article in the *Harvard Educational Review* (1969), which is fully cited at the end of Chapter 4. The other quotation from Jensen, referring to differential mobility among siblings, comes from an unpublished work by him, *Educability and Group Differences.* The data he is summarizing is in M. Young and J. B. Gibson's "Social Mobility and Fertility" (in *Biological Aspects of Social Problems,* edited by J. E. Meade and A. S. Parkes. Edinburgh: Oliver & Boyd, 1965).

CHAPTER FOUR

Nature and Nurture

The problem with nature and nurture is to decide which — inheritance or environment — is primary, for the I.Q. is exclusively the result of neither one alone. Advocates of environment — the clear majority of those who express themselves publicly on the subject — must explain why I.Q.'s usually stay about the same during most people's lives and also why high or low I.Q.'s tend to run in families. Those facts could easily be construed as signs of a genetic basis for the I.Q., although neither is as decisive as laymen tend to make them. A moment's reflection shows that either environment or heredity can lay claim to both stability and family resemblance. While the hereditarian obviously can call on the fixity of the germ plasm, the environmentalist may argue that I.Q.'s remain the same to the extent that environments remain the same. Moreover, the environmentalist may claim that if you are lucky enough to be well-born, then your I.Q. will show the benefits of nurturing, which, in turn, gives you an advantage in the competition for success. If, on the other hand, you are blighted with poor surroundings, your mental growth will be stunted and you are likely to be stuck at the bottom of the social ladder. According to the environmental view, parents bequeath to their children not so much the genes for intelligence as a setting to promote or retard it.

In one plausible stroke the environmentalist arguments seem to explain, therefore, not only the stability of the I.Q. but also the similarity between parents and children. The case is further strengthened by arguing that early training fixes the I.Q. more firmly than anything we know how to do later. And then to cap it off, the environmentalist may attest that the arbitrary social barriers in our society trap the underprivileged in their surroundings while guarding the overprivileged in theirs. Anyone who accepts this series of arguments is unshaken by Jensen's reminder that compensatory education has, at least so far, failed in the United States, for the answer seems to be ready and waiting. To someone who believes in the environmental theory, the failure of compensatory education is not disproof of his theory, but rather a sign that we need more and better special training earlier in a person's life.

To be sure, it seems obvious that poor and unattractive surroundings will stunt a child's mental growth. To question it seems callous. But even if it is plausible, how do we know it is true? By what evidence do we test the environmentalist or hereditarian doctrines? And, even more fundamentally, how sound are the facts themselves that each theory strives to explain? Is the I.Q. stable, and how strong are family resemblances?

As for stability, we know that, on the average, the correlation between a person's I.Q. at separated times in life is .8 or better, so long as he is above the age of seven and below the age of senescence. Below seven, the correlations plummet, unless they are taken close together in time. The correlation between I.Q. at two years and eighteen years or beyond is below .4, while between eight and eighteen years it is above .8. After about ten, it reaches the limits imposed by the reliability of the test itself, in the vicinity of .9–1.0. Sometimes these correlations are misinterpreted, leading to the mistaken observation that "eight-year-olds have 80 per cent of the mental capacity of adults," or the like. But a correlation coefficient does not measure proportional size, it measures predictiveness. An eight-year-old may still have a lot of mental growth ahead — well in excess of 20 per cent — but his relative standing in intellectual capacity among his peers has nevertheless become stable enough to give the .8 correlation.

While a correlation of .8 over most of one's life, starting at about seven years, fully warrants the reputation of stability, it clearly does not mean rigid fixity. Changes of thirty points or more over the school years are not unknown, just uncommon enough to happen to fewer than 10 per cent of the children. In contrast, changes of one to ten points are commonplace, probably occurring in around 70 per cent of the cases.

More than likely, some of these shifts in I.Q. reflect imperfections in the tests themselves, rather than actual changes in intellectual capacities. Yet, test error does not explain all of the inconsistency of the I.Q. Studies have shown that children who are rated as aggressive, independent, and competitive are somewhat more likely to post gains than children rated the opposite. Moreover, children from educationally advanced homes also show a statistical bias towards gains in I.Q. Children from such homes have higher I.Q.'s to begin with, but when their I.Q.'s shift, the changes tend to be in their favor. Finally, boys have been found more commonly among the gainers than girls.

While all of those changes in I.Q. accord with common impressions of how the environment favors some people — e.g., aggressive, well-born males — over others — e.g., retiring, indigent girls — they could equally well reflect inborn factors, given only the data summarized so far. Or, more plausibly, they could be the outcome of some combination of nature and nurture. Sex differences in the stability of I.Q. may be genetic, environmental, or both; social-class differences, likewise, and personality factors may be the effect, as well as the cause, of changes in a child's intellectual standing among his peers.

In summary, the I.Q. from about the age of seven on measures only an approximately stable feature of a person. There are many small changes in I.Q. thereafter, and there are also a few quite large ones. We can guess that some changes reflect nothing more profound than the imprecision of the test itself; that some others reveal natural and inborn spurts and laggings in mental growth just as in physical growth; but that some arise from environmental events promoting or retarding mental development, whatever those happen to be. The relative constancy of the I.Q. does not, in other words, answer our question about environment and heredity. As a practical by-product, it does, however, caution against placing too high a reliance for too long a time on a single I.Q. test in early childhood. Whether because of the test unreliability, the irregularity of mental growth, or the accidents of the environment, a child's score gets dated just like the outcome of a medical examination and should be renewed from time to time.

As a child grows older, his I.Q. stabilizes and also gets more like his parents' I.Q.'s, as numerous studies in many countries during the past half-century have shown. But, like the constancy of I.Q., family resemblance is also a relative matter, far from perfect. A representative study, published in 1940 by Herbert Conrad and Harold Jones of the University of California at Berkeley, reported the I.Q.'s of about 1,000 people in 269 families scattered over nine rural counties in New England. About 700 were children (mostly over seven years old) and the remainder were their parents. The correlations of the I.Q.'s of siblings or of individual parents and their children edged just over .5, a moderate but not overwhelming degree of family resemblance. A correlation of .5 says that if we know that one child in a family has an I.Q. of, for example, 130, the best bet for his father or his sister is about 115. The I.Q. has a standard deviation of about 15 points, and the correlation coefficient measures the proportional change in units of standard deviations. Thus, an I.Q. of 130 signifies 2 standard deviations above the mean of 100, which is multiplied by .5 (the correlation coefficient) to predict the best guess for the child's parent or sibling at 1 standard deviation above the mean.

The environmentalist's first response to this correlation might well be to question why it is not higher. If I.Q.'s reflect the environment primarily, why should the members of the immediate family not resemble each other more? And the environmentalist answer might be that nine rural counties in New England, being of relatively homogeneous character compared to the diversity of environments in society as a whole, underestimate family resemblances. Given only small environmental differences between families, the correlations *within* families will be artificially depressed because of the range effect on correlation, or so the environmentalist might argue. For one reason or another, however, the sibling correlations for I.Q., as well as those for parents and children, most often fall in the vicinity of .5 or just above, in almost all studies of representative samples of people, even where wide differences in environment are likely. The family resemblances in I.Q. among siblings and between children and their parents appear to be stubbornly moderate, of about the same order of magnitude as for clearly inherited traits, like height. For relatively straightforward inherited traits such as height, the expected correlations, barring certain genetic complexities, between a parent and his or her child, or between siblings, is .5, because such pairs of people most likely share about 50 per cent of their genes. In contrast, the sibling correlations for scholastic achievement are usually considerably higher — .7 to .8 in some studies. Home environment makes the children's school grades more alike than their I.Q.'s, or their height.

For I.Q.'s, Conrad and Jones chased down the patterns of correlations within families — between sisters, between brothers, between sisters and brothers, between fathers and sons, or mothers and daughters, and so on. The main upshot was that almost all were about the same, except for minor fluctuations that could have been largely, if not wholly, owing to the imprecision of the tests. The correlation between mothers and their children equaled that between fathers and theirs, pretty much without respect to whether the children were boys or girls. The correlation between siblings of the same sex was slightly, probably insignificantly, lower than between siblings of different sex.

If home environment had been exerting much effect on the children's I.Q.'s, then certain patterns of correlation might have been expected, or so Conrad and Jones surmised. Perhaps, they said, the mother's I.Q. should have been more predictive than the father's, since she has greater contact with the children during the presumably formative early years, or perhaps like-sex siblings should have been more alike in I.Q. than brother-sister pairs, since pairs of brothers or pairs of sisters tend to interact more. While the authors recognized that the environmentalist account is not irrevocably committed to those particular patterns, or the various others they hypothesized, they felt that if the environment were really important, it should leave some sort of traceable pattern. The uniformity of all the correlations impressed them as indirect evidence against the environmental account, especially since the alternative — heredity — had no particular trouble explaining the facts. If I.Q. were mainly inherited, then mothers and fathers might be expected to contribute equally to their children, and siblings might be expected to be intercorrelated without regard to sex. However, Conrad and Jones realized that their data supported a genetic hypothesis mainly by failing to support any plausible environmental hypothesis. To make a strong case for the genetic hypothesis requires something more than circumstantial evidence from resemblances among parents and children sharing a common home environment.

A more direct test of the impact of home environment would be to follow the I.Q.'s of foster children as they grow up, to see whether they come to resemble their foster parents, from whom they get their cultural advantages or disadvantages, or their natural parents, from whom they get their genes. Just such a crucial study was reported by Marjorie Honzik, also of Berkeley, in 1957. Using children raised by their natural parents, she tracked the growing correlations between childhood I.Q. and natural mother's and father's educational level. The correlations, she found, rose from near zero when the children were about two years old, up to somewhere in the range of .3–.4 when the children were seven years old or older. That growth curve is what one might have predicted simply from knowing three facts: the relative stabilization of children's I.Q.'s at about seven years, the sizable correlation between parents' I.Q.'s and their own educational level, and, finally, the moderate correlation between parents' and children's I.Q.'s. Acting together, those three factors suggest that children's I.Q.'s will, by the age of seven, become moderately correlated with their parents' education. Note that the correlation between parents' education and their children's I.Q.'s falls somewhat short of the correlation between the I.Q.'s of parents and children (.3–.4 versus .5). The difference may be saying that parents influence their children's I.Q.'s in some manner other than, or in addition to, the cultural ambience they provide, perhaps by their genetic legacy.

The next part of Honzik's study provided strong evidence for that possibility. She compared the foregoing correlations with those for children raised by foster parents (using data from a study done by other workers). The results of the comparison appear in Figure 5A, for mothers and children, and Figure 5B, for fathers and children. For either fathers or mothers, childhood I.Q. becomes increasingly correlated with the *natural* parent's education, even when the child is being raised in a foster home by foster parents. At no age did the children's I.Q.'s show a significant correlation with their foster parents' educational level.

As it happened, the foster parents covered a broader range of educational levels than did the natural parents of the adopted children in this study, so that the education of the foster parents had the opportunity to be a more potent influence in the foster homes. Nevertheless, the diversity of the foster parents' educational backgrounds accounted for virtually none of their adopted children's spread of I.Q.'s. There seems to be no plausible environmental way to explain the curves in Figures 5A and B.

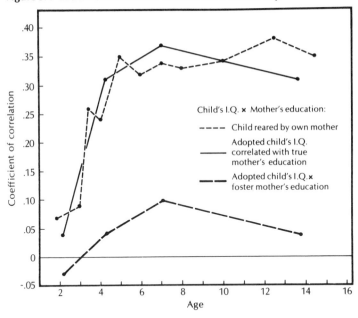

Figure 5A Education of mother in relation to child's I.Q.

Child's I.Q. × Mother's education:

- - - - Child reared by own mother

——— Adopted child's I.Q. correlated with true mother's education

━━━ Adopted child's I.Q.× foster mother's education

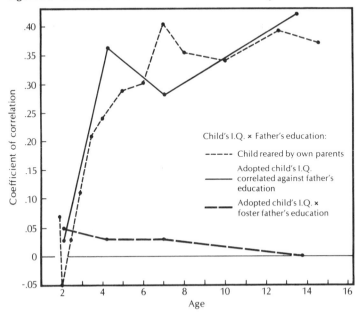

Figure 5B Education of father in relation to child's I.Q.

Child's I.Q. × Father's education:

- - - - Child reared by own parents

——— Adopted child's I.Q. correlated against father's education

━━━ Adopted child's I.Q. × foster father's education

Correlation coefficients between children's I.Q.'s and: 1) their natural parents' education when they were reared by natural parents; 2) their natural parents' education when they were reared by foster parents; and 3) their foster parents' education when they were reared by foster parents.

Parent-child resemblance, as assessed by Honzik, withstood separation virtually undiminished, even when the children were placed in their adoptive homes sometime before the age of six months and had been separated from their true mothers before that. Does this experiment say that environment exerts *no* control over I.Q.? The judicious answer to that question is no. Separation before six months of age still leaves as much as fifteen months between the moment of conception and the end of direct maternal contact. Possibly, there are significant environmental influences during those early weeks and months, although we do not know of any big enough to account for the correlation between maternal education and children's I.Q.'s, let alone for the correlation with the education of fathers who, more often than not, probably had no contact whatever with their illegitimate offspring (which is what most of the children in the sample were). Nongenetic ingredients of the I.Q. cannot be entirely ruled out by this study, impressive a case as it is for heredity.

While the foster children did not show any correlation with their foster parents' education, other studies have turned up small but real correlations between the I.Q.'s of foster parents and children. Later on, that finding will receive more attention, but for now it is worth noting as a possible sign of environmental influence on I.Q. Honzik drew her figures on foster children and their natural and adoptive parents from an earlier study by Marie Skodak and Harold Skeels at the State University of Iowa. Those authors pointed out that, in spite of the lack of correlation between foster parents and children, the adopted children had substantially higher I.Q.'s than their natural mothers. 63 of the 100 children's mothers received an I.Q. test after they had decided to give their babies up for adoption. Their average I.Q. was 86, but their children later tested at 106, a full twenty points higher.

The twenty-point jump in the Skeels and Skodak study is widely cited by environmentalists as proof of how much a good foster home can contribute to a child's I.Q. Ironically, it comes ultimately from the same study that made the potent case for inheritance summarized in Figures 5A and B. Can the two be reconciled? The answer is to recognize that one need not choose absolutely between nature and nurture, for many traits, among them the I.Q., express the influence of both. The strong genetic evidence summarized in Figures 5A and B can coexist with the twenty-point jump, with appropriate qualifications on the latter.

If environment had no effect whatever, we would still have expected the children to have higher I.Q.'s than their mothers, because of statistical regression. Since the mothers fell below the population average of 100, and since the correlation between mothers and children is less than perfect, some regression back towards 100 is in order. In fact, Skeels and Skodak found a correlation of about .4 between the I.Q.'s of true mothers and the children they surrendered for adoption, for the 63 cases given comparable tests. Straight regression back towards the mean therefore predicts that the children should make it to 94.4, as follows:

1) Mothers are at -14, relative to the population mean of 100 (i.e., I.Q. 86).
2) Multiply the mother's deviation from the mean by the correlation: $-14 \times .4 = -5.6$,
3) which gives the expected deviation for the children, and therefore their predicted I.Q.'s on purely statistical grounds: $100 - 5.6 = 94.4$.

The children, averaging 106, were actually 11.6 points higher. The apparent environmental contribution, then, is not twenty points, but 11.6, assuming that the fathers did not average over 100 in I.Q. If they averaged over 100, then the environmental contribution would be smaller. And, by the same token, if they averaged less, the environmental contribution would be larger. Other uncertainties further becloud a positive assessment of the environmental contribution. Were the mothers' I.Q.'s fairly gauged, under the trying circumstances of carrying a child already promised away? Possibly their I.Q. scores were artificially depressed, thereby creating an inflated discrepancy with their children. Skeels and Skodak were reasonably confident the scores were right, but the question remains essentially unanswered. Were the babies typical offspring of their mothers or were they somehow special? It is for the *average* child of mothers with I.Q. 86 that statistical regression foretells an I.Q. of 94.4. If, in the process of selection and placement, the more "promising" babies got picked, the statistical case gets somewhat complicated. The 100 babies in the study tested at I.Q. 117 by the age of two years two months, so they were atypical in that sense but, as noted above, infant I.Q. is only poorly correlated with later I.Q. As with the question of the untested fathers, the question of infant selection must remain unanswered.

Taking the apparent 11.6-point environmental effect at face value would lead one to search in the foster families for the explanation. Figures 5A and B already tell us that the educational level of neither foster parent can be credited with the rise. The foster parents averaged something better than a high school education, while the true parents (based on those known) had less than ten grades of school. Yet educational level did not make the difference in I.Q., otherwise the pattern of correlations in Figures 5A and B would have revealed it. The foster fathers also had a generally higher occupational level than the (known) true fathers. On a standard seven-level scale, going from professional (level I) down to day laborers (level VII), the foster fathers averaged slightly higher than level III (skilled trades), while the true fathers averaged about halfway between level VI (slightly skilled) and level VII. Placement in one of the higher-level foster homes caused only a slight benefit in I.Q. The I.Q.'s of the children (at age ten and beyond) placed in one of the top three levels averaged 109, while those placed in one of the bottom four levels averaged 106.

Neither the educational nor the occupational level of the foster homes, then, accounted for the 11.6-point benefit that may have turned up in the study. Skeels and Skodak felt that intangible factors in the foster homes — not reflected in gross indices of education and occupation — were crucial, but they were not able to anchor their impression to testable hypotheses. That does not, of course, mean they were wrong, but only that the environmental account remained somewhat vague, notwithstanding the apparent benefit of foster rearing in their study. In contrast, the true mothers whose I.Q.'s were under 70 had children whose I.Q.'s ended up about twenty-five points lower than those whose mothers tested at 105 or over — a clear effect, almost certainly genetic to some degree.

Skodak and Skeels provided a list of the 100 adopted children, giving for each the I.Q., the foster father's occupation, and, when known, the natural father's occupation. To an environmentalist, it would seem obvious that the child's I.Q. should reflect the foster father's occupational level, if anybody's. In contrast, the hereditarian would maintain that since occupation is correlated with I.Q. and since I.Q. is genetically transmitted, there should be a correlation between the natural father's occupation and the children's I.Q.'s, even though the children were separated from their mothers in infancy and probably never had any contact with their fathers. Skeels and Skodak did not calculate these correlations (or, at least, did not publish them), but from the data given, it has now been done.

Out of the 100 cases, 71 had sufficiently clear definitions of both foster and natural father's occupation to permit assessing the levels on a seven-point scale (as described above). The correlation in level between foster and natural fathers turned out to be just about zero — a statistically insignificant .02. The correlation between the children's I.Q.'s and their foster father's occupational level also fell near zero — .06. That low correlation, in and of itself, seriously damages the environmental theory. But the outcome is worse still for environmentalists. The correlation between the children's I.Q.'s and their natural father's occupational level was .29. Recall that the natural mother–child correlation for I.Q. in this study was only .4, and also bear in mind that occupational level does not correlate perfectly with one's own I.Q., so that it should correlate less with one's children's I.Q. In clear violation of an environmental theory, and in clear confirmation of the hereditarian, occupational level of natural fathers predicts the children's I.Q.'s substantially better than that of foster fathers, which virtually does not predict at all.

The combination of the foregoing two studies — Honzik's and Skeels and Skodak's — points to some hereditary ingredient in tested intelligence, but it does not permit any sort of estimate of the relative weight of the ingredient. Numerous other studies, drawing on other sorts of evidence, similarly tell us that the genes are doing something without saying just what, or how much. But precisely because the evidence is so varied, it is worth considering at least some of it. It is usually possible to discount a particular experiment, or a certain sort of evidence, if one is disposed to do so, but at some point the mass of evidence prevails.

In their study, Conrad and Jones noted that the parents themselves were correlated in I.Q. by about .5, just about as much as either was with their children. Biologists call the tendency for likes to interbreed "assortative mating," and it will figure prominently in the discussion from time to time. For now, it is noted only to make a relatively obvious point about parent-child resemblances. The more two parents resemble each other in a given trait, the more either one of them will resemble their children. Thus, the parent-child resemblance for hair color is likely to be greater than average when mother and father are both blonds, or to be greater than average for height if both are extremely short or extremely tall. In the case of I.Q., it is known that the children of first cousins are more highly correlated with their parents than children in general. First-cousin marriages, or inbreeding in general, can be thought of as global assortative mating, involving all traits and not just those that ordinarily enter into the selection of a spouse, like I.Q. or height. Or, inversely, the ordinary assortative mating between couples can be thought of as selective inbreeding, involving only a relatively few genes as compared with the total possible. From either standpoint, the children of first-cousin marriages, coming as they do from pairings that have greater genetic overlap, might be expected to correlate more highly with either parent. And the evidence shows that the parent-child correlation for parents who are first cousins exceeds the usual .5 substantially.

But, so far, the facts could equally well be interpreted using the environmental theory. If first-cousin couples are genetically more similar than average, they may well also be more similar in outlook, attitude, and cultural values. Hence, they may share a relatively common approach to child-rearing, which, the environmentalist could argue, would tend to bring their children to their own level of I.Q. The result would be the elevated parent-child correlation seen in the children of first-cousin couples.

The environmental account runs into trouble, however, because of yet another genetic consequence of inbreeding. For many genetic traits, in all sorts of creatures, biologists have found what they call "inbreeding depression," which means that the trait in question tends to be less adequate when produced by inbred matings. Thus, in a particular experiment, maize was found to yield, in bushels per acre, less than half when inbred than when randomly pollinated, or, in another experiment, fruit flies were found less viable when allowed to inbreed. One reason for inbreeding depression (and its mirror image "hybrid vigor") is that dominant genes tend to be more beneficial than recessive ones, and inbreeding gives the recessive ones a chance to combine and express themselves. It has long been known that, in human beings, the children of incestuous (sibling or parent-child) matings are heir to numerous hazards, particularly feeblemindedness. Given the enormity of the social transgression, however, it could be argued forcefully that incestuous matings usually provide woefully poor surroundings for a growing child, not to mention the likely peculiarities, both social and physical, of such parents. Being so atypical, incestuous matings can hardly be a persuasive source of evidence for the genetic basis of intelligence, although the findings appear to be readily compatible with such an account.

Some human inbreeding is, however, not at all atypical in Japan, where it is estimated that 4 to 5 per cent of marriages are between first cousins, at least at the time covered in an exhaustive study published in 1965 by William Schull and James Neel, geneticists at the University of Michigan. Marriage between cousins occurs at all levels of society and has no social stigma attached to it. In fact, under certain circumstances, given the traditional Japanese allegiance to one's family, cousin marriages often get special approbation. Nevertheless, the offspring of such marriages show approximately an 8 per cent depression in their I.Q.'s, as compared with children from noncousin marriages who are drawn from the same social classes so as to correct for sampling. On purely genetic grounds that cannot be explained here, an 8 per cent depression for first cousins predicts a deficit of about 20 I.Q. points for the children of incestuous (parent-child, sibling) matings. What little quantitative evidence there is falls approximately in that range, resulting in the extraordinary high incidence of feeblemindedness associated with incest, even when the parents have normal intelligence.

In addition to I.Q., inbreeding depression for the offspring of first cousins was found in the Japanese children's school grades, particularly in languages, mathematics, science, and physical education. The children were also slightly shorter, lighter, more subject to certain diseases, and had a slightly higher risk of mortality. A diehard environmentalist might be tempted to argue that the effects on I.Q. and school performance were the indirect outcome of the changes registered by the more physiological measures. But, as a rule, the psychological measures showed the largest effects of all, and, moreover, the children of first cousins were already lagging behind the controls in the age at which they first walked and talked, rather well before the environment, as ordinarily thought of, has had much of a chance to take its toll.

The Japanese study contains evidence for suppression of I.Q. when there seems to be no plausible environmental culprit. The obverse can be found in the intelligence testing of deaf children — which shows no suppression of I.Q. even when there seems to be more than enough to blame in the environment. A student of the psychology of the deaf, McCay Vernon, has summarized the results from over forty years of testing of deaf and hard-of-hearing children and finds that deafness, in and of itself and not associated with some broader neurological deficit, seems to lead to no depression of measured intelligence on nonverbal tests. Deaf children's test scores span the normal range, averaging at about the population average, independent of the severity of hearing loss or the age (including prenatal) at which the loss first occurred. It would be hard to imagine many more catastrophically deprived cultural environments than those suffered by some congenitally deaf children, yet, if they are otherwise neurologically normal, they grow up to have essentially normal scores on the performance (i.e., nonverbal) parts of intelligence tests, which, in normal children, are highly correlated with the overall score. The obvious inference is that the mental capacities measured by those tests are sufficiently robust to withstand the inevitable cultural deprivations of a soundless environment. By the same token, it follows that the scores reflect relatively stable, perhaps innate, attributes of the children.

While all of the studies outlined so far point to some genetic contribution to intelligence, they still do not measure the contribution with any precision. They, and many other studies, simply say that a child's I.Q. reflects something more than the social and cultural setting in which he grows up, and that the something more could easily be genetic, since it results in true parent–child correlations of about the right size for genetic traits. To get any more exact about the matter, to estimate the *size* of the genetic contribution (and, complementarily, of the environmental contribution) takes certain special kinds of data, and, sometimes, special kinds of statistical analysis.

The simplest possible means of assessing the inherited factor in I.Q. is to study identical twins, for only environmental differences can turn up between people with identical genes. In an article recently published in the periodical *Behavior Genetics*, Professor Jensen surveys four major studies of identical twins who were reared in separate homes. Most of the twins had been separated by the age of six months, and almost all by the age of two years. The twins were Caucasians, living in England, Denmark, and the United States — all told, 122 pairs of them. The overall I.Q. of the 244 individuals was about 97, slightly lower than the standard 100. Identical twins tend to have slightly depressed I.Q.'s, perhaps owing to the prenatal hazards of twindom. The 244 individuals spanned the range of I.Q.'s from 63 to 132, a range that brackets most of humanity— or to be more precise, 97 per cent of the general population on whom intelligence tests have been standardized.

Being identical twins, the pairs shared identical genetic endowments, but some of their environments were as different as those of random pairs of children in the society at large. Nevertheless, their I.Q.'s correlated by about .85, which is more than the usual .5 between ordinary siblings or even the .55 or so between fraternal twins growing up together with their own families. It is, in fact, almost as big as the correlations between the heights and weights of these twins, which, in the largest of the four twin studies summarized by Jensen, were ascertained to be .94 and .88 respectively. Even environmentalists would expect separately raised twins to look alike, but these results show that the I.Q.'s match almost as well. Of course, if the environment alone set the I.Q., the correlations should have been much smaller than .85. It would, however, be rash to leap to the conclusion that the .85 correlation is purely genetic, for when twins are placed into separate homes, they might well be placed into similar environments, not to mention their common uterine and early infant environments. The children had been separated not for the edification of psychologists studying the I.Q., but for the weighty reasons that break families up — illness, poverty, death, parental incapacity, and so on — and the accidents of separation may not have yielded well-designed experiments. Some of the pairs were no doubt raised by different branches of the same family, perhaps assuring them considerable environmental similarity anyway. In such cases, the correlation of .85 would not be purely genetic, but at least partly environmental. Fortunately for our state of knowledge, one of the four studies examined by Jensen included ratings of the foster homes in terms of the breadwinner's occupation. Six categories sufficed: higher professional, lower professional, clerical, skilled, semiskilled, unskilled. Now, with this classification of homes, we know a little about whether the twins were raised in homes with a similar cultural ambience. To the extent that the environment in a home reflects the breadwinner's occupation, the answer is unequivocally negative, for there was literally no general correlation in the occupational levels of the homes into which the pairs were separated. At least for this one study — which happened to be the largest of the four — the high correlation in I.Q. resulted from something besides a social-class correlation in foster homes, most likely the shared inheritance.

Twins raised apart differ on the average by about 6.5 points in I.Q. Two people chosen at random from the general population differ by 17 points. Only 4 of the 122 pairs of twins differed by more than 17 points. Ordinary siblings raised in the same household differ by 12 points. Only 19 of the 122 twin pairs differed by more than that. And finally, fraternal twins raised in the same home differ by an average of 11 points, which was exceeded by only 23 of the 122 pairs. In other words, more than four times out of five the difference between identical twins raised apart fell short of the average difference between fraternal twins raised together by their own parents.

At the same time, those separated twins were not so similar in schoolwork. From two of the four studies, it was possible to compare the impact of separation with that of a shared home environment on both I.Q.'s and school achievement. The average difference in I.Q. between twins raised together was about 5 points, while for the separated twins it was about 6.5 points. This shows that whatever it is in the environment that causes the I.Q.'s of twins to diverge to the extent that they do, it has already taken most of its toll by the time the twins are separated in infancy. Growing up together causes an average 5-point difference; being separated adds a mere additional 1½ points on the average, even though these twins were separated into uncorrelated homes, as far as socioeconomic level was concerned. For those same children, school achievement showed a rather different picture. Measuring on a scale set to be numerically comparable to I.Q., the twins raised together differed by only an average of about 2.5 points. Separation in infancy produced an average difference of about 10.5 points. In other words, twins raised together perform in school even more closely than they do on I.Q. tests, but separation pushes the school performance much farther apart than it does the I.Q. The difference tells us that school performance responds to the environment substantially more than does the I.Q., although neither one is solely the outcome of either nature or nurture.

The I.Q. behaves more like a person's height than his scholastic performance as far as sensitivity (or, rather, insensitivity) to home environment is concerned. Table 4 reproduces part of a chart presented by Jensen (based, in turn, largely on the work of Cyril Burt in England) showing the correlations among various sorts of kinfolk for height, I.Q., and scholastic achievement. Although there are minor uncertainties about the precise value of some of the figures in the table, the pattern is quite clear. Separation into different homes tends to decrease substantially the correlation in people's scholastic achievement, while depressing the correlations of I.Q. only slightly, and of height, not at all. The main surprise in the table is the .27 correlation between unrelated people in the same home (i.e., foster siblings), which is reduced to zero for pairs of people taken at random in the general population. Later on, the unexpectedly high correlation between foster siblings, from a genetic standpoint, will be reconsidered. At this stage, it poses no serious challenge to the conclusion that I.Q. and height are more alike in their insensitivity to changes in the home environment than either is like scholastic achievement.

While these data suggest that height and I.Q. are relatively more genetic than school performance, they by no means prove it, for, given only these data, it could still be that height or I.Q., or

| | Correlation | | SCHOLASTIC |
	HEIGHT	I.Q.	ACHIEVEMENT
Identical twins together	.96	.97	.95
Identical twins apart	.94	.89	.72
Fraternal twins	.47	.55	.88
Siblings together	.50	.52	.86
Siblings apart	.54	.49	.55
Unrelated together	0	.27	.56
Unrelated apart	0	0	0

TABLE 4

Correlations between Relatives for Three Traits

both, are strictly environmental, but the relevant environmental factors have almost nothing to do with home surroundings. Under that supposition, separation would have little impact, but it would take great ingenuity to think of such environmental factors, under the constraint that the other correlations in the table would also need to be accounted for environmentally.

The average difference in I.Q. between the separated twins was about 6.5 points, as noted before. However, many of the pairs, in fact, almost 40 per cent of them, had differences exceeding that average. The largest difference of all was 24 points, separating two girls pseudonymously famous in the psychological literature as Gladys and Helen, whose I.Q.'s were 92 and 116, respectively. Much has been made of this one case by environmentalists, for Gladys was raised in isolated surroundings and had only three grades of education, while her twin sister finished college. Less extreme cases further support the conclusion that twin differences are often, though not always, larger between pairs that had the larger differences in educational advantages in the homes in which they were raised.

It may sound to the untrained ear as if the foregoing conclusion argues against a large genetic factor in I.Q., as it has seemed to more than a few psychologists who have written on the subject. But that is not the case at all. Between identical twins who share a common set of genes (except for some embryological subtleties that will be overlooked here), any difference is an environmental difference, for it can be nothing else. The 24 points separating Gladys and Helen, by biological necessity, is therefore nongenetic, hence environmental. It adds nothing to the environmental case, as such, to find an environmental correlate of the 24 points, although it may be useful to know what in the environment affects I.Q. — especially if it really is something we can influence, like education.

The differences between the 122 separated twin pairs form a distribution, shown in Figure 6, ranging from 5 cases of zero all the way to Gladys and Helen at 24 points difference. The shaded region superimposed shows how many out of a sample of 122 pairs of people chosen at random might be expected to differ in I.Q. by 0, 1, 2, 3, 4, 5, to 39 points, in 1-point intervals. The dashed curve is theoretical, generated mathematically by known properties of the distribution of intelligence in the general population, rather than by an actual sampling of random pairs of people. Differences of zero points can, on the average, be expected slightly more often than 4 times in 122; differences of exactly 39 points,

Figure 6

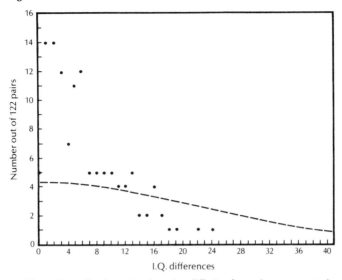

The points tally the 122 twin pairs, differing by various amounts in I.Q. The curve shows how 122 randomly drawn, unrelated pairs of people would differ.

Figure 7

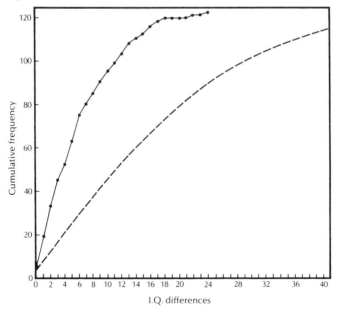

Each point on the upper curve shows how many pairs of twins out of the 122 differed in I.Q. by up to the value directly below on the horizontal axis. The dashed curve shows what would be expected of randomly drawn, unrelated pairs of people.

slightly less often than once in 122. In between, the expected numbers slope off gradually. In marked contrast, the twin differences bunch at the low values. Even the famous 24 points separating Gladys and Helen turns up less often among twins (just once in 122 pairs) than it should have by chance (more than twice in 122).

Figure 7 presents the comparison between the twins and random pairs another way. The steeper curve shows how many twins differed by given numbers of I.Q. points *or less*. Gladys and Helen, in other words, are represented by the very last point, where the entire sample of 122 pairs on the vertical axis intersects a difference of 24 points on the horizontal axis. The other curve is again theoretical, showing how random pairs would spread out. Among random pairs, we would, on the average, find more than 30 who differed by 24 points or more, for the tally up to and including a difference of 24 points is only 89 pairs. On the random curve, a difference of 39 points, 15 greater than that between Gladys and Helen, still would fail to encompass about 9 pairs out of 122.

The differences between the twins, while vastly compressed as compared to random pairs of people, are what would be expected if the environmental buffeting of people's I.Q.'s conformed to the usual normal distribution, showing the effects of numerous random influences. In fact, one of the sources of difference doubtless resides in test unreliability, for the same person taking different forms of the same I.Q. test on two occasions shows an average discrepancy of over 4 points. In other words, separated twins, growing up apart, differ from each other by less than twice as much as people do from themselves because of test unreliability.

Aside from sheer test unreliability, the sources of twin differences correlate at least moderately with the cultural surroundings in which the children get raised. However, there appears to be a substantial physiological, perhaps prenatal, component in the already small environmental factor. It has been shown that the twin heavier at birth tends to end up with the higher I.Q., and, among girls, the one younger at menarche does too, on the average. Identical twins who have relatively large physical differences of any sort — in fingerprint patterns, direction of the crown whorl of the hair, general health — appear to be the pairs who have the larger differences in I.Q. Gladys and Helen, for example, had not only quite different educational careers, but Gladys (I.Q. 92) was plagued by poor health, and the two girls had markedly different fingerprint patterns. The nongenetic ingredients in I.Q., at least among the separated twins, apparently combine cultural and straightforward physiological, perhaps prenatal, factors. All told, however, the nongenetic influences — social, cultural, pre- and postnatal, physiological, and so on — appear to account for only about 10 per cent of the spread of I.Q.'s among the 244 people in the twin study. Of the other 90 per cent, about 5 per cent can be blamed on test unreliability and about 85 per cent on the variety of genetic endowments.

The figures just cited — 10 per cent for environment, 85 per cent for heredity, and 5 per cent lost in the imprecision of testing — come from Jensen's reanalysis of the twin data and should be generalized further only carefully, for there may be limits on their applicability. Before noting some of those limits, it may be pertinent to observe that Jensen's conclusions about the relative contributions of nature and nurture to the I.Q.'s of those twins fall approximately into line with the conclusions of the original investigators. An 85 per cent contribution for inheritance is neither the highest nor the lowest assignment among the group of studies, but a weighted intermediate that reflects the fact that the largest study (Burt's) came up with the highest estimate (87 per cent).

There are three main ways to overestimate the genetic contribution to I.Q. in the population as a whole when the estimate is from studies of separated twins. The first obvious, and already noted, possibility is the inadvertent placement of the twins into correlated environments, subjecting them to similar experiences and therefore enhancing their resemblance in I.Q. Although the evidence suggests only a minor effect of such placement, it cannot be ruled out altogether. The second source of overestimation of the role of the genes is that the twins do not encounter the full range of environments in society at large, since they may be spared the worst ones by the process of adoption. If the worst environments happened to be especially potent in influencing the I.Q., and if the separated twins really did not encounter them as much as people in general, then the population of separated twins might be significantly unrepresentative and would consequently convey a somewhat inflated impression of the relative importance of heredity. On the basis of internal evidence concerning both the environments themselves and the range of I.Q. scores among the twins, this factor probably accounts for no more than a slight inflation, but an inflation nonetheless. The third possible source of overestimation has already been noted — the shared pre- and immediately postnatal environment. While there is some evidence that identical twins in utero tend more to make things different for each other than to make them similar, the common early environment may be making the twins more alike in I.Q. than can properly be ascribed entirely to just their genes. However, the existing data tend to rule out the early postnatal, as well as the prenatal, environment as a homogenizing influence. Stephen Vandenberg has tallied the eventual I.Q. differences between a sampling of twins separated at various ages in infancy and childhood. For pairs separated between the ages of one day and two months (inclusive), the eventual I.Q. difference averaged 3.4 points; for pairs separated between one year and six years (inclusive), the eventual I.Q. difference was 9.5 points. While it would be rash to argue from the small number of cases involved in this particular comparison that common early home environment makes twins more *different,* there is certainly little factual basis for arguing the reverse. Of course, twins who are not separated at all in childhood do grow up to be slightly closer in I.Q. than separated pairs, which shows that overall home environment exerts some equalizing influence.

Within the limitations already noted, the study of separated twins suggests something in the vicinity of an 85 per cent hereditary component to intelligence as measured by tests. Moreover, the facts about foster children, inbreeding depression in Japan, the normality of the I.Q.'s of deaf children, and so on, also betray a sizable, if not precisely assessable, genetic factor. Yet, the studies noted so far comprise only a minute fraction of the evidence for a large, approximately 75 per cent (plus or minus 10 per cent) genetic ingredient in mental capacity. In fact, the hereditarian's most impressive argument is simply to note the convergence of dozens, if not hundreds, of studies over the past sixty years. With only occasional, and usually explainable, exceptions, to which due regard will be given, all investigations of the relative contributions of nature and nurture have found the first to be predominant. Unfortunately, a full summary, with the necessary technicalities, would be inappropriate in a work of this sort, and so the discussion will strive to anticipate common questions and misapprehensions, to give at least a flavor of the data and their treatment, and, finally, to suggest the remaining limitations, complexities, and uncertainties of the genetics of human intelligence.

Some of Jensen's critics have argued that because environment and inheritance are intertwined, it is impossible to tease them apart. The criticism may seem persuasive to laymen, for nature and nurture are indeed intertwined, and in just the way that makes teasing them apart most difficult. For intelligence — unlike, for example, skin color — the main agents of both nature and nurture are likely to be one's parents. One inherits skin color from one's parents, but the relevant environment does not come directly from them but from sun, wind, age, and so on. For skin color, resemblance to parents signifies (albeit not infallibly) inheritance; for intelligence, resemblance is usually ambiguous. Nevertheless, analysis is possible even with I.Q., as Jensen and his predecessors have shown. The most useful data for the purpose are the correlations between I.Q. and kinship, as exemplified by the separated-twin studies, which set genetic similarity high and environmental similarity low. Foster children in the same home define the other extreme of kinship and environment. If environment had no bearing at all on intelligence, then the I.Q.'s of such unrelated children should correlate slightly at most (and only to the extent caused by a special factor mentioned shortly). In contrast, if environment were all, then the correlation should approach the value for natural siblings. Actually, the I.Q.'s of foster children in the same home correlate, according to Jensen, by about .25 (less than half the value for natural siblings). However, even the correlation of .25 cannot be credited entirely to the children's shared environment. Bear in mind that adoption agencies try to place "comparable" children in the same home, which means that there may be more than just their common surroundings making them alike. Suppose, for example, that adoption agencies tried to put children with similar hair color in any given family. They could check on the natural parents, and perhaps even on the grandparents, and make a reasonable guess about the baby's eventual hair color. The foster children in a given home would then often have similar hair color; they would be unrelated by blood, but the similarity would be more genetic than environmental. By trying for a congenial match between foster child and foster parents — in appearance and in mental ability — adoption agencies may make the role of environment look more important than it probably is.

In between foster siblings and identical twins come the more familiar relations, and these too have been scrutinized. Table 5 comes from Jensen's widely discussed article, published in the *Harvard Educational Review* in 1969, about a year before the study of twins just summarized. This table almost certainly summarizes more sheer data, over a broader range of conditions, than any other chart in the field of quantitative psychology. It presents the correlation in mental capacity between various kinfolk culled from fifty-two independent studies (virtually all by workers other than Jensen himself) over a period of more than two generations, in eight countries spread over four continents, from a variety of mental tests administered to tens of thousands of individuals of

If intelligence were purely genetic, the I.Q.'s of second cousins would correlate by .14 and that of first cousins by .18 (the reasons for those peculiar percentages are well beyond the scope of this discussion, so they are offered without proof). Instead of .14 and .18, the actual correlations are .16 and .26 — too large for genetic influence alone, but in the right range. Uncles' (or aunts') I.Q.'s should, by the genes alone, correlate with nephews' (or nieces') by a value of .31; the actual value is .34. The correlation between grandparent and grandchild should, on genetic grounds alone, also be .31, whereas the actual correlation is .27, again a small discrepancy. And finally for this brief survey, the predicted correlation between parent and child, by genes alone, is .49, whereas the actual correlation is .50 using the parents' adult I.Q.'s and .56 using the parents' childhood I.Q.'s — in either case too small a difference to quibble about. All in all, Table 5 says that (1) the more closely related by blood two people are, the greater the correlation between their I.Q.'s, and (2) the correlations fall in the right range from the purely genetic standpoint, although, generally speaking, slightly above the genetic predictions for people who may be assumed to share a more or less similar environment. By evaluating the total evidence, including data not in the table, and by a procedure too technical to explain here, Jensen concluded (as have most of the other experts in the field) that the genetic factor is worth about 80 per cent and that only 20 per cent is left to everything else — the social, cultural, and physical environment, plus illness, prenatal factors, and what have you. It should be noted that the separated-twin studies alone give close to the same answer as the data on the various relations. While one might argue that the twin studies spuriously inflated the genetic component because of the common uterine environments or the inadvertent correlations in the homes into which they were separated, it seems highly implausible that a wholly different set of accidents should inflate, to just about the same degree, the apparent genetic component in assessments of or-

dinary siblings, uncles and nephews, grandparents and grand-
children, and so on.

A highly technical discussion of the genetic contribution to
intelligence (and other psychological traits like neuroticism, in-
troversion-extroversion, and scholastic achievement) was published in 1970 by J. L. Jinks and D. W. Fulker of the University
of Birmingham in England. Using a variety of analytic techniques,
Jinks and Fulker concluded that the relative contribution of the
genes to measured intelligence falls between about 70 and 85
per cent, depending mainly on the intelligence test used, since
some testing procedures apparently succeed better in getting at
innate intelligence than others. They show, as did Jensen, the
convergence of the overwhelming body of data on measured intelligence to a figure in the vicinity of 80 per cent or higher for
the genetic contribution to scores on standard I.Q. tests. For
example, using data just from the comparison of identical twins
raised apart and together, the estimate of the genetic contribution was 87 per cent; extending the comparison to include
fraternal twins raised together, along with the identical twins
raised apart and together, yielded an estimate also of 87 per cent;
a comparison based on data from identical twins raised together
along with data on ordinary siblings raised apart and together
produced an estimate of 82 per cent.

Jinks and Fulker's most complete analysis for the genetic and
environmental contributions to I.Q. is partly reproduced in Table
6, using data based on identical twins raised apart and together,
fraternal twins raised together, siblings raised apart and together, and unrelated foster children raised together. The theoretical correlations follow from setting the genetic contribution at
83 per cent, leaving 17 per cent to the environment. The minor
disparities in the actual correlations shown in Table 5, from
Jensen, and Table 6, from Jinks and Fulker, result from differences
in averaging across different studies, inclusion of somewhat different collections of data, and variations in the use of corrections

for test unreliability. The disparities cannot, however, mask the substantial agreement between fact and theory. Only for identical twins raised apart and foster children raised together does the discrepancy rise as high as 1 per cent or higher. For the separated twins, the 3 per cent difference could easily be just a sampling problem, for Jinks and Fulker used a rather high (87 per cent) estimate of the actual correlation. Had they used Jensen's lower

	OBTAINED CORRELATION	THEORETICAL CORRELATION	DIFFERENCE BETWEEN OBTAINED AND THEORETICAL
Identical twins together	.92	.9274	—.0074
Identical twins apart	.87	.8376	+.0324
Fraternal twins together	.54	.5326	+.0074
Siblings together	.53	.5326	—.0026
Siblings apart	.44	.4428	—.0028
Unrelated together	.27	.0897	+.1803

TABLE 6

Theoretical and Obtained Correlations for Intelligence Scores

estimate (85 per cent) of the correlation between separated twins, the discrepancy would have been only 1.2 per cent. On the other hand, the 18 per cent discrepancy for foster siblings cannot be discounted so easily. Although the numbers of cases involved are small in comparison with most of the other entries, it is probably true that foster children resemble each other somewhat more in I.Q. than would be predicted from the rest of the data bearing on kinship correlations. Whether this is owing to selective placement leading to inadvertent genetic similarity, some peculiarity of the home environments of foster children, some as yet not understood form of environmental action in general, or just a statistical fluke that will iron itself out with more data, cannot now be answered. Omitting the data on foster children would raise the estimate of the genetic contribution from 83 to 87 per cent. In any event, even taking the relatively high correlation of the foster children at face value does not change the essential findings for the population at large, which is that genes provide the main source of variation in I.Q. among individuals.

The analysis by Jinks and Fulker carried well beyond that simple statement. They were able to establish that the 17 per cent environmental contribution is about evenly divided between variations within the home and variations from home to home. In other words, if every family were suddenly to provide the same environment for nurturing I.Q. as every other family, the spread of people's scores would decrease about 9 per cent, since environmental differences between families account for about that much of the variation. In contrast, if families continued to differ from each other as much as they do now on the average, but the parents in each family somehow managed to give equal advantages (or disadvantages) to all of their children, the spread of I.Q.'s would decrease by 8 per cent, since environmental individual differences within families account for that much of the variation. Usually, we think of the environmental variations between families in our society as being large, reflecting the span of social classes, while the environmental variations within families are depicted as small, but as regards the I.Q., they are both small and just about equal to each other in impact. It may be hard to believe, but the facts say that the average differences in the nurturing of I.Q. within families just about equal the average differences from family to family in society at large. This does not exclude exceptionally good or bad individual cases, for it expresses only the overall average. Nor does it say that for other important traits and achievements — such as psychic well-being or scholastic performance — parents are comparably impotent. The I.Q. proved to be the most inherited facet scrutinized by Jinks and Fulker, with neuroticism and schoolwork more, though by no means altogether, responsive to the environment. However, the data bearing on those other dimensions fall far short of the I.Q. in both quality and quantity and have limited applicability at this time.

The relative wealth of data on I.Q., and their overall consistency, enabled Jinks and Fulker to approximate some of the genetic details of the transmission of intelligence. For example, they estimated, by methods too technical to outline here, that intelligence as measured by I.Q. tests is encoded at numerous genetic locations in the germ plasm. Apparently, the score on an intelligence test reflects a genetic endowment embodied in something between twenty and one hundred genes, contributing in ways that we mostly do not know and acted on somehow by the physical and social environment. Here and there, particularly for genes that can result in catastrophic mental disability, the hereditary picture is being sketched in with some detail. At the moment, however, most of those twenty to one hundred genes are known only as undifferentiated contributors to intelligence, accounting for about 80 per cent of the variation among people.

Other clues in the data reveal that genes for high I.Q. are somewhat dominant over genes for low I.Q., just as the genes for brown eyes dominate over those for blue, only not so completely. Genetic dominance shows up, for example, as inbreeding depression, otherwise there would be no hereditary penalty in I.Q. for marriage among kinfolk. Dominance also shows up in the departures from the normal distribution of I.Q. in the population as a whole, making it slightly biased towards high scores. Finally, dominance expresses itself as a tendency for siblings to be more highly correlated with each other than parents are with their children, except for assortative mating, which counteracts this difference by causing parents and children to be more alike than they would otherwise. By drawing on the relevant items of data, the amount of assortative mating and the amount and direction of genetic dominance have been teased out of the mass of information. In general, the husband-wife correlation for I.Q. falls in the .4 to .6 range, while dominance for high scores is substantial, but not complete, as if some of the genes involved just blended while others behaved more like brown and blue eye color, giving one result or the other, but virtually nothing in between. Where the genes for I.Q. fail to blend, the one for higher I.Q. usually dominates. That high I.Q. would dominate over low I.Q. makes good biological sense, since it indicates that over the eons man's I.Q. has been subjected to natural selection favoring high intelligence.

Nature and nurture have so far been discussed as if their contributions to the variations in I.Q. simply get added to each other: 83 per cent for nature, 17 per cent for nurture, according to Jinks and Fulker, or 80 per cent for nature, 20 per cent for nurture, according to Jensen, but inevitably adding up to 100 per cent. It is natural to wonder whether so complex a thing as mental capacity can really be viewed as the simple sum of environment and heredity. The apparent implausibility of such convenient simplicity is, however, based more on a misunderstanding of statistical theory than on well-grounded empirical skepticism. The question of nature and nurture finally boils down to the study of variation. Granted that I.Q.'s vary among people, to what extent does the variation correlate with the differences in their surroundings on the one hand and with the differences in their genetic makeup on the other? No one disputes the existence of all three kinds of variation — in I.Q., environment, and inheritance — only their interconnections. In effect, the environmentalist says that among a group of people, the various I.Q.'s reflect the various surroundings more or less without regard to the genes. In contrast, the nativist says the reverse — that different I.Q.'s reflect different genetic endowments rather than different environments. The study of quantitative genetics contrives to answer such riddles, but the answers it gives are themselves something of a puzzle to laymen (and apparently also to a fair number of social scientists). A brief didactic excursion appears, therefore, to be in order, starting not with the overheated subject of I.Q., but with a trait to which we are not emotionally committed to begin with.

Suppose we wanted to know the heritability of skin color. We would not need science to tell us that dark or fair complexions run in certain families or larger groups. Nor must we be told that nongenetic elements also enter in, as when a person is tan from the sun or pale with illness or yellow from jaundice or red with rage or blue with cold. The task of quantitative genetics is to come up with a number that says how large a role inheritance plays in the total amount of variation in skin color that we see in a particular group of people at a particular time. If the number is large, then skin color is largely heritable; if very small, then the heritability is negligible. If the number is large, then there will be marked family resemblances; if small, then members of given families will be no more alike than unrelated people. To convey such information, the number must reflect which group of people we choose to study. Consider first the United States, with its racial and ethnic diversity. Much skin variation here is related to ancestry, hence genetic, whether black, white, yellow, red, or Mediterranean, Nordic, Alpine, or some blend. Family resemblances in skin color are quite strong in America, so the heritability should come out large. Now contrast this with an isolated village in Norway, full of Scandinavians with generations of pale-skinned ancestors. In the Norwegian town, whatever little variation there is in skin color is likely to be environmental, due to circumstances of life rather than to the accident of inheritance. As regards skin color, children will be no more like their parents than their nonrelatives, so heritability should come out low.

The hardest thing to grasp about heritability is that it says something about a trait in a population as a whole, not about the relation between particular parents and their offspring. Skin color turns out to be more heritable in the United States than in Norway, even though the physiological mechanisms of inheritance are surely the same. In the Norwegian town, a swarthy father and mother (who probably got that way from exposure to the weather) are likely to have children as fair-skinned as their neighbors. In the American town, however, it is more likely that the swarthiness of swarthy parents is genetic and will be passed on to the children. Although heritability is not the strictly physiological concept that laymen imagine it to be, it is uniquely useful for talking about the nature-nurture question, for it tells us whether traits run in families within a broader population of individuals.

A trait may change its heritability with changing circumstances, even though the genes themselves are not changing. Consider the heritability of contracting the disease tuberculosis, an example noted by Jensen and others. We think of tuberculosis as purely contagious; in the past it was thought to run in families, and both are right. Tuberculosis is caused by a germ, but especially so in people who are constitutionally susceptible. Before people knew about the dangers of contagion, virtually everyone was exposed to the germs, but not everyone got sick. Only the susceptible ones got sick. If susceptibility was at all genetic, then the main factor deciding whether a given person got TB was what he inherited, not his environment. The disease would therefore have seemed to run in families, and the heritability was correspondingly high. But now, a person who inherits a susceptibility may escape infection just because he takes the common precautions against exposure. People have learned to cover their mouths when they cough, or avert their heads when someone else fails to do so, and we do not readily use a stranger's drinking cup or towel. The likelihood of getting TB now depends on variation in *both* the genetic and the environmental factors, and so the heritability is less than it used to be. Yet, a given individual either gets tuberculosis or not by the same combination of events now as two hundred or two thousand years ago — if he has the susceptibility and has been exposed to the germ.

The technical measure of heritability is a number between o

and 1.0, or a percentage between 0 and 100, that states how much of the variation in a trait is due to genetic factors. How it is calculated need not detain us here. It is enough to know that a heritability of .5 means (deferring some technical complexities for a moment) that the variation is due half to genetic factors and half to other factors; a heritability of .2 means that only a fifth of the variation is genetic, and so on. Some actual heritabilities of traits in animals may be helpful. In piebald Holstein cattle, for example, the amount of white in the fur has a heritability of about .95, a value so high that it is almost right to say the environment plays no role here. In contrast, milk yield has a heritability of only .3. White in the fur, therefore, breeds more true than milk production. In pigs, the thickness of body fat has a heritability of .55, while the litter size has a heritability of only .15.

There are two main technical complexities worth considering, for they often come up in discussion of the heritability of I.Q. Perhaps, it might be said, different genetic patterns react differently to given environments. For example, suppose the average I.Q. difference between separated identical twins were found to depend on whether the twins, as a pair, had high or low I.Q.'s. Figure 8 shows hypothetical findings of that sort. In Figure 8A, the difference between the pairs spreads as the twin pairs' average I.Q. rises. In Figure 8B, just the opposite trend is shown. Either result exemplifies what statisticians would call "interaction" of heredity and environment, for each shows a departure from the simple additivity of the two sources. Since identical twins differ only in the extent to which they have had different environments acting on them, the gap between the lines estimates the environmental gap between pairs of people at different levels of I.Q. The gap increases with higher I.Q.'s if people's ability to benefit from better environments, in the sense of gaining I.Q. points, is itself aided by a higher I.Q. The gap diminishes with higher I.Q.'s if the opposite is the case — i.e., if people with lower I.Q.'s can benefit more from better environments. Another way to look at this is to consider the slopes of the lines. A steep slope

Figure 8

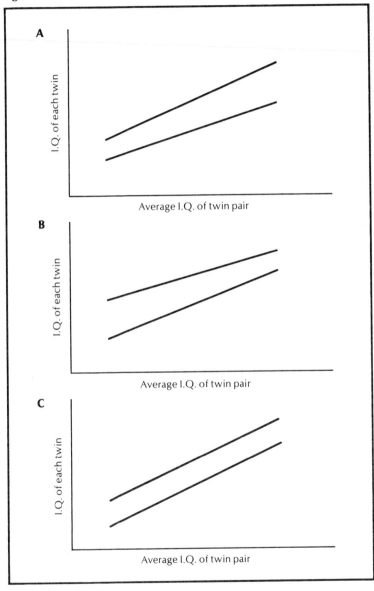

Statistical interaction of heredity and environment is exemplified in
A and B; the findings for twins are summarized in C.

covers a broader range of I.Q.'s than a shallow one. Figures 8A and B each contain a steep slope and a shallow one. In Figure 8A, the upper line is steep and the lower is shallow, while in Figure 8B it is the reverse. However, since these are twin pairs, the upper line, by design, plots the twin in each pair that had the better environment. The hypothetical interaction depicted in Figure 8A therefore says that good environments expand the range of I.Q.'s, while in Figure 8B good environments contract the range. The actual data, however, say neither, for the gap between separated twins is essentially uncorrelated with the I.Q. level of the pair. Figure 8C shows the fitted straight lines for the 122 pairs of separated twins described earlier. Wherever pairs of twins placed on the I.Q. scale, the difference between them averaged around six to seven. The slight convergence of the two lines (which is probably undetectable in this drawing) has no statistical significance. From any practical standpoint, they are parallel, which means that the data from the twins reveal no interaction (in the technical sense) of heredity and environment.

The scarcity of evidence for interaction does not mean that interaction is forever impossible, only that it is not accounting for much now. It is, in fact, entirely possible that science could uncover ways of raising people's I.Q.'s by special sorts of environments, tailor-made for them. A world in which each person enjoyed something approaching his optimal environment — let us assume a different environment for each — might register large interaction and little overall variation in I.Q. That is, however, not our world, and we have as yet hardly an inkling of how to get from here to there, or even of whether or not the way exists in any practical sense.

But even if interaction (again in the technical sense) accounts for little, suppose people with the genetic advantages also ended up with the environmental ones too, and those with genetic shortages also had the poorer environments. Then, it could be argued, the differences between people would be accentuated, and might be falsely blamed entirely on their genes. This complexity, known in the trade as "covariance," is doubtless the most common criticism leveled at efforts to separate the environmental and inherited contributors to I.Q. Presumably, if that sort of covariance were significant, society might try to minimize it, and thereby reduce the intellectual differences between people.

In one sense, covariance must be large indeed. Children with high I.Q.'s simply behave differently from those with low I.Q.'s, and thereby the two types of children (and the adults they grow into) create different environments for themselves. For example, when an elementary school enlarges its library, not all the children read more. In general, those with the higher I.Q.'s will profit more and may show the benefits in the form of still higher test scores. The school administrator may think the school library causes interaction, for it appears to operate selectively on the children, but a more insightful analysis is to recognize that the library simply fails to become part of some children's, particularly the low-I.Q. children's, environment. It may be that those children would gain just as many, if not more, I.Q. points from reading as their more intellectual schoolmates, if only they would read. The practical question about covariance in this case is what needs to be done to break it down, to get the favorable behavior in all the children, so that the differences in I.Q. might diminish. Obviously, if environmental rearrangements put an end to such covariance, I.Q. differences might become less of a problem than they are now.

The usual assumption about covariance centers on the home environment. Parents with higher I.Q.'s, it is said, inadvertently (or deliberately) pass on to their children both the right genes and the right customs and habits for gaining high test scores, while people with low I.Q.'s do the opposite. Since most studies of natural families combine both influences, it may seem hard, if not impossible, to tell how much covariance families arrange. Note, however, that much of the data already summarized — on identical twins raised together and apart, on siblings raised together and apart, and on the greater similarity of identical twins growing up apart than fraternal twins growing up together — already show that covariance of home environment and genetic endowment can hardly account for much, otherwise the results would make no sense.

The information bearing most directly on this sort of covariance comes from studies of foster children when adequate information about the adoptive and natural parents is available. Studies already summarized (see Figures 5A and B) show that foster children grow up more highly correlated in I.Q. with their natural parents' education than with that of the adoptive parents who raised them. A still more persuasive case for the relative unimportance of home-genetic covariance can be found in a study published in 1928 by Barbara Burks of Stanford University. The study compared 214 foster children and their adoptive parents (the "experimental" group) to a carefully matched collection of 105 children being raised by their own parents (the "control" group). The control group was chosen to mimic the experimental group for the age and sex of the children, and for the locality, type of neighborhood, occupation, and ethnic characteristics of the family. Moreover, enough was known about the true fathers of the adopted children to show that there was little if any selective placement as regards fathers. There was no correlation between the occupational level or the cultural rating of the foster fathers and the occupational level of the true fathers. All the children in the experimental group were adopted before the age of twelve months and more than 60 per cent of them did not know they were adopted at the time of the study. The distribution of intelligence-test scores covered about the same range, with close to the same average, for the foster parents and the control parents raising their own children. To the extent possible for naturalistic studies of human beings, Burks succeeded in crossing a broad range of genetic endowments with a broad range of home environments. If covariance were crucial, the study would have shown it.

First, in keeping with the studies of foster children summarized earlier, the foster children's I.Q.'s correlated with their natural parents' I.Q.'s more than with their foster parents'. Even though the natural parents and the foster parents were uncorrelated as regards cultural or social-class characteristics, the true father–child or true mother–child correlations were in the .5 range. In contrast, the foster father–child correlation was essentially zero, while the foster mother–child correlation was about .2. The control-group correlations, for parents raising their natural children, were only slightly higher than the true parent–child correlations in the experimental group, comprising adopted children. The study clearly and unequivocally showed that the home environment, when disentangled from the genetic connection between ordinary parents and their children, accounts for relatively little of the variation in children's I.Q.'s

Subjecting Burks's results to the statistical procedures of quantitative genetics yields an estimate of heritability in the familiar .8 range, even though the design of her study carefully eliminated the covariance of genetic endowment and home environment. From this, and from other comparable results, it can be concluded that covariance of this variety accounts for little concerning the I.Q. in most circumstances. That, of course, is again not to say that in a radically different world, covariance might not be highly significant, or even that in certain limited instances in our own society, it is unimportant. From her analysis, Burks could properly say that "nearly 70 per cent of schoolchildren have an actual I.Q. within 6 to 9 points of that represented by their innate intelligence." But unusually good or unusually poor environments, so rare as to affect something less than 1 per cent of the total population, might be promoting or retarding the I.Q.'s of the people encountering them as much as 20 points.

Burks's sample was drawn from the white, primarily native American or western European population living around San Francisco and Los Angeles. The families spanned all social classes, from those of unskilled laborers to successful professionals and businessmen. Nevertheless, in racial, ethnic, linguistic, and, no doubt, cultural terms, the study omitted significant parts of the vastly diversified American population. Since heritability measures a population trait, it is quite possible that the estimates are off somewhat. It could well be that there are sources of environmental variation left out of Burks's study, or, for that matter, the other studies in the literature reviewed here. Including them might reduce the heritability estimate. Much of Jinks and Fulker's analysis is, for example, based on data collected in England by Cyril Burt. If one assumes that the intellectual environment in England is more homogeneous than in America, then Burt's data will set too high a value on heritability for the American population.

These uncertainties inhere in *any* population statistic — birth and mortality rates, crime rates, and so on — not just in the estimation of the genetic contribution to tested intelligence. Population statistics are not like the timeless constants of physical science, fixed by properties somehow inherent in nature. They are, rather, more like the actuarial data of the insurance business — more or less approximate, contingent, and, above all, changeable features of populations. Both insurance companies and quantitative geneticists are well advised to keep taking soundings.

The fact that a number of independent studies point to a particular narrow range of values for the heritability of I.Q. suggests a robustness to the estimate that should not be overlooked. However, it should not be overinterpreted either, for, while independent, the studies may nevertheless share common methodological weaknesses. For example, the poorest, most culturally deprived sectors of the population tend to be omitted, or at least underrepresented, in most assessments of heritability. If those unfortunate people happen to show most fully the impact of environment, their omission from the population sampled raises the heritability. In contrast, if the unsampled ones have unusual genetic endowments (i.e., unusually poor as regards I.Q.), their omission from the population sampled lowers the heritability, because it excludes some of the variations in genetic endowment. At the moment, there is little basis for deciding which of the biases, if either, is operating on the estimates of heritability of I.Q. in America. It is therefore pointless to argue over second and third decimal places. Instead, the proper conclusion is that a value in the vicinity of .7 to .85 describes the genetic contribution to variations in I.Q. over a large chunk of at least the American and western European population at the present time and for the past couple of generations.

The scientific literature, of which Jinks and Fulker's and Jensen's papers are but good recent examples, leaves little doubt about the heritability of I.Q. among North American and western European whites, whom most data on the subject describe. In fact, there is little dispute on this score even among those who seem to be objecting most vigorously. It is the relation between heritability and group, especially racial, differences that really raises the hackles. Given the well-established, roughly fifteen-point black-white difference in I.Q. (as documented exhaustively by Audrey Shuey in her 1966 summary of several hundred studies), the argument turns on whether the difference arises in the environment or the genes. If intelligence were entirely genetic, then racial differences would be genetic simply because they could be due to nothing else. Conversely, if the genes were irrelevant, then the racial difference would have to be due to the environment, again because there would be no alternative. As it is, I.Q. reflects both a person's genes and his environment. The racial issue really poses the nature-nurture question all over again, but this time for a particular finding — the higher scores of whites over blacks on I.Q. tests.

Using the procedures of quantitative genetics, most experts estimate that I.Q. has a heritability between .7 and .85, but this is based almost entirely on data from whites. We may, therefore, say that 70 to 85 per cent of the variation in I.Q. among whites is due to the genes. Notwithstanding some preliminary reports of slightly lower heritabilities for blacks, we still cannot make a comparable statement for them. But let us simply assume, for the sake of discussion, that .8 is the heritability for whites and blacks taken together. What could we say about the racial difference in I.Q. then? The answer is that we could still say nothing positive about it. Recall that the concept of heritability applies to a population as a whole. All we could say is that the differences between people, on the average and without regard to color, are 80 per cent inherited. But within this broad generality, particular differences could and would be more or less inherited. Take, for example, the differences in I.Q. between identical twins. Even with the average heritability equal to .8, all twin differences have to be totally environmental, since their genes cannot differ. Or conversely, consider the differences between foster children in a given foster family. Because they are growing up in the same home, their I.Q. differences could easily be relatively more genetic than those of people taken at random. When this line of reasoning is applied to a racial (or ethnic) difference in I.Q., the only proper conclusion is that we do not know whether it is more genetic, less genetic, or precisely as genetic as might seem to be implied by a heritability of .8.

Although there are scraps of evidence for a genetic component in the black-white difference, the overwhelming case is for believing that American blacks have been at an environmental disadvantage. To the extent that variations in the American social environment can promote or retard I.Q., blacks have probably been held back. But a neutral commentator (a rarity these days) would have to say that the case is simply not settled, given our present stage of knowledge. To advance this knowledge would not be easy, but it could certainly be done with sufficient ingenuity and hard work. To anyone who is curious about the question and who feels competent to try to answer it, it is at least irritating to be told that the answer is either unknowable or better not known, and both enjoinders are often heard. And there is, of course, a still more fundamental issue at stake, which should concern even those who are neither curious about nor competent to study racial differences in I.Q. It is whether inquiry shall (again) be shut off because someone thinks society is best left in ignorance.

Social policy must, of course, be made in light of existing knowledge, even when it is far from perfect or complete. In recent years, efforts have been made to rectify disproportions of racial, ethnic, and sexual groups in schools and occupations, usually on the assumption that, except for prejudice, all groups would be represented with proportionate-to-population frequency in virtually all common occupations and professions. While prejudice doubtless does hold people back unfairly, not to mention illegally, the use of such equalizing quotas may, in time, create unfairness of its own. Only if it is indeed true that all groups of people have essentially equal talents and capacities can we justly use quotas. For if there are relatively stable group differences in mental or physical capacity — between the sexes or the races or the nationalities — then the presumption of equality, when translated into quotas, is bound eventually to discriminate against the qualified individual from time to time. At the moment, while significant and intractable group differences in occupational qualifications have not yet been proved to exist, it must, in fairness, also be said that they have not been proved to be absent.

The measurable differences between blacks and whites, or between men and women, on certain subtests in the typical intelligence test may be partly or wholly environmental in origin, slated to vanish or diminish if and when society learns how to treat people evenly and fairly. And even if the differences were substantially genetic — which, after all, they could be, given existing knowledge — all known groupings of people, by race, sex, and so on, overlap substantially. Even with the present black-white difference in I.Q., for example, millions of American blacks test higher than the median American white; millions of American whites test lower than the median American black. No rational and fair social policy could discriminate on the basis of the average racial difference in test scores. Quotas against the individuals in certain groups on the supposition of group differences are therefore no less inappropriate, and certainly no less destructive, than quotas predicated on group equality.

At present, the most that the existing knowledge can tell us is that people had best be treated individually, without regard to race, ethnic or geographical origin, sex (except where sex is itself at issue), or whatever. Otherwise, we risk replacing the pernicious quotas and social barriers of the past with a new set, conceived in a spirit of generosity, but pernicious nevertheless, albeit on a smaller scale.

Setting aside group differences, the conclusion about intelligence is that, like other important though not necessarily vital traits, it is highly heritable. It is not vital in the sense that it may vary broadly without markedly affecting survival, although it no doubt affects one's life-style. Does it do us any practical good to know how heritable intelligence is? We are not, for example, on the verge of Galton's vision of eugenics, even though we now have the mental test that he thought was the crucial prerequisite. For good or ill, and for some time to come, we are stuck with mating patterns as people determine them for themselves. No sensible person would want to entrust human breeding to those who control today's states. There are, however, practical corollaries of this knowledge, more humble than eugenics, but ever more salient as the growing complexity of human society makes acute the shortage of high-grade intellect, as the final chapter spells out.

Heritability is first and foremost the measure of breeding true, useful for predicting how much of some trait the average offspring in a given family will have. For example, disregarding the complications of genetic dominance and covariance, to predict the I.Q. of the average offspring in a family:

1. Average the parents' I.Q.'s.
2. Subtract 100 from the result.
3. Multiply the result of (2) by .8 (the heritability).
4. Add the result of (3) to 100.

Thus, given a mother and father each with an I.Q. of 120, their average child will have an I.Q. of 116. Some of their children will be brighter and some duller, but the larger the family, the more nearly will the average converge onto 116. With parents averaging an I.Q. of 80, the average child will have an I.Q. of 84. The formula predicts something the experts call "regression toward the mean," the tendency for children to be closer to the general population average (in this case, I.Q. 100) than their parents. And in fact, *very bright* parents have children who tend to be merely *bright*, while *very dull* parents tend to have them merely *dull*. The amount of regression for a trait depends on the heritability — with high heritability, the regression is smaller than with low. Also, for a given trait the regression is greater at the extremes of a population than at its center. In other words, ordinary parents are more like their children (on the average) than extraordinary ones (whether extraordinarily high or low). All of these characteristics of the "generation gap" follow directly and completely from the simple formula given above. Thus, when the parents average 120, the regression effect is only four I.Q. points, but if they averaged 150, the regression effect would be ten points. In comparison, height, with its heritability of .95, would show smaller regression effects than I.Q., since the multiplier in step 3 of the formula is closer to 1.0. But even so, very tall parents tend to have children who are merely tall, and very short parents tend to have them merely short. As long as the heritability of a trait falls short of 1.0, there is some regression effect.

First impressions notwithstanding, regression towards the mean is not driving mankind closer to an I.Q. of 100 with each succeeding generation. Regression is a logical peculiarity of imperfect correlation, not an empirical finding of psychology or biology. If the mid-parent (i.e., average of mother and father) and child I.Q.'s correlate by .8 (which is higher than the correlation between either parent alone and his or her children), then there is regression either way. In other words, given a family whose average child has I.Q. 120, the best bet for his parents is 116, just as parents averaging 120 will have children averaging 116. The way out of the apparent paradox is to see that the more imperfect (i.e., the smaller) the correlation between parents and children, the more nearly independent are their I.Q.'s. In the limiting case, if the correlation were zero, the most likely average I.Q. for the children in any family would be 100 (the population average), whatever their parents scored. But by the same token, knowing the children's scores would predict nothing about their parents, so the best guess would be I.Q. 100 for them too.

Some of the foregoing examples assumed, for simplicity's sake, that the two parents had equal I.Q.'s This is obviously not typical, but it is true that couples are more alike than the principle of random mating would assume. They are, in fact, often more alike in I.Q. than brothers and sisters are, although the husband-wife correlations in I.Q. vary from study to study, ranging from just over .2 to Jensen's figure of .6. Whether this shows that intelligence really matters in mate selection or that our society tends to put people with similar I.Q.'s close together in school and work is an interesting question, but not one to answer here. In any case, assortative mating is considered biologically important if the trait is highly heritable, like intelligence. To see why, imagine a microworld containing only four people: a smart man, a dull man, a smart woman, and a dull woman. Let us suppose further that the two smart people have the same high I.Q. and the two dull people the same low one. Now consider random mating, with the smart man married to the dull woman and the dull man to the smart woman. Given the equal average I.Q. in the two pairs of parents, the average child in each family would have the same I.Q. (which could have been predicted by the heritability formula given above if the I.Q.'s were known). Each family would have some bright and some dull children, but the two families would contribute, on the average, an equivalent offspring, except to the extent that the mother's or father's I.Q. is environmentally more important (a possibility for which there is little or no evidence). Now imagine the same microworld with assortative mating — the smart man married to the smart woman and the dull man to the dull woman. Now the children in the two families will no longer have the same average I.Q., for there will be a smart family and a dull one. In just one generation of this microworld, assortative mating would begin to create a hierarchy of intellectual classes. Although the I.Q. of all the children in both families averaged together would be the same whether or not the mating was assortative, the range of I.Q.'s is larger when it is assortative. Random mating tends to bunch the I.Q.'s around middling values, while assortative mating spreads them out towards the extremes, but neither, by itself, does anything to the overall average.

The effects of assortative mating are therefore more evident the further out into the extremes of I.Q. one looks, as some of Jensen's figures show. If mating were random with respect to intelligence, then there would be about 10,000 people per million with I.Q.'s greater than 130. Given assortative mating, the figure is about 23,000. With random mating, there would be about 240 people per million with I.Q.'s greater than 145. As it is, the frequency is about 1,350. And finally, there are about twenty times as many people with I.Q.'s above 160 because of assortative mating than there would be if it were random. This is all very fine, but the trouble is that assortative mating works just as well at the bottom end of the population as at the top.

For each gift of an extra-high-I.Q. child, the mechanism of assortative mating may exact the price of an extra-low one. It may be a good exchange, if the social benefits of more bright people override the social costs of more dull ones, but this kind of social bookkeeping is, at the moment, still pure fantasy. There is, however, one certain social effect of assortative mating, and that is on reproduction itself. It has been shown that, contrary to common impression, the lowest birth rate is for people at the bottom of the I.Q. scale (below about 80) and the highest rate is for people near the top (above about 130). (The *families* are bigger at the bottom end — which explains the common impression —

but there are also many more there who remain unmarried and childless.) Assortative mating tends to put the low-I.Q., relatively infertile, sector of the population together and removes them to some degree from the breeding population. At the same time, it yields more high-fertility, high-I.Q. individuals than does random mating. If each generation is more fertile at the top of the scale, the net effect should be an upward drift in the average intelligence of successive generations. We will, of course, not see the drift in I.Q. scores as long as the testers keep restandardizing the scale around an average of 100. And the improvement is probably too slight anyway to be detected in the course of one lifetime. Nevertheless, any barrier to the free selection of spouses that may impede assortative mating — such as laws against miscegenation or taboos against ethnic or religious intermarriage — may be socially undesirable in the long run, at least in its effects on intelligence.

Intelligence may also be drifting up or down for environmental reasons from generation to generation, notwithstanding the high heritability. Height, for example, is said to be increasing — presumably because of diet and medicine — even with its .95 heritability. We can easily tell whether there has been a change in height, for the measures are absolute, and there is the tangible evidence of clothing, furniture, coffins, and the skeletons themselves. For intelligence, however, we have no absolute scales, only relative ones, and the tangible remains of intelligence defy interpretation. But if height has changed, why not intelligence? After all, one could argue, the I.Q. has a heritability of only .8, perhaps even .7, measurably lower than that of height, so it should be even more amenable to the influence of the environment. That, to be sure, is correct in principle, but the practical problem is to find the right things in the environment to change — the things that will nourish the intellect as well as diet does height. The usual assumption, that education and culture are crucial, is running into evidence that the physical environment — for example, early diet — might be more important.

Suppose we do find an environmental handle on I.Q. — something, let us say, in the gestating mother's diet or in preschool education. What then? Presumably society would try to give everyone access to the favorable factors, within the limits of its resources. Intelligence would increase accordingly. But that would not end our troubles with I.Q. Recall that heritability is a measure of relative variation. Right now, about 80 per cent of the variation in I.Q. derives from the genes. If we make the relevant environment much more uniform (by making it better for more people), then an even larger proportion of the variation in I.Q. will be attributable to the genes. The average person would be smarter, but intelligence would run in families even more obviously and with less regression towards the mean than we see today. It is likely that the mere fact of heritability in I.Q. is socially and politically important, and the more so the higher the heritability. Because the I.Q. measures something *both* heritable *and* necessary for important social consequences, it cannot be dismissed *either* as an insignificant biological curiosity *or* as a wholly arbitrary cultural value. A mere biological curiosity it is not, because of its social predictiveness; a purely cultural artifact it is not, because of its heritability.

Notes to Chapter Four

Francis Galton, in *Natural Inheritance* (London: Macmillan, 1889), tried to work out the quantitative hereditary relationships among various members of a family for measurable traits, such as height and eye color, as well as for more intangible or complex characteristics, such as artistic talent or tendency towards various diseases. Although he showed his accustomed insightfulness, the subject of quantitative, or population, genetics came into its own only after the efforts of several highly gifted mathematical biologists in the twentieth century. Several long series of works by two British scientists, R. A. Fisher and J. B. S. Haldane, and one American, Sewall Wright, shaped the fundamental concepts of the subject, which have now been elaborated by many other gifted theorists. An excellent recent presentation, including an extensive bibliography of both the historical and contemporary sources is J. F. Crow and M. Kimura's *An Introduction to Population Genetics Theory* (New York: Harper & Row, 1970). Narrower in scope, and less detailed and up to date, but highly useful on the concept of heritability is D. S. Falconer's *Introduction to Quantitative Genetics* (New York: Ronald, 1960).

Although both Fisher and Wright occasionally concerned themselves with the inheritance of human intelligence, the main early extensions of quantitative genetics to this topic were made by Cyril Burt and his collaborators in a series of papers over several decades. The especially relevant, more contemporary, ones are:

Burt, C. and Howard, M. "The Multifactorial Theory of Inheritance and Its Application to Intelligence." *British Journal of Statistical Psychology* 9 (1956): 95–131.

Burt, C. and Howard, M. "Heredity and Intelligence: A Reply to Criticisms." *British Journal of Statistical Psychology* 10 (1957): 33–63.

Burt, C. "The Inheritance of Mental Ability." *American Psychologist* 13 (1958): 1–15.

―――. "The Genetic Determinations of Differences in Intelligence: A Study of Monozygotic Twins Reared Together and Apart." *British Journal of Psychology* 57 (1966): 137–153.

―――. "Quantitative Genetics in Psychology." *British Journal of Mathematical and Statistical Psychology* 24 (1971): 1–21.

―――. "Inheritance of General Intelligence." *American Psychologist* 27 (1972): 175–190.

Burt's twin study (see Burt, 1966, cited above) was one of the four brought together by Arthur R. Jensen in his article "I.Q.'s of Identical Twins Reared Apart" (*Behavior Genetics* 1 [1970]: 133–146). The other three are:

Newman, H. H.; Freeman, F. N.; and Holzinger, K. J. *Twins: A Study of Heredity and Environment.* Chicago: University of Chicago Press, 1937.

Shields, J. *Monozygotic Twins Brought Up Apart and Brought Up Together.* London: Oxford University Press, 1962.

Juel-Nielsen, N. "Individual and Environment: A Psychiatric-Psychological Investigation of Monozygous Twins Reared Apart." *Acta psychiatrica et neurologica Scandinavica,* Monograph Supplement 183 1965.

The first of Jensen's articles that called wide public attention to his work, and which contains a survey of the data on the inheritance of intelligence as well as a discussion of compensatory education is his "How Much Can We Boost I.Q. and Scholastic Achievement?" (*Harvard Educational Review* 39 [1969]: 1–123). A second article dealt with some of the comments by several writers responding to an invitation by the *Harvard Educational Review*: "Reducing the Heredity-Environment Uncertainty" (*Harvard Educational Review* 39 [1969]:

209–243). These two articles by Jensen, as well as some of the commentaries, have been issued as Reprint Series No. 2 by the *Harvard Educational Review*.

A somewhat more technical, but highly useful, discussion of the heritability of I.Q. and other traits can be found in J. L. Jinks and D. W. Fulker, "Comparison of the Biometrical Genetical, MAVA, and Classical Approaches to the Analysis of Human Behavior" (*Psychological Bulletin* 73 [1970]: 311–349).

Other workers, besides Burt and Jensen, have compiled the correlations in I.Q. among relatives of various degrees of kinship, and the most complete other source is L. Erlenmeyer-Kimling and L. F. Jarvik, "Genetics and Intelligence: A Review" (*Science* 142 [1963]: 1477–1479). The 30,000 correlation pairs in that study have recently been supplemented by a table of figures, credited to Erlenmeyer-Kimling, that appears on page 352 of J. P. Guilford's *The Nature of Human Intelligence* (New York: McGraw-Hill, 1967).

The main study of parent-child and sibling correlations cited in the chapter is H. S. Conrad and H. E. Jones's "A Second Study of Familial Resemblance in Intelligence: Environmental and Genetic Implications of Parent-Child and Sibling Correlations in the Total Sample" (*Yearbook of the National Society for the Study of Education* 39 (II) [1940]: 97–141).

Parent-child resemblances in the context of foster and natural parenthood are dealt with in:

Burks, B. S. "The Relative Influence of Nature and Nurture upon Mental Development: A Comparative Study of Foster Parent–Foster Child Resemblance and True Parent–True Child Resemblance." *Yearbook of the National Society for the Study of Education* 27 (I) (1928): 219–316.

Skodak, M. and Skeels, H. M. "A Final Follow-up Study of One Hundred Adopted Children." *Journal of Genetic Psychology* 75 (1949): 85–125.

Honzik, M. P. "Developmental Studies of Parent-Child Resemblance in Intelligence." *Child Development* 28 (1957): 215–228.

Related to the question of parent-child resemblance is the question of chronological stability in I.Q. A general study of human stability in development is B. S. Bloom's *Stability and Change in Human Characteristics* (New York: Wiley, 1964). Stability as regards I.Q. is discussed in:

Honzik, M. P., McFarlane, J. Q., and Allen, L. "The Stability of Mental Test Performance between Two and Eighteen Years." *Journal of Experimental Education* 17 (1948): 309–324.

Bayley, N. "Consistency and Variability in the Growth of Intelligence from Birth to Eighteen Years." *Journal of Genetic Psychology* 75 (1949): 165–196.

Hilden, A. H. "A Longitudinal Study of Intellectual Development." *Journal of Psychology* 28 (1949): 187–214.

Bayley, N. "Some Increasing Parent-Child Similarities during the Growth of Children." *Journal of Educational Psychology* 45 (1954): 1–21.

Sontag, L. W., Baker, C. T., and Nelson, V. L. "Mental Growth and Personality Development: A Longitudinal Study." *Monograph, Society for Research in Child Development* 23 (2) (1958): 1–85.

Inbreeding depression, described in some technical detail in the textbook by Crow and Kimura cited above, turned up for I.Q. in W. J. Schull and J. V. Neel, *The Effects of Inbreeding on Japanese Children* (New York: Harper & Row, 1965). A brief discussion of incest and I.Q. can be found in S. G. Vandenberg, "What Do We Know Today About the Inheritance of Intelligence and How Do We Know It?" (*Intelligence: Genetic and Environmental Influences*, edited by R. Cancro. New York: Grune & Stratton, 1971). The same chapter by Vandenberg also discusses twin data on intelligence and other issues in the evaluation of the genetic contribution to I.Q. An assessment of the inherited factor in particular mental abilities, rather than in I.Q. in general, is part of Vandenberg's "The Nature and Nurture of Intelligence" (in *Genetics*, edited by D. C. Glass. New York: Rockefeller University Press and Russell Sage Foundation, 1968). Both the Cancro and Glass collections contain other useful contributions on inheritance in relation to intelligence.

Assortative mating is discussed in principle in Crow and Kimura, cited above. In relation to intelligence, see R. J. Garrison, V. E. Anderson, and S. C. Reed, "Assortative Marriage" (*Eugenics Quarterly* 15 [1968]: 113–127); and B. K. Eckland, "New Mating Boundaries in Education" (*Social Biology* 17 [1970]: 269–277). The closely related matter of differential fertility and I.Q. is the subject of J. V. Higgins, and E. W. and S. C. Reed's "Intelligence and Family Size: A Paradox Resolved" (*Eugenics Quarterly* 9 [1962]: 84–90); and S. C. Reed's "The Evolution of Human Intelligence: Some Reasons Why It Should Be a Continuing Process" (*American Scientist* 53 [1965]: 317–326).

The normality of I.Q. among deaf people is discussed in M. Vernon's "Fifty Years of Research on the Intelligence of Deaf and Hard-of-Hearing Children: A Review of Literature and Discussion of Implications" (*Journal of Rehabilitation of the Deaf* 1 (4) [1968]: 1–12).

Audrey Shuey's summary of racial differences in I.Q. is in *The Testing of Negro Intelligence* (2nd ed. New York: Social Science Press, 1966).

CHAPTER FIVE

The Specter of Meritocracy

The specter of Communism is haunting Europe, said Karl Marx and Friedrich Engels in 1848. They could point to the rise of egalitarianism for proof. From Jefferson's "self-evident truth" of man's equality to France's *égalité* and beyond that to the revolutions that swept Europe as Marx and Engels were proclaiming their *Manifesto*, the central political fact of their times, and ours, has been the rejection of aristocracies and privileged classes, of special rights for "special" people. The vision of a classless society was the keystone of the Declaration of Independence as well as the *Communist Manifesto*, however different the plan for achieving it.

Against this background, the main significance of intelligence testing lies in what it says about a society built around human inequalities. The message is so clear that it can be made in the form of a syllogism:

1. If differences in mental abilities are inherited, and
2. If success requires those abilities, and
3. If earnings and prestige depend on success,
4. Then social standing (which reflects earnings and prestige)

will be based to some extent on inherited differences among people.

The syllogism has five corollaries which make it more relevant to the future than to the past or present.

Corollary A: As the environment becomes generally more favorable for the development of intelligence, its heritability will increase, as Chapter 4 showed. Regardless of whether this is done by improving educational methods, diet for pregnant women, or whatever, the more advantageous we make the circumstances of life, the more certainly will intellectual differences be inherited. And the greater the heritability, the greater the force of the syllogism.

The heritability increases because as everyone approaches the optimal environment, only their genes distinguish them. The total amount of intellectual variation would be reduced to the extent that environmental factors had been causing it, but what remains would be stubbornly intractable. As far as we know, this obdurate residue would be substantial: the best current guess for the heritability of the I.Q., an estimate of how much of the total variation in intelligence resides in the genes, hovers around 80 per cent. Hence, getting down to the bare genetic bones would reduce the current variation by only 20 per cent. For abstruse, but straightforward, statistical reasons, the 20 per cent reduction in the variation would change the standard deviation by only about 1½ I.Q. points, from about 15–16, where it is now, to about 13.5–14.3, if the environmental differences were totally wiped out. This means that if 95 per cent of the population now falls between I.Q. 78–132 (which is about right), elimination of *all* environmental differences would leave a range of 81.4–128.6 for those 95 per cent, which is not much compression.

That little computation makes some assumptions, however, the main one being that the environment optimal for one is the environment optimal for all. By this assumption, giving everyone the best possible surroundings would make environments extremely alike, not just extremely good. Since the assumption may be somewhat faulty, we ought to consider the consequences of a different one — that different people learn best in radically different environments. In that case, making environments extremely good need not also make them alike. And if it does not make them alike, heritability might not increase even as the overall level of competence rose. With environments tailor-made for individuals, the range of intellectual differences between people might diminish to a far greater extent than the 20 per cent that follows from the first assumption, for each genetic shortcoming would have some chance of environmental compensation. And with the narrower spread of intelligence, its correlation with success may plummet (recall the range effect on correlation). In the syllogism's terms, the weakening of the second premise diminishes the force of its conclusion.

It therefore makes a good deal of difference which assumption is more nearly correct — will environmental amelioration tend more towards uniform or towards specialized treatment? The question obviously calls for speculation, for firm answers are not to be had. The second possibility appeals more, for it promises an end to broad differences in capacity with no unwholesome side effects. It is a fitting long-term goal. In the meantime, however, amelioration demands a certain amount of increasing uniformity. Most of the environmental diversity in the world today cannot be defended on educational grounds. Eliminating large classes in school, poor libraries, shabby physical surroundings, teeming ghettos, undertrained teachers, inadequate diet, and so on, remain laudable goals, but we should recognize that they have the corollary effect of increasing heritability. In the short term, therefore, the syllogism will become more potent as the right environment for intellectual development is made more generally available. The day of specialized environments for each person, improving them all to the point where differences approach insignificance, seems remote.

These days, there is great pressure to reduce individual differences, perhaps even by withholding educational advantages from gifted people and lavishing them on the less well endowed. Educators may not think they are advocating any such selective deprivation, but, in effect, they do so when they assume that an educational system must strive to blot out individual differences at all costs — and that goal has become commonplace. The problem comes from not appreciating the crucial distinction between the reduction of individual differences by tailoring environments for individuals and by selective deprivation. The first must raise the average level of the population, for it optimizes the environment for all; the second may lower it, for it sets equalization as its goal, instead of optimization. Yet both can eliminate at least some of the troublesome spread of ability, so that, lacking the wherewithal for the first, we may be tempted to settle for the second.

It may help to recast the alternatives in medical terms, since the equivalent problems seem to evoke less obscurantism. Doctors blame some of the differences in people's health on differences in care and some on differences in constitution. In response to social pressure to reduce the differences, the first step would be to improve the care of people who had been suffering some deprivation. To the extent that the existing differences in health had been due to poor facilities or surroundings, this step would make the average person healthier and would reduce the range of differences. At the same time, however, it would increase the heritability of health, for the lingering differences would be relatively more dependent on constitutional factors, and those are to a considerable extent genetic. Thus far, the analogy takes us to the point of this corollary, which is that environmental amelioration increases heritability. Now suppose further that medicine went beyond a general improvement of facilities to individualized preventive medicine. People might be tested at birth, let us say, and their diets, medication, perhaps even place of residence would be designed to offset their constitutional weaknesses. Obviously this is as much a fantasy as the analogous scheme for education, but medical and psychological science may in time deliver the necessary information. With individualized preventive care, the outcome would be an increase in the health of the average person, a major reduction in overall variation from person to person, and no necessary increase in the heritability, which are the analogues to the benefits of individualized compensatory education. As before, no one could decently object. However, part of the same result could be achieved simply by depriving healthier people of some part of their medical care and diverting it to the unhealthy. This, too, would reduce the differences between people and would not necessarily cause any increase in heritability. However, the health of the average person might well deteriorate. For that reason, and because it would seem both arbitrary and immoral, many people (particularly the healthy ones) would surely object strenuously. In the case of health care, the difference between individualized preventive medicine and selective deprivation is plain.

To return to the issue at hand, there are doubtless many unsatisfactory educational practices in the United States, unequally inflicted on the population. Getting rid of such inequities by correcting the deficiencies has increased heritability as an unwelcome corollary, but can hardly be forsaken on those grounds. In contrast, individualized instruction on a large scale (at present more a goal than an actual option) could raise people's overall intellectual level, reduce the differences between them, and perhaps avoid any increase in heritability. But this happy alternative tends to be confused with an at best dubious, at worst unsavory, program of compensatory deprivation, which would also reduce individual differences, but do so at the expense of those who are fortunate enough to have been well endowed to begin with. Not only would such selective deprivation be unfair, but it would be a waste our society can ill afford.

Corollary B: All modern political credos preach social mobility. The good society should, we believe, allow people to rise (and, by implication if not by frank admission, fall) according to their own efforts. The social barriers of the past — race, religion, nationality, title, inherited wealth — are under continuous assault, at least in principle. The separation of church and state, the graduated income tax, the confiscatory inheritance tax, the laws against discrimination and segregation, the abolition of legal class and caste systems all manifest a desire to accelerate movement on the social ladder. The standard wisdom of our time avows that people should be free of "unfair" impediments and divested of "unfair" advantages in all their endeavors. But the syllogism becomes more potent in proportion to the opportunities for social mobility, for it is only when people rise and fall by their own merit that they can be sorted out according to inherited differences. Actual social mobility is blocked by innate human differences after the social and legal impediments are removed.

Estimates of upward social mobility during the past fifty years or more have revealed a stubborn tendency to hover around 30 per cent in Asia (Japan), Europe, and America. On the average, something less than one boy in three (the studies have focused on male occupational status) has been able to rise above his father's occupational status. Downward social mobility has also seemed to be stuck within a range, albeit somewhat broader and lower than for upward. To the surprise of some, and the dismay of many, society continues to recruit its class members preferentially. By some ideal of democracy or simple fairness, the children of all classes should be equally spread over the occupational continuum when they grow up. The fact that they clearly are not has been taken as proof that our society (as well as all others that have been examined) must be favoring some children and holding back others.

While deliberate and inadvertent favoritism may be causing some of the social immobility, there are other obstacles to the democratic ideal. Occupational success is correlated with I.Q., and fathers' and sons' I.Q.'s are also correlated, largely for genetic reasons. Those two facts by themselves impose a brake on the democratic ideal of unhampered intergenerational traffic in social class, as will be spelled out henceforth. This is not to deny the massive environmental handicaps of, for example, the children of migrant workers or the comparable advantages of young Rocke-fellers or Rothschilds. But however visible, disturbing, or enviable those extremes, only a small fraction of the population falls unam-biguously in either class. For the preponderant remainder, it is not so obvious what controls mobility, or the lack of it.

Both correlations — between I.Q. and the usual occupational scale, and between fathers' and sons' I.Q.'s — are intermediate: in the vicinity of .5. Even if there were no environmental favorit-ism whatsoever, we would need an intermediate amount of mo-bility to maintain the status quo. The father-son correlation in I.Q. of .5 produces, as a general principle, regression halfway back to-wards the population average (i.e., 100), for reasons covered in Chapter 2 and exemplified by data in Chapters 3 and 4. A man whose I.Q. of 130 helped land him a high position in industry will therefore have sons whose I.Q.'s center on 115 — and an I.Q. of 115 predicts a job on a lower rung of the social ladder. Hence, right here there may be some downward mobility, as well as an eventual vacancy on the upper rung, perhaps to be filled by some-one upwardly mobile. Of course, all this is in terms of an *average* son, of which any given family may have no instance, for statis-tical principles apply only in the aggregate.

Suppose there were no mobility at all — the sons staying at the same occupational level as their fathers, who would be at the same level as their fathers, and so on. Because of regression to-wards the mean, the I.Q. at each occupational level in this rigid caste society would converge on the population average. As those class differences approached the vanishing point, the correlation between I.Q. and occupational success would approach the van-ishing point also. One generation of this process is shown in Tables 7A and B, from an English study published in 1961 by Cyril Burt. Table 7A shows the I.Q.'s of a representative sample of 1,000 men from all occupational levels. The six levels differ slightly from the usual socioeconomic index since they are based more on the re-quired intellectual competence in the jobs than on income or

A. DISTRIBUTION OF INTELLIGENCE ACCORDING TO OCCUPATIONAL CLASS: ADULTS

	50–60	60–70	70–80	80–90	90–100	100–110	110–120	120–130	130–140	140+	Total	Mean I.Q.
I. Higher Professional									2	1	3	139.7
II. Lower Professional							2	13	15	1	31	130.6
III. Clerical				1	8	16	56	38	3		122	115.9
IV. Skilled			2	11	51	101	78	14	1		258	108.2
V. Semiskilled		5	15	31	135	120	17	2			325	97.8
VI. Unskilled	1	18	52	117	53	11	9				261	84.9
TOTAL	1	23	69	160	247	248	162	67	21	2	1000	100.0

B. DISTRIBUTION OF INTELLIGENCE ACCORDING TO OCCUPATIONAL CLASS: CHILDREN

	50–60	60–70	70–80	80–90	90–100	100–110	110–120	120–130	130–140	140+	Total	Mean I.Q.
I. Higher Professional						1		1	1		3	120.8
II. Lower Professional				1	2	6	12	8	2		31	114.7
III. Clerical			3	8	21	31	35	18	6		122	107.8
IV. Skilled		1	12	33	53	70	59	22	7	1	258	104.6
V. Semiskilled	1	6	23	55	99	85	38	13	5		325	98.9
VI. Unskilled	1	15	32	62	75	54	16	6			261	92.6
TOTAL	2	22	70	159	250	247	160	68	21	1	1000	100.0

TABLE 7

prestige, although all three are highly correlated. Nevertheless, the occupational levels in this table show a somewhat steeper gradient of I.Q. than one usually encounters — covering a span of almost 55 I.Q. points. As is typical of all such tallies, the spread of I.Q. is much broader at the bottom of the ladder than at the top, in keeping with the conclusion that I.Q. is necessary, even if not sufficient, for occupational success.

Table 7B shows the I.Q.'s of the children whose fathers were tallied in the foregoing table. The children from the various classes still differ in average I.Q., but regression towards the mean has taken its predicted toll. Instead of a 55-point spread across the classes, it is now about half that — 28 points — which is just what it should be given the father-child correlation of .5 in I.Q. Table 7B shows another feature of regression, the increased variability at every occupational level in the I.Q.'s of the children as compared to their fathers.

Now, what would happen if the children were locked into their fathers' levels? In one generation, the I.Q. gradient would have been sharply reduced. The next generation would reduce it further, and so on, as long as mobility were prohibited. In just a few generations, there may be no trace of the sizable correlation between I.Q. and occupational level that permeates Table 7A (and the society that it describes). The persistent, perhaps even growing, occupational differences in I.Q. therefore show that there must be at least enough mobility across socioeconomic classes to sustain them.

The children in Table 7B did not stay at their father's level. They moved up or down, as Burt also showed, depending on whether they were more or less well endowed with intellect than their fathers, and on whether they were motivated towards occupational success. Beyond those two ingredients, other factors like home surroundings and caliber of schooling seemed to make only minor contributions to individual success.

A certain amount of mobility therefore follows naturally from the parent-child regression in I.Q. and from the correlation between I.Q. and status. The question is, how much of American mobility is pure statistical necessity and how much is extra social fluidity. It has, in fact, been estimated that roughly 50 per cent of the mobility from generation to generation can be pinned on the way I.Q. is transmitted from fathers to their children. Since we know that the transmission is mainly (perhaps increasingly, see corollary A) genetic, it follows that mobility itself flows within genetic constraints. Other genetic factors besides I.Q. would also contribute their share to mobility, but not even a guess at their magnitude is possible now.

The 50 per cent estimate should be taken as a stab in the dark rather than as a known quantity. The missing detailed statistical information on I.Q. and occupational status over several generations is hard to come by, and, given the unsettled climate of discussion on the subject, likely to become harder still. Moreover, it would require continual updating, for the patterns of mobility are likely shifting for various reasons. First, the correlation between occupational status and I.Q. may change. If the correlation gets bigger, it would take more mobility in each generation to undo the leveling effect of the regression in I.Q. from father to child. Table 7 presents a concrete case in point. The children clearly are more scattered around the table than their fathers. To produce as high a correlation between I.Q. and status for the children as there was for their fathers calls for a certain amount of mobility. The higher the correlation that the children are recovering, the greater the amount of mobility called for. With smaller correlations, the required mobility would decrease. In the limiting case, with no correlation between I.Q. and occupation, the leveling effect of regression becomes irrelevant to mobility, for nothing would need to be undone.

Second, the father-child correlation in I.Q. might increase, perhaps because of increased assortative mating for I.Q. (see Chapter 4). The greater the correlation, the less the regression towards the mean. As a result, it would take less mobility to sustain the current distribution of I.Q.'s across occupations. In the limiting case, with a perfect correlation, there would be no regression, hence no mobility would be called for on this count. A reduced father-child correlation would have the reverse effect, increasing mobility.

Third, the labor market for I.Q. may be changing (which also concerns corollary D). Jobs towards the lower end of the occupational scale may be disappearing and being replaced by jobs towards the upper end. Among its other effects, such a shift increases the amount of upward mobility, since it creates high-level vacancies to be filled by offspring recruited from lower levels. A shift in the other direction, towards the bottom of the scale, also increases mobility, except it would be downward mobility. By all indications, however, changes in the occupational structure favor upward mobility.

Fourth, population growth itself may be a source of mobility. If any sector of the social scale suddenly changes its fertility, it exerts pressure for mobility out of its level. Thus, overreproduction at the lower end of the scale exerts pressure towards upward mobility. However, if the upper classes continued to breed at their old rate, and no new jobs were being created, any new upward mobility would be balanced by equal downward mobility and new unemployment, perhaps correlated with I.Q. (see corollary C). Overreproduction at the upper end of the scale exerts pressure towards downward mobility, but the upshot may be not much different. Either way, the average I.Q. at each occupational level could remain constant, but with greater mobility up and down. The exact effects of differential reproduction depend upon its precise details — how much, from which levels, and with what changes in the job market — except that it is likely to churn up additional mobility.

The foregoing list of factors affecting mobility is not exhaustive. It does not even handle, for example, obvious complications like family wealth or education in "exclusive" schools. Nevertheless, it shows that a given rate of mobility sustains a status quo, whether or not unfair impediments or advantages contribute also. It also shows how the mobility may rise or fall as a natural outcome of changes that do not seem particularly fair or unfair — increased assortative mating, a large role for intelligence in occupational success, a reduced birth rate within some social class, and so on. The theme that runs throughout is that mobility flows along the channels cut by the occupational requirements for I.Q. (among other personal traits), which, in turn, flows largely via the germ plasm. Moreover, to restate the point of this corollary, as the contribution of fundamentally irrelevant factors like family connections, inherited wealth, race, and religion diminish, the inherent factors, like occupational demands for inborn capacity, will take on increasing importance.

Corollary C: It was noted earlier that there are many bright but poor people even in affluent America. The social ladder is tapered steeply, with far less room at the top than at the bottom. For reasons discussed later, income (or wealth) redistribution would not be a viable remedy. The best hope for rescuing the people at the bottom is to take the taper out of the ladder, which is to say, to increase the aggregate wealth of society in such a way that there is more room at the top. This is, of course, just what has been happening since the Industrial Revolution. But one rarely noted by-product of poverty is that it may minimize the inherited differences between classes by assuring that some bright people will remain at the bottom of the ladder. As the syllogism implies, when a country gains new wealth, it will tend to be gathered most efficiently by the hands of the natively endowed. New wealth has usually diffused throughout a society, sometimes increasing the earnings of those at the bottom of the ladder by as large a factor as those at the top. However, in addition to that diffuse effect, new wealth also enriches certain individuals — for their business acumen or their cunning or their creativity or, no doubt, sometimes for their obsequiousness or their dumb luck. However, premise 2 asserts that success requires mental capacity, which should be as true of the successes that create the new wealth as it has been of the old. Whenever the new wealth enriches people from the lower classes, it will recruit for the upper classes precisely those who have the edge in native ability.

This conclusion does not assume that the virtuous inevitably become the wealthy, or vice versa for that matter. It merely extrapolates the past and present forward. Up till now, the highly gifted have enjoyed an advantage in the creation and gathering of new wealth. The advantage, while neither absolute nor enormous, has been statistically unmistakable. If we suppose that *new* wealth (not just a redistribution of existing resources) continues to favor the gifted as much as it has in the past, then those from the lower social echelons who have the requisite ability will be favored most. Simple arithmetic tells us that removing the higher I.Q.'s from the lower classes must reduce the average score of those remaining. Whatever else this accomplishes, it will also increase the I.Q. (hence, the genetic) gap between upper and lower classes, making the social ladder even steeper for those left at the bottom.

The inverse of this corollary is also worth noting. Suppose that a society suddenly suffers a loss of wealth. How would the losses be distributed? If we assume that the reduced goods are still subject to premise 2, then the loss will tend to show up as increased numbers of gifted but poor people, as in a major depression. Other things equal, the average score for the lower classes would rise and the I.Q. gap between the classes would therefore diminish.

It is, of course, possible that other things would not be equal. For example, it may be that the I.Q. required for success would rise as wealth shrank. In that case, poverty might not narrow the I.Q. gap between upper and lower classes, for only *highly* superior people would stay on top, instead of merely the superior ones. However, in the absence of information to the contrary, the safest assumption is the one that assumes least — namely that the psychological requirements for success would remain the same even as wealth contracted, but a smaller fraction of those who could meet the requirements would actually get a chance to do so.

The superficial impressions jibe, for the successful people in poor countries seem to be cut from more or less the same cloth as those in wealthy countries in mental capacity and drive. They do not, at any rate, seem markedly brighter.

The precise size of the I.Q. gap between classes depends on a host of specific details that would be out of place here, even assuming that they are available someplace. Questions of income distribution, shifting criteria for success, patterns of taxation, the level of wealth taken as the base line, the spread of I.Q. and its correlation with economic success, the very definitions of upper and lower classes, all these elements would enter into any numerical estimate of how changes in wealth might affect the class separation in I.Q. Moreover, the class separation in I.Q. cannot be fully summarized as a single gap between two arbitrary classes. There are actually many levels on the social ladder, not just two, and the spacing of rungs can be varied endlessly by particular circumstances. However, at a qualitative level, the corollary appears unassailable. For any foreseeable society, the lower classes will be a reservoir of human abilities of the type that make for success. This is simply a way of saying that the lower classes span the full range of ability. When new wealth creates more room at the top (as it sometimes does, even if not often enough by some standards), the gifted ones are likely to ascend first.

Corollary D: Technological advance may change the marketplace for I.Q. Even if every single job lost in automating a factory is replaced by a new job someplace else in a new technology, it is possible that some of those put out of the old jobs will not have the I.Q. for the new ones. Technological unemployment is not just a matter of "dislocation" or "retraining" if the jobs created are beyond the native capacity of the newly unemployed. It is much easier to replace men's muscles with machines than to replace their intellects. Already the shifts in the labor force across single generations show a trend toward the occupations with higher prestige — managerial, professional, and white-collar — and away from semiskilled and unskilled labor. The proportion of unskilled and semiskilled laborers in the total work force has, in fact, been decreasing for at least three generations in America, perhaps longer. If the I.Q. requirements for given jobs are not changing — and there is no evidence for any obvious trend — then the labor market must already be shifting towards higher values.

The computer visionaries believe that their machines will soon be doing our thinking for us too, but in the meantime, backhoes are putting ditchdiggers out of work. And if some stay out of work, most likely they will be ones who lack the qualifications for the new jobs, including some level of I.Q. or its prime correlate, education.

To be sure, not all automation pushes the labor market the same way. In some lines of work — the baking industry, for example — new technology may have a net effect in the opposite direction, displacing relatively large numbers of skilled bakers and creating still larger numbers of semiskilled positions — slicing- and packaging-machine operators, truck drivers, and so on. Perhaps the same is true of furniture-making, which has little use for master carpenters anymore. In the long run, however, what counts is the overall impact on the labor market, which seems to be the reverse of that on the baking business.

Each occupation requires some minimum mental capacity (see Chapter 3), a hurdle usually cleared with points to spare in the past. But if technology is, on balance, shifting those minima upward — as it does, for example, by replacing ditchdiggers with backhoe operators — there must come a time when people will be unemployed simply because the job market has shifted too far up to provide slots for all of them. The time may not be upon us yet. It would be hard to prove one way or the other, for unemployment always has multiple causes, some of them readily curable by familiar economic measures. Nevertheless, sooner or later, if and when technology has truly replaced the drawers and the hewers and the other simple vocations, the tendency to be unemployed may run in the genes of a family about as certainly as the I.Q. does now.

Corollary E: The syllogism deals manifestly with intelligence. The invention of the intelligence test made it possible to gather the data necessary to back up the three premises. However, there may be other inherited traits that differ among people and contribute to their success in life. Such qualities as temperament, personality, appearance, perhaps even physical strength or endurance, may enter into our strivings for achievement and are to varying degrees inherited. The meritocracy concerns not just inherited intelligence, but all inherited traits affecting success, whether or not we know of their importance or have tests to gauge them.

Schooling, measured simply as years completed or by grades earned, is the prime competitor to I.Q. as a predictor of success in our society. Sometimes, people interpret the predictiveness of schooling as a refutation of the importance of I.Q., hence of inheritance. They note that schooling lends itself more readily to environmental change for social purposes than I.Q., even if not so readily as was thought at the beginning of the recent surge of compensatory education. At any rate, schools can be improved in tangible ways, and since occupational and social success correlate highly with schooling, such improvements should play handsome returns all around, this argument holds.

What the foregoing argument overlooks is that, up till now, schooling has itself been heritable, largely because of its intimate connection with I.Q. Those with higher intellectual endowments have tended to persevere in school and have earned better grades along the way. Later, they go on continuing to win more than their share of life's other rewards. In other words, we should not say that schooling, rather than I.Q., leads to success, but that distinction in school is the common, albeit not infallable, sign in childhood and youth of high ability.

While not as heritable as I.Q., schooling predicts individual success better, at least according to studies of young men. And it undeniably lends itself more to social manipulation than I.Q. The unique availability of quality, free education was, and is, the road to success climbed by thousands upon thousands of poor children, to their advantage and our country's. But the conclusion that more schooling is all we need to accelerate the process to any desired degree does not follow from the facts, however much we want to believe it.

To see why, one must ponder further the fact that a particular poor child climbs the educational ladder on his or her way up, while classmates with the same apparent opportunities do not. It is customary these days to blame something in the environment outside school — in the home or on the streets perhaps. No doubt, homes and streets often deserve the blame they get and ways should be sought to improve them, for the potential benefits are great. However, the intimate tie between schooling and I.Q. — as recounted in Chapters 3 and 4 — tells us that school simply cannot teach all children uniformly, at least not school as we have known it. The correlation between I.Q. and school performance means that they covary, and since the I.Q. expresses inborn potential, so does schooling, although to a lesser degree. A school that revealed no innate differences would most likely have ceased teaching much that is generally useful. Education has been a step on the way up while it has taught useful skills and, as a by-product, has spotted the able, motivated individual who will probably continue his winning ways. If and when it ceases to do either, it will quickly cease predicting success. If schools are to continue being useful, they must retain their power to discriminate (among individuals, that is), however heavy that has come to weigh nowadays.

The syllogism seems to deal with "mental abilities" as if they came in a bunch — inherited as an undifferentiated cluster and then contributing to success according to how large the cluster is. Yet, Chapter 2 showed that the testing of intelligence has uncovered many subabilities, dozens and dozens of them by some reckonings. Is there an inconsistency here? May there not be many different sorts of "success" in our society, tapping many different sorts of abilities? Thus, the verbally endowed would talk to get ahead, while the numerical ones would count, and the mechanical ones would fabricate. If almost everyone did at least something well, could there not be so many independent paths to success of various sorts that the one-dimensional conception of the syllogism would be refuted? The answer is that the paths are, alas, not independent, as Chapter 2 also pointed out. The single Spearmanian factor g accounts for about half the variation among people in mental ability. It may account for an even larger share of the mental abilities that enter into the determination of status. Just two or three additional broad factors — such as the verbal, the numerical, and the mechanical — encompass still more of the relevant mental endowment. While the numerous minor (in the statistical sense) abilities may dictate a person's most favorable occupation, success in society, for most lines of work, does indeed correlate with a small number of traits. This overlooks the uncommon occupations that call on highly special talents or attributes, as in professional sports or music and art or modeling, which may have relatively lesser correlations with the broad factors. For ordinary occupations, as plied by the vast majority of working people, the syllogism applies — all the more so because the patterns of assortative mating tend to enmesh further the very traits that contribute to success. People tend to marry within their class, and by doing so, they pair off corresponding genetic endowments. The more or less unitary social continuum of success feeds back into germ plasm, creating greater uniformity of ability, temperament, and perhaps even such an irrelevancy as appearance, at each status level than there might have been on genetic grounds alone.

The syllogism and its corollaries point to a future in which social classes not only continue but become ever more solidly built on inborn differences. As the wealth and complexity of human society grow, there may settle out of the mass of humanity a stratum that is unable to master the common occupations, cannot compete for success and achievement, and is most likely to be born to parents who have similarly failed. In Aldous Huxley's *Brave New*

World, it was malevolent or misguided science that created the "alphas," "gammas," and the other distinct types of people. But nature itself is more likely to do the job or something similar, as the less well-known but far more prescient book by Michael Young, *The Rise of the Meritocracy*, has depicted. Young's social-science-fiction tale of the antimeritocratic upheavals of the early twenty-first century is the perfect setting for his timely neologism, "meritocracy." The troubles he anticipated, and that the syllogism explains, may already be catching the attention of alert social scientists such as Edward Banfield, whose book *The Unheavenly City* describes the increasingly chronic lower class in America's central cities. While Sunday supplements and popular magazines crank out horror stories about genetic engineering, our society may be sorting itself willy-nilly into inherited classes. What troubles most about this prospect is that the growth of an increasingly hereditary meritocracy will arise out of the successful realization of contemporary political and social goals. The more we succeed in achieving relatively unimpeded social mobility, adequate wealth, the end of drudgery, and a uniformly wholesome environment, the more forcefully does the syllogism apply.

Are there alternatives short of turning back to the past, which minimized the syllogism largely by social immobility, poverty, drudgery, and squalor? The first two premises of the syllogism cannot easily be challenged, for they are true to some extent now and are likely to become more so in the foreseeable future. The heritability of intelligence will grow as the conditions of life are made more uniformly wholesome; intelligence will play an increasingly important role in occupational success as the menial jobs are taken over by machines. In time, science may foster a genuine educational technology to compensate for the significant cognitive differences among people, thereby obviating premise 1 on inherited mental capacity. At the moment, however, the prevailing orthodoxy on human equality has slowed, if not stalled, forward progress. Or, we may anticipate a future when technology has advanced so far that the sort of mental capacity measured by

I.Q. tests contributes to success no more than the size of one's biceps does now, thus taking the sting out of premise 2 on the correlation between success and intelligence.

In the interim, however, it may seem more plausible to block the third premise by preventing earnings and prestige from depending upon successful achievement. The socialist dictum, "From each according to his ability, to each according to his needs," can be seen as a bald denial of the third premise. It states that whatever a person's achievement, his reward (economic, social, and political) is unaffected by his success. Instead, the dictum implies, people will get what they need however they perform, but only so long as they fulfill their abilities. But life under the dictum has not been notably free of pressure. Those in power soon discover that they must insist on a certain level of performance, for what the dictum neglects is that "ability" is, first of all, widely and innately variable, and second, that it expresses itself in labor only for some sort of gain. In capitalist countries, the gain is typically in material wealth, but even where the dictum rules (if only in principle), social and political influence, or relief from threat, would be the reward for accomplishment. Human society has yet to find a working alternative to the carrot and the stick. Meanwhile, the third premise assures the formation of a social continuum.

Classlessness is elusive because people vary and because they compete for gain — economic and otherwise. There is a recurrent dream of a human society populated by selfless workers dedicating themselves to "the good of the people," and expecting no special benefits for their best efforts. The dream would be irresistible were it not for its persistent tendency to become a nightmare when acted upon. The record of past efforts at classless states would by itself deter the judicious, for their span is typically distinguished by economic disaster and inhuman cruelty. Mankind stubbornly refuses to organize itself like a beehive, with altruism the apparent central motive. But, then, the altruistic worker bee is a sterile female, a biological nonentity except insofar as she has evolved over eons to serve the community and its fecund (and rather selfish) queen — not at all like the raw material out of which human societies must be fashioned. The threat of terror or the promise of admiration and gratitude prove to be the main human alternatives to instinctive altruism. Our few tens of thousands of years of social life have only begun to instill in us the altruistic impulses that the social insects have evolved in their tens of millions of years of mutual interdependence, as E. O. Wilson has so vividly described in *The Insect Societies.*

Mankind, while invincibly and inherently egocentric, can be impelled by more than just the crasser rewards. Society can encourage us to strive for honor, respect, a sense of pride, responsibility, as well as for money. But whatever goals we adopt, the main rewards go to those who somehow earn them, so that the syllogism applies anyway. The tendency to respect, honor, praise, remunerate, and perhaps even envy people who succeed is not only ingrained, but is itself a source of social pressure to contribute to one's limit. It is the form in which the social contract must be drafted for egocentric (although not necessarily egotistical) creatures like us.

It was noted before that the premium given to lawyers, doctors, engineers, and business managers is not accidental, for such jobs are left to incompetents at our collective peril. There are simply fewer potentially competent physicians than barbers. The gradient of occupations is, then, a natural, essentially unconscious, expression of the current social consensus. Whether or not the gradient is right, or good, or permanent, it directs human effort one way or the other, in accordance with prevailing, often shifting, notions of how effort is best invested. And beneath the gradient is a scale of inborn ability, which is what gives the syllogism its unique potency.

Imagine, for example, what would happen if the gradient of gain were inverted by government fiat. Suppose bakers and lumberjacks got the top rewards, while engineers, physicians, lawyers, and business executives got the bottom. This is harder to imagine

than one might guess, for it requires inverting the scale of prestige, respect, social standing, and the resulting sense of social
utility — as well as the scale of income. Soon thereafter, the scale
of I.Q.'s would also invert, with the competition for the newly
desirable jobs now including people with the highest I.Q.'s. (For
simplicity's sake, only I.Q. is mentioned, but there may be, and no
doubt are, other factors that contribute to success, for recall that
I.Q. is only necessary not sufficient.) With their competitive advantage, the top I.Q.'s would once again collect at the top of the
social ladder. But no government (let alone people themselves) is
likely to conduct such an experiment, for it is not a sensible allocation of a scarce resource like high-grade intelligence. Nor could
a government long equalize the gains from all occupations. The
lure of greater rewards (financial and otherwise) for certain jobs
directs the flow of talent as the consensus dictates, like a labor
pump. Without the pump, society would annul its influence over
the allocation of talent, which it cannot and should not do. This
does not mean that the scale of compensation must stretch from
opulence to racking poverty to accomplish society's valid purposes. A gentler slope might do; it might even do better. On the
other hand, the scale cannot be totally flattened with impunity,
however humanitarian the impulse to do so. Someplace between
those extremes falls the right balance between the needs of society in general and compassion for those who fare poorly, but
where that ideal is, nobody knows. We should manipulate the
strength of the pump with care.

Social reformers sometimes argue that society can rely on peoples' inner satisfactions to produce the necessary division of labor.
To be sure, work often affords inherent pleasures, above and beyond the rewards that society attaches to it. The musician may
play for himself, as well as for his audience. The seaman may sail
for the love of the sea, not just for his pay. The carpenter may
enjoy the feel of the wood and the mastery he has over it. But
musicians or sailors or carpenters do not often escape society's
control. The social rewards are built around the inherent qualities

of work, augmenting here, diminishing there. A job judged worthy earns an extra bonus if it is also disagreeable or dangerous — like a fireman rushing through the flames to make a daring rescue or a house painter working from a scaffold high above the ground. But for a job that is a delight in itself — like spending the summer on the beach as a lifeguard — no one expects much pay. Society clearly needs brave firemen and conscientious lifeguards, who, it finds, can be engaged at different rates.

It is as if the work at each level of social status draws something like a fixed total gain — the higher the status, the higher the gain — which is equal to the sum of the social rewards (in their various forms, like money, prestige, and so on) plus (or, if the work is disagreeable, minus) its intrinsic qualities. Obviously, since people differ somewhat in their enjoyment of any given occupation, as well as in their appreciation of the social rewards, the setting of total gain must necessarily be imprecise. If they differed enough — so that one man's meat were truly another man's poison as a general rule — there would be neither competition for the "better" jobs nor any broad agreement about which were better. But the existence of general agreement in society shows that the differences between people are not large enough to wreck the system, although it doubtless gets shaken from time to time when values are shifting, as they seem to be now. In the ideal case, the people most drawn to any job would be those for whom the intrinsic consequences are most positive (or least negative), since simple arithmetic shows they stand to gain most. Among those, the ones who land the job would be the most able among the competitors, producing the familiar correlation between status and ability.

A few people evidently escape the social pulls and pushes, occasionally to society's material benefit, although rarely to their own. We are grateful that Gregor Mendel and Béla Bartók continued with their science and music respectively, in spite of the message of indifference they were apparently getting from their fellowman. But our admiration for, and fascination with, such rare instances should not obscure their rarity. As for the rest of us, we seem to be stuck with the conclusion of the syllogism. The data on I.Q. and social-class differences show that we have been living with a partly inherited stratification of our society for some time. The signs point to more rather than less of it in the future, assuming that we are not plunged back into a state of primeval poverty by some cataclysm or do not turn back to rigidly and arbitrarily privileged classes. Wiping out the trappings of privilege — the differences in inherited wealth, schooling, neighborhood, and so on — would not wipe out the social differences between families, although it would reduce them at first. The remaining family differences would be the genetic ones, which clearly are smaller than the genetic plus environmental distinctions we live with now. However, the increase in mobility that we gain by eliminating arbitrary social barriers is self-limiting, perhaps even self-reversing. Recall that familial regression towards the mean, which is a biological source of social mobility, depends upon the heritability and that improving environment raises the heritability, which reduces the mobility. Moreover, without arbitrary social barriers, assortative mating for inherited attributes like I.Q. would probably rise, further reducing familial regression and blocking mobility still more. The higher the heritability and assortative mating, the closer will human society approach a virtual caste system, with families sustaining their position on the social ladder from generation to generation as parents and children grow more nearly alike in their essential features.

The opportunity for social mobility across classes assures the biological distinctiveness of each class, for the unusual offspring — whether more or less able than his (or her) closest relatives — would quickly rise above his family or sink below it, and take his place, both biologically and socially, with his peers. The traffic is significant these days, for the lower classes produce, in sheer numbers, more people with high I.Q.'s than the upper classes (see Chapter 3) simply because they are so large a proportion of the total population. It is not uncommon now for lower-class families to have close blood ties reaching into the upper layers of status, and vice versa, somewhat softening the impact of the chasm between the classes. However, if the size of the lower class diminishes, if the heritability rises, and if the gap in ability between top and bottom widens — all of which seem more than likely — the traffic across the most separated classes would subside into a trickle. Further alienation at the bottom and indifference at the top are the obvious hazards; the less obvious ones may be worse.

If all this is a fair picture of the future, then we should be preparing ourselves for it instead of railing against its dawning signs. Greater wealth, health, freedom, fairness and educational opportunity are *not* going to give us automatically the egalitarian society of our philosophical heritage. They will instead give us a society sharply graduated, with ever greater innate separation between the top and the bottom and ever more uniformity within families as far as inherited abilities are concerned. Naturally, we find this vista appalling, for we have been raised to think of social equality as our goal. The vista reminds us of the world we had hoped to leave behind — aristocracies, privileged classes, unfair advantages and disadvantages of birth. But it is different, for the privileged classes of the past, based on religion, title, property, race, even physiognomy, were probably not much superior biologically to the downtrodden, which is why revolutions had a fair chance of success. By removing arbitrary barriers between classes, society achieves the laudable goal of allowing people of different races, religions, and ethnic backgrounds to earn any level of status, but, simultaneously, it fosters biological barriers to mobility. When people can freely take their natural level in society, the upper classes will, virtually by definition, have greater capacity than the lower.

The measurement of intelligence is one of the yardsticks by which we may assess the growing meritocracy, but other tests of human potential and performance should supplement the I.Q. in describing a person's talents, interests, skills, and shortcomings. The biological stratification of society looms whether we have tests to gauge it or not, but with them a more humane and tolerant grasp of human differences is possible. At the moment, that seems our best hope, for the information could help us in our search for effective compensatory education. Unfortunately, the odds are against that worthy cause as long as the egalitarian orthodoxy can portray the quest for understanding as apostasy.

Notes to Chapter Five

Deliberate, selective deprivation of resources as a solution to educational diversity may seem like a farfetched danger, but an article in the *New York Times* on Sunday, 19 November 1972, shows it may not be. Under the title "Trying to Equalize Schools" (Section E, page 7), Gene I. Maeroff describes a proposal made by the New York State Board of Regents which "recommended that citizens in wealthy school districts be prohibited from raising their school expenditures above a certain level — even if the taxpayers in those districts are willing to shoulder the burden." It may be that such compensatory deprivation would be used simply to equalize school expenditures per pupil across school districts varying in wealth. However, if the Board of Regents hopes to equalize school performances by equalizing expenditures, would it be willing to recommend the next step if the first step fails to reach that goal? The article does not say whether the Board of Regents would favor pushing per capita expenditures in wealthy districts *below* the level in the poorer ones.

The idea that mobility in an open-class society may have limitations imposed by inherited intellectual differences between the classes turned up recently in B. K. Eckland's "Social Class Structure and the Genetic Basis of Intelligence" (in *Intelligence: Genetic and Environmental Influences*, edited by R. Cancro. New York: Grune & Stratton, 1971). It is, however, by no means a new idea. C. A. Anderson, J. C. Brown, and M. J. Bowman, "Intelligence and Occupational Mobility" (*Journal of Political Economy* 60 [1952]: 218–239), make an attempt to estimate what part of the intergenerational traffic can be attributed to the father-child correlation in I.Q. A similar task is addressed in C. Burt's "Intelligence and Social Mobility" (*British Journal of Statistical Psychology* 14 [1961]: 3–24). In addition, R. B. Cattell devotes a chapter to "intelligence and society" in his *Abilities: Their Structure, Growth and Action* (Boston: Houghton Mifflin, 1971), covering substantially more ground than the limitations on mobility. A comparably broad, much earlier discussion of inheritance and society, without any emphasis on intelligence, can be found in R. A. Fisher's *The Genetical Theory*

of Natural Selection (1929. Reprint [rev. ed.]. New York: Dover, 1958).
Fisher wrote as a biologist rather than as a social scientist.

The recognition of inherited factors in human society in general has been part of modern biology since its launching by Darwin in the mid-nineteenth century. A brief paper by T. Dobzhansky, "Genetics and the Social Sciences" (in *Genetics*, edited by D. C. Glass. New York: Rockefeller University Press and Russell Sage Foundation, 1968) makes the general point that social movement often carries genetic material with it. A lengthy discussion of the same essential point, plus much else, applied to the whole of human history (and prehistory) can be found in C. D. Darlington's *The Evolution of Man and Society* (New York: Simon & Schuster, 1969).

On mobility itself, the point of departure for modern writers is P. A. Sorokin's *Social Mobility*, 1927, reprinted as part of his *Social and Cultural Mobility* (Glencoe, Ill.: Free Press, 1959). A landmark analysis of the amount of intergenerational traffic in various countries is S. M. Lipset and R. Bendix, *Social Mobility in Industrial Society* (Berkeley: University of California Press, 1959). For mobility in just one country, a widely cited work is D. V. Glass, ed., *Social Mobility in Britain* (London: Routledge, 1954). The essentials of social stratification, presupposed in most studies of mobility, can be found in a chapter entitled "Stratification" in R. Brown's *Social Psychology* (New York: Free Press, 1965).

Is technology changing the labor market for I.Q., and, if so, is it raising or lowering it? The common wisdom on the matter is equivocal. On the one hand, it is obvious that the easiest thing to replace about labor is the sheer muscle power, which would imply a market for a higher average I.Q. On the other hand, technology supposedly mechanizes and dehumanizes labor, making people into mere cogs, which suggests a market for a decreasing average. The apparent inconsistency is readily explained: technology has many effects, including the two just characterized. On balance, however, the indications are that the average I.Q. called for with technological change is rising. Blue-collar jobs, which tend to have the lowest I.Q. requirements, are converted into white-collar jobs, requiring somewhat higher scores. At the same time, white-collar jobs tend to be shifted in the blue-collar direction, with many intellectual functions of the old jobs mechanized away by the technology of the office. However, the two trends appear to be unequal in magnitude, for the average I.Q. of office workers does not seem to be dropping noticeably as their ranks are enlarged with recent importations from the blue-collar level. The evidence for the foregoing can be found in a chapter by R. S. Weiss, E. Harwood, and D. Riesman, "Work and Automation: Problems and Prospects" (in *Contemporary Social Problems*, 3rd. ed., edited by R. K. Merton and R. Nisbet. New York: Harcourt Brace Jovanovich, 1971); and in J. T. Dunlop, ed.,

Automation and Technological Change (Englewood Cliffs, N. J.: Prentice Hall, 1962), particularly the chapter by E. Clague and L. Greenberg, "Employment." A useful case study from the steel industry can be found in C. R. Walker's *Toward the Automatic Factory: A Case Study of Men and Machines* (New Haven, Conn.: Yale, 1957). It may be that the skill or ability required at any given occupational level is not trending either up or down — as concluded in H. A. Simon's *The Shape of Automation: For Men and Management* (New York: Harper & Row, 1965) — but the sheer numbers towards the upper end of the occupational ladder are sharply increasing. The well-advertised danger of an undereducated labor force is another way of saying that the labor market has shifted towards high I.Q.'s.

The creation in modern societies of a managerial or power elite has been noted to the point of tedium. A useful, by no means tedious, account can be found in D. Bell's "The Post-Industrial Society: The Evolution of an Idea" (*Survey*, no. 2 [79], 1971). That this modern development cuts across capitalist and socialist countries is suggested by a comparison between J. Burnham, *The Managerial Revolution* (New York: John Day, 1941), and M. Djilas, *The New Class: An Analysis of the Communist System* (New York: Praeger, 1957). A discussion of both sorts of economy and their possible future development is contained in the remarkable book by J. A. Schumpeter, *Capitalism, Socialism, and Democracy* (New York: Harper, 1942), which recognizes the tendency for human talent to flow towards the greater challenges, consequently, the greater rewards. The thirty years since the book's publication have fulfilled an impressive fraction of Schumpeter's prognostications, particularly as regards the evolution of capitalist societies. The future was also the concern in M. Young's *The Rise of the Meritocracy* (Penguin paperback, 1958). Alternatives to meritocratic societies are set forth in lavish detail in E. O. Wilson's *The Insect Societies* (Cambridge: Harvard University Press, 1971).

Bibliography

Anderson, C. A.; Brown, J. C.; and Bowman, M. J. "Intelligence and Occupational Mobility." *Journal of Political Economy* 60 (1952): 218–239.

Ball, R. S. "The Predictability of Occupational Level from Intelligence." *Journal of Consulting Psychology* 2 (1938): 184–186.

Banfield, E. C. *The Unheavenly City.* Boston: Little, Brown, 1968.

Bayley, N. "Consistency and Variability in the Growth of Intelligence from Birth to Eighteen Years." *Journal of Genetic Psychology* 75 (1949): 165–196.

――――. "Some Increasing Parent-Child Similarities During the Growth of Children." *Journal of Educational Psychology* 45 (1954): 1–21.

Bell, D. "The Post-Industrial Society: The Evolution of an Idea." *Survey* 79 (1971): 102–168.

Binet, A., and Henri, V. "La psychologie individuelle." *L'Année psychologique* 2 (1895): 411–465. Reprinted and translated in Herrnstein, R. J., and Boring, E. G. *A Source Book in the History of Psychology.* Cambridge, Mass.: Harvard University Press, 1965. Pp. 428–433.

――――. *L'étude expérimentale de l'intelligence.* Paris: Schleicher frères, 1903.

Bloom, B. S. *Stability and Change in Human Characteristics.* New York: Wiley, 1964.

Bolton, T. L. "The Growth of Memory in School Children." *American Journal of Psychology* 4 (1891–92): 363–380.

Boring, E. G. "Intelligence as the Tests Test It." *The New Republic* 34 (1923): 35–36.

Brown, R. *Social Psychology.* New York: Free Press, 1965.

Bruner, J. S.; Olver, R. R.; and Greenfield, P. M., *et al. Studies in Cognitive Growth.* New York: Wiley, 1966.

Burks, B. S., "The Relative Influence of Nature and Nurture upon Mental Development: A Comparative Study of Foster Parent–Foster Child Resemblance and True Parent–True Child Resemblance." *Yearbook of the National Society for the Study of Education* 27 (1928): 219–316.

Burks, B. S.; Jensen, D. W.; and Terman, L. M. *Genetic Studies of Genius, III: The Promise of Youth: Follow-up Studies of a Thousand Gifted Children*. Stanford: Stanford University Press, 1930.

Burnham, J. *The Managerial Revolution*. New York: John Day, 1941.

Burt, C. *Mental and Scholastic Tests*. London: King, 1921.

———. *The Factors of the Mind*. New York: Macmillan, 1941.

———. "Alternative Methods of Factor Analysis and Their Relations to Pearson's Method of 'Principal Axes.'" *British Journal of Psychology, Statistical Section* 2 (1949): 98–121.

———. "The Inheritance of Mental Ability." *American Psychologist* 13 (1958): 1–15.

———. "Class Differences in General Intelligence: III." *British Journal of Statistical Psychology* 12 (1959): 15–33.

———. "Intelligence and Social Mobility." *British Journal of Statistical Psychology* 14 (1961): 3–24.

———. "The Gifted Child." *British Journal of Statistical Psychology* 14 (1961): 123–139.

———. "The Genetic Determination of Differences in Intelligence: A Study of Monozygotic Twins Reared Together and Apart." *British Journal of Psychology* 57 (1966): 137–153.

———. "Quantitative Genetics in Psychology." *British Journal of Mathematical and Statistical Psychology* 24 (1971): 1–21.

———. "Inheritance of General Intelligence." *American Psychologist* 27 (1972): 175–190.

Burt, C. and Howard, M. "The Multifactorial Theory of Inheritance and Its Application to Intelligence." *British Journal of Statistical Psychology* 9 (1956): 95–131.

———. "Heredity and Intelligence: A Reply to Criticisms." *British Journal of Statistical Psychology* 10 (1957): 33–63.

Cancro, R., ed. *Intelligence: Genetic and Environmental Influences*. New York: Grune & Stratton, 1971.

Cattell, J. McK. "Mental Tests and Measurements." *Mind* 15 (1890): 373–381.

Cattell, R. B. *Abilities: Their Structure, Growth, and Action*. Boston: Houghton Mifflin, 1971.

Conrad, H. S., and Jones, H. E. "A Second Study of Familial Resemblance in Intelligence: Environmental and Genetic Implications of Parent-Child and Sibling Correlations in the Total Sample." *Yearbook of the National Society for the Study of Education* 39 (1940): 97–141.

Conway, J. "Class Differences in General Intelligence: II." *British Journal of Statistical Psychology* 12 (1959): 5–14.

Cox, C. M. *Genetic Studies of Genius, II: The Early Mental Traits of Three Hundred Geniuses*. Stanford: Stanford University Press, 1926.

Cronbach, L. J. *Essentials of Psychological Testing*. 3rd ed. New York: Harper & Row, 1970.

Crow, J. F., and Kimura, M. *An Introduction to Population Genetics Theory*. New York: Harper & Row, 1970.

Darlington, C. D. *The Evolution of Man and Society*. New York: Simon & Schuster, 1969.

Darwin, C. *On the Origin of Species by Means of Natural Selection, or the*

Preservation of the Favoured Races in the Struggle for Life. London: John Murray, 1859.

Djilas, M. *The New Class: An Analysis of the Communist System*. New York: Praeger, 1957.

Dobzhansky, T. "Genetics and the Social Sciences." In *Genetics*, edited by D. C. Glass. New York: Rockefeller University Press and the Russell Sage Foundation, 1968. Pp. 129–142.

Duncan, O. D. "A Socioeconomic Index for All Occupations." In *Occupations and Social Status*, edited by A. J. Reiss, Jr., *et al*. Glencoe: Free Press, 1961.

———. "Ability and Achievement." *Eugenics Quarterly* 15 (1968): 1–11.

Dunlop, J. T., ed. *Automation and Technological Change*. Englewood Cliffs, N.J.: Prentice Hall, 1962.

Eckland, B. K. "New Mating Boundaries in Education." *Social Biology* 17 (1970): 269–277.

———. "Social Class Structure and the Genetic Basis of Intelligence." In *Intelligence: Genetic and Environmental Influences*, edited by R. Cancro. New York: Grune & Stratton, 1971. Pp. 65–76.

Erlenmeyer-Kimling, L., and Jarvik, L. F. "Genetics and Intelligence: A Review." *Science* 142 (1963): 1477–1479.

Falconer, D. S. *Introduction to Quantitative Genetics*. New York: Ronald, 1960.

Fisher, J. "The Twisted Pear and the Prediction of Behavior." *Journal of Consulting Psychology* 23 (1959): 400–405.

Fisher, R. A. *The Genetical Theory of Natural Selection*. Reprint. New York: Dover, 1958.

Flavell, J. H. *The Developmental Psychology of Jean Piaget*. Princeton, N.J.: Van Nostrand, 1963.

Galton, F. *Hereditary Genius: An Inquiry into Its Laws and Consequences*. London: Macmillan, 1869.

———. *Inquiries into Human Faculty and Its Development*. London: Macmillan, 1883.

———. "Family-Likeness in Eye Colour." *Proceedings of the Royal Society of London* 40 (1886): 402–415.

———. "Co-relations and their Measurement, Chiefly from Anthropometric Data." *Proceedings of the Royal Society of London* 45 (1888): 135–145.

———. *Natural Inheritance*. London: Macmillan, 1889.

Garrison, R. J.; Anderson, V. E.; and Reed, S. C. "Assortative Marriage." *Eugenics Quarterly* 15 (1968): 113–127.

Gilbert, J. A. "Researches on the Mental and Physical Development of School Children." *Studies of the Yale Psychological Laboratory* 2 (1894): 40–100.

Glass, D. C., ed. *Genetics*. New York: Rockefeller University Press and the Russell Sage Foundation, 1968.

Glass, D. V., ed. *Social Mobility in Britain*. London: Routledge, 1954.

Goodenough, F. L. *Mental Testing: Its History, Principles, and Applications*. New York: Rinehart, 1949.

Guilford, J. P. *The Nature of Human Intelligence*. New York: McGraw-Hill, 1967.

Guilford, J. P., and Hoepfner, R. *The Analysis of Intelligence*. New York: McGraw-Hill, 1971.

Harrell, T. W., and Harrell, M. S. "Army General Classification Test Scores for Civilian Occupations." *Educational and Psychological Measurement* 5 (1945): 229–239.

Harvard Educational Review, Reprint Series No. 2, 1969.

Herrnstein, R. J. "I.Q." *The Atlantic Monthly,* September 1971, 43–64.

Herrnstein, R. J., and Boring, E. G. *A Source Book in the History of Psychology.* Cambridge, Mass.: Harvard University Press, 1965.

Higgins, J. V.; Reed, E. W.; and Reed, S. C. "Intelligence and Family Size: A Paradox Resolved." *Eugenics Quarterly* 9 (1962): 84–90.

Hilden, A. H. "A Longitudinal Study of Intellectual Development." *Journal of Psychology* 28 (1949): 187–214.

Honzik, M. P. "Developmental Studies of Parent-Child Resemblance in Intelligence." *Child Development* 28 (1957): 215–228.

Honzik, M. P.; McFarlane, J. W.; and Allen, L. "The Stability of Mental Test Performance between Two and Eighteen Years." *Journal of Experimental Education* 17 (1948): 309–324.

The Humanist, January–February 1972.

Huxley, A. *Brave New World.* Garden City, N. Y.: Doubleday, 1932.

Jensen, A. R. "How Much Can We Boost I.Q. and Scholastic Achievement?" *Harvard Educational Review* 39 (1969): 1–123. (Also, *Harvard Educational Review,* Reprint Series No. 2, 1969, 1–123.)

———. "Reducing the Heredity-Environment Uncertainty." *Harvard Educational Review* 39 (1969): 449–483. (Also, *Harvard Educational Review,* Reprint Series No. 2, 1969, 209–243.)

———. "I.Q.'s of Identical Twins Reared Apart." *Behavior Genetics* 1 (1970): 133–146.

———. "Hierarchical Theories of Mental Ability." In *On Intelligence,* edited by W. B. Dockrell. London: Methuen, 1970.

———. *Educability and Group Differences.* London: Methuen, forthcoming.

Jinks, J. L., and Fulker, D. W. "Comparison of the Biometrical Genetical, MAVA, and Classical Approaches to the Analysis of Human Behavior." *Psychological Bulletin* 73 (1970): 311–349.

Johnson, D. M. "Applications of the Standard-Score I.Q. to Social Statistics." *Journal of Social Psychology* 27 (1948): 217–227.

Juel-Nielsen, N. "Individual and Environment: A Psychiatric-Psychological Investigation of Monozygous Twins Reared Apart." *Acta psychiatrica et neurologica Scandinavica.* Monograph Supplement 183, 1965.

Kagan, J. "I.Q.: Fair Science for Dark Deeds." *Radcliffe Quarterly,* March 1972.

Lipset, S. M., and Bendix, R. *Social Mobility in Industrial Society.* Berkeley: University of California Press, 1959.

Medvedev, Z. A. *The Rise and Fall of T. D. Lysenko.* Translated by I. Michael Lerner. New York: Columbia University Press, 1969.

Miller, G. A. *Psychology: The Science of Mental Life.* New York: Harper & Row, 1962.

Newman, H. H.; Freeman, F. N.; and Holzinger, K. J. *Twins: A Study of Heredity and Environment.* Chicago: University of Chicago Press, 1937.

Oden, M. H. "The Fulfillment of Promise: 40-Year Follow-up of the Terman Gifted Group." *Genetic Psychology Monographs* 77 (1968): 3–93.

Pearson, K. "Mathematical Contributions to the Theory of Evolution, III:

Regression, Heredity and Panmixia." *Philosophical Transactions of the Royal Society of London* 187 (1896): 253–318.

Peterson, J. *Early Conceptions and Tests of Intelligence.* Yonkers, N.Y.: World Book, 1925.

Philippe, J. "Jastrow — Exposition d'anthropologie de Chicago — Test psychologiques, etc." *L'Année psychologique* 1 (1894): 522–526.

Reed, S. C. "The Evolution of Human Intelligence: Some Reasons Why It Should Be a Continuing Process." *American Scientist* 53 (1965): 317–326.

Schull, W. J., and Neel, J. V. *The Effects of Inbreeding on Japanese Children.* New York: Harper & Row, 1965.

Schumpeter, J. A. *Capitalism, Socialism, and Democracy.* New York: Harper, 1942.

Shields, J. *Monozygotic Twins Brought Up Apart and Brought Up Together.* London: Oxford University Press, 1962.

Shuey, A. *The Testing of Negro Intelligence.* 2nd ed. New York: Social Science Press, 1966.

Simon, H. A. *The Shape of Automation: For Men and Management.* New York: Harper & Row, 1965.

Skodak, M., and Skeels, H. M. "A Final Follow-up Study of One Hundred Adopted Children." *Journal of Genetic Psychology* 75 (1949): 85–125.

Sontag, L. W.; Baker, C. T.; and Nelson, V. L. "Mental Growth and Personality Development: A Longitudinal Study." *Monographs of the Society for Research in Child Development* 23 (1958): 1–85.

Sorokin, P. A. *Social Mobility.* 1927. Reprinted as part of Sorokin, P. A. *Social and Cultural Mobility.* Glencoe, Ill.: Free Press, 1959.

Spearman, C. "The Proof and Measurement of Association between Two Things." *American Journal of Psychology* 15 (1904): 72–101.

———. " 'General intelligence,' Objectively Determined and Measured." *American Journal of Psychology* 15 (1904): 201–293.

———. *The Abilities of Man.* New York: Macmillan, 1927.

Stern, W. *Die psychologische Methoden der Intelligenzprufung.* Leipzig: Barth, 1912.

Stewart, N. "A.G.C.T. Scores of Army Personnel Grouped by Occupation." *Occupations* 26 (1947): 5–41.

Terman, L. M. *Genetic Studies of Genius, I: Mental and Physical Traits of a Thousand Gifted Children.* 2nd ed., Stanford University Press, 1926.

Terman, L. M., and Oden, M. H. *IV: The Gifted Child Grows Up: Twenty-five Years' Follow-up of a Superior Group.* Stanford University Press, 1947.

———. *V: The Gifted Group at Mid-Life: Thirty-five Years' Follow-up of the Superior Child.* Stanford University Press, 1959.

Thomson, G. H. *The Factorial Analysis of Human Ability.* Boston: Houghton Mifflin, 1939.

Thorndike, R. L., and Hagen, E. *Ten Thousand Careers.* New York: Wiley, 1959.

Thurstone, L. L. "Multiple-Factor Analysis." *Psychological Review* 38 (1931): 406–427.

———. *The Vectors of Mind.* Chicago: University of Chicago Press, 1935.

———. "Primary Mental Abilities." *Psychometric Monographs,* no. 1 (1938), 1–121.

————. *Multiple-Factor Analysis*. Chicago: University of Chicago Press, 1947.

————. "Psychological Implications of Factor Analysis." *American Psychologist* 3 (1948): 402–408.

Tyler, L. J. *The Psychology of Human Differences*. 3rd ed. New York: Meredith, 1965.

Vandenberg, S. G. "The Nature and Nurture of Intelligence." In *Genetics*, edited by D. C. Glass. New York: Rockefeller University Press and the Russell Sage Foundation, 1968. Pp. 3–58.

————. "What Do We Know Today about the Inheritance of Intelligence and How Do We Know It? In *Intelligence: Genetic and Environmental Influences*, edited by R. Cancro. New York: Grune & Stratton, 1971. Pp. 182–218.

Vernon, M. "Fifty Years of Research on the Intelligence of Deaf and Hard-of-Hearing Children: A Review of Literature and Discussion of Implications." *Journal of Rehabilitation of the Deaf* 1 (1968): 1–12.

Vernon, P. E. *The Structure of Human Abilities*. London: Methuen, 1950.

Walker, C. R. *Toward the Automatic Factory: A Case Study of Men and Machines*. New Haven, Conn.: Yale, 1957.

Wechsler, D. *The Measurement and Appraisal of Adult Intelligence*. 4th ed. Baltimore: Williams & Wilkins, 1958.

Weiss, R. S.; Harwood, E.; and Riesman, D. "Work and Automation: Problems and Prospects." In *Contemporary Social Problems*, edited by R. K. Merton and R. Nisbet. 3rd ed. New York: Harcourt Brace Jovanovich, 1971. Pp. 545–600.

Wilson, E. O. *The Insect Societies*. Cambridge, Mass.: Harvard University Press, 1971.

Yerkes, R. M. "Psychological Examining in the United States Army." *Memoirs of the National Academy of Sciences*, no. 15 (1921).

Yoakum, C. S., and Yerkes, R. M. *Army Mental Testing*. New York: Holt, 1920.

Young, M. *The Rise of the Meritocracy*. Baltimore: Penguin paperback, 1958.

Young, M., and Gibson, J. B. "Social Mobility and Fertility." In *Biological Aspects of Social Problems*, edited by J. E. Meade and A. S. Parkes. Edinburgh: Oliver & Boyd, 1965.

INDEX

(SDS), 11, 15, 19, 21, 25, 27, 31, 32, 37, 39, 40, 47–50; 1972 annual convention, 26–30, 41; "public statement," 28, 30
syllogism, 197–198

Taussig scale, 140
technology, 10, 207, 210–211, 215–216, 223–224
Terman, L. M., 129–138, 140–141
Thomson, G. H., 108–109
Thorndike, R. L., 140
Thurstone, L. L., 94–98, 107–110
Time, 12, 15
tuberculosis, 177
twins. *See* I.Q., twin studies
Tyler, L. J., 139–140

unemployment, 210–211
University Action Group (UAG), 15, 21, 25, 47–50; leaflets, 16–18, 22–23, 37, 44. *See also* Students for a Democratic Society

Vandenberg, S., 166, 196
verbal factor, 97–98, 102–103, 112
Vernon, M., 55, 157, 196
Vernon, P. E., 109

Walker, C. R., 224
Washington Post, 24
Watson, J. B., 6
Wechsler, D., 108–109
Weismann, A., 45
Weiss, R. S., 223
Wilson, E. O., 217, 224
Wright, S., 193–194

Yerkes, R. M., 76
Yoakum, C. S., 76
Young, M., 141, 215, 224